Tracing Architecture

Tracing Architecture
The Aesthetics of Antiquarianism

Edited by

Dana Arnold and Stephen Bending

Blackwell
Publishing

First published as Volume 25 number 4 of *Art History*, 2002

350 Main Street, Malden, MA 02148-5018, USA
108 Cowley Road, Oxford OX4 1JF, UK
550 Swanston Street, Carlton South, Melbourne, Victoria 3053, Australia
Kurfürstendamm 57, 10707 Berlin, Germany

First published 2003 by Blackwell Publishing Ltd

Library of Congress Cataloging-in-Publication Data applied for

ISBN 1-4051-0535-6

A catalogue record for this title is available from the British Library

Set by MHL Typesetting Ltd

For further information on
Blackwell Publishing, visit our website:
http://www.blackwellpublishing.com

CONTENTS

1

INTRODUCTION

Tracing Architecture: the aesthetics of antiquarianism

Dana Arnold and Stephen Bending

Walter Benjamin's theory of art in the age of mechanical reproduction has been influential in its account of mass production, a consequent disjunction between art and its 'aura' and a concomitant democratization of the image in the late nineteenth century.[1] Benjamin looks to lithography, to photography and to film at the turn of the last century; however, mass production was of course not new in the nineteenth century and the previous hundred years saw a widespread and increasingly commercial marketing of prints alongside major advances in the technology of printmaking.[2] These developments brought with them fresh opportunities for the mass distribution of images but also new problems as the aesthetic sphere opened up to a wider public audience and the very proliferation of the image brought its authority increasingly into question.

This volume considers the interrelationship between antiquarianism and aesthetic practices before the era in which Benjamin finds true mass production but when the role and significance of the print in the dissemination of antiquarian studies comes to the fore. The essays concentrate on British attitudes to antiquity, which are commonly presented in an isolated nationalistic context, but here the discovery of the ancient world through the medium of print is explored as a Europe-wide phenomenon, where the visual language of the printed image transcended national boundaries. In this way printed images of the monuments of antiquity and the middle ages in Britain and elsewhere – with special emphasis on architecture – are considered as histories in their own right, which present an alternative interpretation of the past to that offered by textual analyses. The relationship between text and image is, quite clearly, not a new concern for art historians as it underpins much of the intellectual fabric of the discipline – after all, we write about images in order to offer a textual exegesis on the visual. Moreover, there have been specific studies of the relationship between visual images and textual histories. On the one hand Francis Haskell's *History and its Images* offers a broad perspective on the role of images in the construction of written histories whilst Alex Potts's *Winckelmann and the Birth of Art History* gives a detailed consideration of the role of text in the construction of histories of art. Although at first these studies may appear to have opposing concerns, both are positioned within the paradigm of textual histories which put the object at one remove from the reader. The importance of printed images has been considered from a range of viewpoints, including Tim Clayton's *The English Print 1688– 1802*, which maps the growth of the print industry and its role in the development of aesthetic attitudes, whereas Barbara Stafford's *Body Criticism: imaging the unseen in enlightenment art and medicine* focuses more on the role of prints as language. Studies which concentrate on the more general practices of antiquarians include *Producing the Past*, edited by Martin Myrone and Lucy Peltz, and the winter 2001 issue of *Eighteenth-Century Studies* on *Antiquarianism, Connoisseurs, and Collectors*. This study re-focuses attention on the images made of the past at a crucial moment, when technology enabled new printing techniques. The essays which follow concern themselves with the new and innovative forms of visual representation which emerged in the eighteenth century and consequently with the relationship between the ever-refining set of cultural values applied to and associated with antiquarianism through the study of both classical and medieval architecture and artefacts. This new visual language made three-dimensional objects widely available in a readable and coherent two-dimensional formula in the period before Benjamin's age of mechanical reproduction. It equipped polite society with the critical faculties necessary to determine the associative values of modern and antique architecture and design. The case studies serve at once to demonstrate the specificity of the chosen examples whilst at the same time presenting a broader contextualizing cultural framework. In this way we are reminded that artefacts were seen as essential pieces of evidence about the past and their reproduction was as essential an element of historical narrative as the reproduction of textual sources and histories.

The eighteenth century is often presented as the emergence of what we would now recognize as a 'public' in the modern sense,[3] as a body of rational individuals, which begins to question the élite's traditional claims to dominance over the interpretation of representation: once released from its role in the service of social representation, it can be argued that art becomes an object of free choice and of changing taste. More than this, it is in the act of discussion that individuals are able to appropriate art and thus the public sets about defining itself crucially by its engagement with the aesthetic as a commodity. The essays in this volume seek to support but also to question this model by asking what kind of rational debate might be operating around these representations and what purposes those debates serve, and they recognize the increasing democratization of aesthetics in the eighteenth century. However, the chapters also consider the ways in which prints are knowingly manipulated either to resist or to exploit the democratizing implications of mass production. In this they suggest that the images being produced are not passive; rather, that they take an active part in defining the membership of that newly emerging public sphere. Equally, if the printed image of an antique past can be co-opted into the rational debates of an emerging public – particularly in order to confirm Enlightenment narratives of civilization – it is also the concern of these essays to demonstrate the visual image's independence from conventional histories and its ability to create new visual histories which might challenge the dominance of textual historiography.

One crucial aspect of this independence from textual historiography is the antique image's ability to aid the individual's visualization of, and engagement with, the past. Susan Stewart has argued that images of the antique attempt to replace the actual past with an imagined past, which is then available for consumption in the modern world.[4] This act of transformation is inevitably also a moment of nostalgia which invites the individual to produce a narrative in which they connect the purity and simplicity of a lost past with the complexity of their own lives in the present. In this sense nostalgia looks not only to the past but is defined by and acts to define the present. In this engagement the original holds an uncertain position as an object from the past and a representation in the present, and that uncertainty is one of the subjects of this volume. Throughout the period, as the following essays demonstrate, images of the antique consistently attempt to grapple with the very materiality of the past. The standard criticism of antiquarians, of course, is that in turning to the detail of physical remains they get lost in the material objects of the past, and in doing so, fail to produce anything of value, or even interest, to others. However, as the writers in this volume demonstrate, the eighteenth and early nineteenth centuries see a series of attempts to co-opt images of a reconstructed past in the aid of quite specific projects in the present. That manoeuvring inevitably unfolds around issues of consumption, accuracy of representation and the problematic relationship between the present and its pasts.

The need to classify in order to clarify for the modern world of course remains central to prints of both medieval and classical antiquities, and it relies upon a confidence in the ability to translate the materialness of the past into a recognizable two-dimensional form. Printed images were commonly upheld as an icon of modernity, one of the few striking demonstrations of modern superiority over the ancient world. Like moveable type, the print enabled multiple access to information and seemed to overcome the barriers of time and space. The assumption that it is possible to 'publish' the monuments of the past as printed images was undoubtedly shared by a wide range of architects and scholars, and yet that confidence masks important divisions in the antiquarian community. Not only was the publication of monuments motivated by radically different agendas, from preserving the memory of decaying artefacts to boosting the value of an individual's collection, but the act of representation required a fundamental choice between textualizing monuments or attempting to reproduce their materiality. This introduces a fundamental dilemma which is a core theme of this volume. On the one hand technologies of printing enabled an almost photographic facsimile which could capture the original monument in all its temporal vulnerability – an aesthetic practice which made time visible. On the other hand, the rejection of facsimile or accurate rendition of the current state of a monument in favour of a representation that decontextualized and/or reconstructed it was an aesthetic practice which instead favoured the mythological and the universal in an attempt to dignify the study of the past.

Maria Grazia Lolla explores the extremes to which that choice might push the individual through the different approaches within a single decade of

Winckelmann's major work, *Monumenti antichi inediti*, and the finally abortive attempt of the Society of Antiquaries to produce a facsimile of the Domesday Book. Winckelmann's great volume is, of course, notorious for the poor quality of its engraved images and its lack of interest in the physicality of the monuments he records. Ostensibly a volume which records the great monuments under his care in the collection of the Pope, Clement XIII, Winckelmann chose instead to make physical monuments totally subservient to verbal texts. Indeed, his insistence on reading the iconography of monuments only in order to illuminate ancient texts saw the production of a volume in which engravings were not only inaccurate and aesthetically dull, but where bas-reliefs, statues and even paintings become almost indistinguishable. Removing ancient monuments from their historical and material contexts, Winckelmann insists that the material past is only of value in so far as its study aspires to the status of poetry. As Lolla argues, this deliberate attempt to resist the materiality of the past may then be understood as an attempt to raise the status of antiquarianism by rejecting a misplaced obsession with physical remains, an obsession which risks losing sight of higher goals amongst the discarded rubbish of an earlier age.

If Winckelmann's radical rejection of physical antiquities represents a rejection also of the engraving's ability to tell us anything useful about the past, the same decade saw an alternative extreme in the attempts of the Society of Antiquaries to reproduce Britain's classic historical document, the Domesday Book. Originally conceived by Parliament, the project had passed on to the Society in 1768. At the heart of the debate was the inevitable question of accuracy. Moveable type was soon found to be unsatisfactory for its inability to reproduce the sheer range of pen strokes, different-sized letters, spacing and so on; moreover, as the questioning of various printers made clear, editorial decisions about which characters were to be forged as type inevitably came between the original and its reproduction. Engraving – the only other real alternative for multiple production – was also found to be wanting, however: as the Society discovered in its exhaustive interviews, a facsimile could not be and could not reproduce all aspects of the original. As Lolla argues, what these debates represent is not simply an obsession with the physical object and its accurate reproduction, but a recognition that a true facsimile (if such a thing were possible) would preserve for the future those things which the current generation was unable to comprehend. If this reverses the values of Winckelmann by insisting on the importance of the original and its accurate reproduction, it also insists that in the future there will be new ways of seeing the past and that the visual object – even if that object is an antique text – holds within it an alternative to the traditions of text-based scholarship. Implicit, then, in the Society's inquiries was a belief in the value of the visual object as distinct from, and as a rival to, a study of antiquity based on textual evidence.

The resonance between both the verbal and the visual and between the opposing aesthetic practices used in the representation of antiquity can be seen to cohere around representations of Paestum and the Graeco-Roman controversy during the eighteenth century. Drawing on the highly influential but disparate images of Paestum, all of which relate to studies produced by Count Gazola, Dana Arnold argues that in the fluidity of these prints' afterlife and social use we can begin to see a visual history which we might separate from the dominance of the verbal. If textual studies tend to produce historical narratives that favour the idea of 'progress' in Western culture, we might also argue that many architectural images follow that model in their insistence on a form of abstraction and reduction which aims to impose order on the 'inexact reality' of the remains of ancient architecture. For Arnold, however, Gazola's images – free from demonstrable sequence or progression – allow us to trace a narrative of visual and emotional history quite independent of such constraints. They express an emotive, psychological response to ruins which is outside of verbal expression and which sets them apart from the rationalist structure used by others to record the temples. In this way images of the temples at Paestum allow us to consider the role that prints – both as individual images and as assemblages or collections of images – played in the construction of visual histories. More obliquely, these images allow us to consider the impact of the printing press – the firm means of mechanically reproducing an image – on the idea of history itself.

One further possibility, in addition to the single print or assemblage of different images of the same subject, was that of the multi-informational image adopted by Piranesi and employed again some decades later by Hoüel in his *Voyage pittoresque*. During the 1750s and 1760s, Piranesi took to illustrating architectural remains by combining on a single sheet different types and scales of representation. There was some precedent for this in cartography and, indeed, in antiquarian publications, but what marks these images out is not only the range of different kinds of information they made available but also the recognition of gaps in historical knowledge and the need to imagine connections which were not otherwise visible. By juxtaposing a mass of competing and sometimes apparently contradictory verbal and visual information, Piranesi offered a lost past which might be brought back into existence by seeing the connections that others had not yet made. As other essays in this volume also demonstrate, Piranesi's method did not prove popular. It was, however, imitated to some extent by Hoüel and, as Susan Dixon argues, the attraction for Hoüel was that in his attempt to describe a total culture – including not only ancient monuments but the geology, ethnography, economics and commerce of a region – the multi-informational image allows for the wide range of subjects with which the pittoresque traveller engages. Notably, as with Piranesi before him, the weight of Hoüel's method falls on the image as the prime means of ordering current knowledge: the text here serves largely in a supporting role as a description of those images. Thus, what is at stake once again is the structure of knowledge and the means of its representation. Piranesi's multi-information images offered the past as a specific time and place and made the artist the discoverer of a lost world. What was deemed lost in the ancient world, however, was to be radically altered by the French at the very beginning of the nineteenth century, as demonstrated in Abigail Harrison Moore's essay, which comes later in the volume.

Returning our attention to antiquarianism in Britain, it may seem that during the eighteenth century there was a clear division between those who supported a return to the architectural styles of ancient Greece and Rome and those who turned instead to the native antiquities of medieval Europe. As Andrew Kennedy argues, however, such a neat division is far from certain and we should be wary of supposing an unbridgeable gap between the architecture based on these perceived aesthetic preferences. Indeed, if it were so, it would seem difficult to explain why several prominent followers of the style associated with improvement and modernity, albeit that this was based on Graeco-Roman architecture, might subscribe to publications on medieval as well as Romano-British antiquities. Focusing on the brothers Samuel and Nathaniel Buck, their programme of recording the antiquities of Britain and the subscribers to their multi-volume works, Kennedy notes that in their publications antiquities could be seen alongside contemporary improvements. While these two elements could be seen as contrary, Kennedy argues that they might also be understood as complementary, essentially parts of one larger national venture. That venture, he suggests, can be seen in a range of works, including the travels of Defoe and the early antiquarian inquiries of William Stukeley. In his tours, Defoe saw the importance of the historic landscape to an understanding of its contemporary face.

Cohering around the itinerary of the individual traveller, the landscape becomes fruitful of instruction once the personal experience of the traveller is itself classified and ordered. Stukeley was to claim that his prints served just this purpose by turning an unmeaning variety into orderly classification. The print here becomes both an index of the historic landscape and of the individual's engagement with that landscape, and if his engravings failed to live up to his hopes, he nevertheless asserted, 'It is evident how proper engravings are to preserve the memory of things, and how much better an idea they convey to the mind than written descriptions.' Stukeley's itineraries recreate the traveller's own experience of travelling across the country and seeing a ruin for the first time. What complicates that, however, is the recognition of the individual's own personal engagement with the materialness of the past and the ambiguity of that engagement, its inability to step outside the modern moment even as it searches for a sense of separation as a welcome relief from an all-too-insistent present. If the prints Stukeley produced finally failed in their attempts to index the historical landscape, Kennedy argues that this was, nevertheless, the task set for themselves by Samuel and Nathaniel Buck. The accusation of being lost in the past was, of course, commonly hurled at those who studied antiquities, and especially British antiquities, but the Bucks' attempt to produce a comprehensive series of views of towns and antiquities should alert us to a sense of the antique as not merely a vestige, but as an integral part of the contemporary world.

William Stukeley's claim that engravings may act as an index of knowledge became increasingly apparent in the insistence of antiquarian scholars on accuracy and systematic display in the latter half of the eighteenth century. Accordingly, Sam Smiles argues that central to antiquarian research from the 1760s onwards is a drive towards images as information, which sees a confidence in empirical observation producing accurate records of visual data, as a means of amending or even supplanting textual sources. Smiles examines a development in eighteenth-century understanding of medieval architecture, when the emergence of empirical observation can be witnessed taking shape as a new investigative methodology. Here, learning to look at medieval buildings, seeing them as repositories of historical data from which inferences can be drawn, is part of a development in antiquarian scholarship from the middle years of the eighteenth century onwards.

The accurate recording and interpretation of visual evidence characterized one of the most important innovations in antiquarian method, bidding by these means to offer a secure stock of material data as a counter-weight to hearsay and traditional written accounts. A detailed consideration of the recuperation of Exeter cathedral's building history, the conjunction of detailed archival records with eighteenth-century scholars able to make proper use of them, places the examination of the building's history at the heart of the antiquarian endeavour. The balance struck there between textual and material evidence helps to illuminate how the methodology of medievalist research changed during the eighteenth century. In particular, it is in the work of Richard Gough, who was himself heavily influenced by Montfaucon's use of illustrations to give clarity and order to what might otherwise appear the confusions of the classical past. He recognized the need to place antiquarian knowledge of the medieval past into an orderly and ordering structure in order to avoid the common complaint that antiquarianism simply reproduced the rubbish and confusion of the random traces from which it drew. However, as Smiles notes, what makes Gough's work radical is not simply the attempt to produce order from chaos, but to move beyond Montfaucon's model by giving visual evidence greater weight than secondary textual sources. Rather than using illustrations to support an apparently known history, Gough argued that empirical observation of visual evidence could challenge the received wisdom of antiquity's textual sources. This inevitably put a huge burden on the antiquarian engraver and Gough was far from alone in bewailing the lack of talented engravers outside London and indeed the lack of engravers with any interest in antiquities at all. It is for this reason that John Carter, the first draughtsman to be appointed by the Society of Antiquaries, was to be a crucial figure. Carter was the first to take up the challenge of Gough's need for visual accuracy and, like Gough, was to insist upon stripping away the affective tropes of picturesque composition in order to create once again that 'neutral' style. As with Gough, however, the crucial point here is that Carter's images ask for more than this, in that they invite judgement of a culture based on their visual impact rather than on the discursive context in which they are placed. For Smiles, then, what this amounts to is a demonstration of the increasing importance of visual illustration as itself a form of knowledge separate from a traditional antiquarian reliance on textual precedent.

As Smiles notes, the stress on visual accuracy was to gain in influence but it was hardly the norm by the end of the eighteenth century, even if accuracy and fidelity were paid increasing lip-service. Francis Grose, the larger-than-life popularizer of antiquities and the force behind well over a thousand antiquarian images, could be found amongst those appropriating the language to their own ends. Grose's many works provided low-cost images of the antiquities of England and Wales, and while he came close to Gough in his claims for the fidelity of those images, Gough and others were emphatically unimpressed. Indeed, it is Grose who perhaps more than others came to represent that picturesque and haphazard approach to the recording of antiquities from which Smiles seeks to distinguish Gough and Carter. It is tempting, therefore, to dismiss Grose as a mere popularizer and a charlatan; but to do so is to miss another crucial aspect of representations of antique monuments in the eighteenth century. Bending argues that while Grose's images fail to meet the standards of a Gough or a Carter, they do open up to a wider national public the antiquities of their native land. As we shall see in Abigail Harrison Moore's discussion of the work of Denon, the use of an apparently 'neutral' method of representation can itself be highly politicized in its exclusion of all but an educated élite. Grose was to aim at a wider market but a market which might not wish to see itself in that way. Central to his venture is at once the commodification of the past and an attempt to represent that commodification as nothing of the kind. As Bending argues, if Grose sets about repackaging the ancient as the modern, the old as the new – a now classic act of consumerism – he works hard also to deny that activity, and does so with the language of scholarship and accuracy. Thus Bending suggests that while Grose seeks to distinguish his publications from other commercial ventures, his cheaply produced and mass-marketed images and texts finally demonstrate an antiquarian past which repeatedly collapses into a commercial present and a distinction between money and aesthetic value which can never be maintained. While Carter and Gough produce high-quality, high-cost images for a self-selecting group, Grose makes the antique past available to a wide audience, and an audience which can find itself a connection with the national past in the very act of consumer aesthetics.

There is no doubt, then, of the importance of the trend in the period towards an increasing interest in the accurate representation of the antique past and the adoption of a style which claims to be 'neutral'. However, it is clear that such claims to neutrality must inevitably carry their own political freight. As Abigail Harrison Moore argues, the work of Dominique-Vivant Denon in Napoleonic France makes that case most forcefully. Denon took part in the massive French operation of mapping and 'making known' the antiquities of Egypt in the period after Napoleon's invasion. Turning once again to a scientific language of neutral observation, Denon sets about reducing, abstracting and restructuring Egypt while also drawing on the European conventions of picturesque aesthetics. Both the use of the picturesque to commodify and appropriate the past, and the language of scientific neutrality, are moves which we have seen before: Denon's work forms part of what we must now understand as an attempt to legitimize the wholesale raiding of Egyptian treasures for the collections of imperial France and the appropriation of a language of conservation and careful management in order to justify French expansionism and indeed France itself as a culturally superior nation. Denon, like many others considered in this volume, constructs an ancient culture which is at once exotically separate from, and yet comfortably supportive of, his own account of the modern world. However, as Harrison Moore demonstrates, this 'neutral' style adopted by Denon in his attempts to bring Egypt to the French public should not necessarily be associated with Benjamin's assumption that mass-production and dissemination inevitably leads to democratization. As Harrison Moore notes, set against that democratizing impulse we must recognize élite culture's attempts to shore itself up and to find new ways of asserting its authority. Thus Harrison Moore argues, the very abstraction and reduction involved in Denon's scientific language could ultimately exclude all but an educated minority: that is, the cultural competence required to read such images inevitably becomes a demonstration not simply of taste but, in Bourdieu's terms, of taste as a means of legitimating social difference.[5] Denon's assumed neutrality brings with it a further assumption that the ancient world can be mapped and known by its visual representations. It brings with it also the problem of what kinds of information can be represented in any particular image. We have seen alternative approaches to this in the various forms of architectural abstraction, picturesque appropriation and verbal assimilation of the image. The belief that ancient cultures hold lessons for the modern world is no doubt perennial, but what that culture might be, and just what might be learned from it, remains constantly troubled. The excavations at Rome and Pompeii and the images which sprang from them undoubtedly produced a new interest in Roman civic life, just as Denon's work offered Egypt to a new French oligarchy in the early years of the nineteenth century. Winckelmann's striking lack of interest in the materiality of the past, as discussed by Lolla, was met by a range of attempts to reproduce that materiality as accurately as possible. In this way attempts to reconstruct the past from its fading traces tend to divide over textual and visual sources.

And we return to Winckelmann, or at least his methods of investigating and representing the past, in the concluding essay in this volume. In his *Specimens of Antient Sculpture*, Richard Payne Knight attempted to produce a chronology of stylistic change in antique sculpture, including architectural sculpture, and was inspired by Winckelmann's methods, but placed the physical object far more firmly at the centre of attention. Knight's project foundered when he failed to recognize the Parthenon sculptures as genuine fifth-century BC work: as Andrew Ballantyne argues, from this point on the authority of his attempted chronology became suspect. However, in the second (posthumous) volume of his commentary Knight was to set out his vision of ancient Greek culture and its worth. Knight argued that mimesis was at the heart of civilization, its driving force and that which moved man on from a state of savagery. Conversely, as Ballantyne notes, this confidence in the forward motion of civilization was tempered by his recognition of the loss that it inevitably entailed. Drawing on Adam Smith's account of the division of labour, with its specialization and mass production, Knight looks back appreciatively to a pre-industrial savage state, a state in which the creativity of everyday life could produce its own works of beauty. However, for Knight, as individual creation is replaced by mass production, and as the mechanical drudgery of the artisan becomes the norm, such harmonious life becomes impossible. There is some irony in this, of course, for the set of fine engraved prints published with his commentary are themselves the mark of an increasingly industrialized process of mass production. Knight can offer his reader not the originals here but a highly sophisticated representation of the original. Working at one remove, the images which accompany Knight's text are in themselves the physical demonstration of a harmonious human community which seems no longer possible; they become objects of nostalgia for the modern world.

The essays in this volume explore the struggles which emerge from a newly forming language of architectural representation. Attempts to publish the monuments of the past in a coherent two-dimensional form consistently face the problem of their own authority, their place in a modern world of consumer aesthetics and the competing chronologies with which they inevitably engage. While frequent attempts were made to adopt a 'neutral' language of objective

9

observation, the essays in this volume demonstrate the multiple ways in which that apparent neutrality is co-opted to the particular ends of the modern world. Equally, while Benjamin's insight into the mass-produced image and the disjunction between the original and its 'aura' might suggest a democratizing force at one with a newly forming public sphere, these essays also point to the ways in which that process can be resisted. Underlying all of this is the problem of accurate representation. What each of these essays demonstrates in a different context is that there remains a radical disjunction between a belief in the empirical observation embodied in accurate measurement and the fundamental unknowableness of the past. Multi-informational images jostle with deeply shaded elevations and peopled perspectives in their attempts to make the past knowable. While those attempts rely at times on the documentary evidence of historical sources, what we also see is the increasing ability of the antique print to tell its own story, a story often quite independent from those textual accounts which had for so long dominated the past.

Notes

1 Walter Benjamin, 'The Work of Art in the Age of Mechanical Reproduction', in *Illuminations*, ed. Hannah Arendt, trans. Harry Zohn, London: Fontana, 1973, pp. 211–44.
2 See Tim Clayton, *The English Print, 1688–1802*, New Haven and London: Yale University Press, 1998.
3 See, for instance, Jürgen Habermas, *The Structural Transformation of the Public Sphere: An Inquiry into a Category of Bourgeois Society*, trans. Thomas Burger & Frederick Lawrence, Cambridge: Polity Press, 1989.
4 Susan Stewart, *On Longing: narratives of the miniature, the gigantic, the souvenir, the collection*, Baltimore: Johns Hopkins University Press, 1984; rpt Durham: Duke University Press; and see also Susan Pearce, *On Collecting: An investigation into collecting in the European tradition*, London: Routledge, 1995.
5 Pierre Bourdieu, *Distinction: A Social Critique of the Judgement of Taste*, trans. Richard Nice, London, 1984.

2

Monuments and Texts:
Antiquarianism and the beauty of antiquity

Maria Grazia Lolla

In the spring of 1767, just about a year before he was murdered in mysterious circumstances,[1] Johann Joachim Winckelmann published his last work, *Monumenti antichi inediti*, or, as he referred to it throughout his correspondence, his 'great Italian work'. Although the book did not get the recognition that its author had hoped for and has been much neglected by modern scholars, *Monumenti antichi inediti* was the book that Winckelmann viewed as the culmination of his scholarly career and on which he staked his hopes of financial independence.[2] It was also the book which, by promising to add another volume of 'previously unpublished monuments' to an already copious list, encapsulated one of the most ordinary and most problematic aspects of antiquarianism: its commitment to publishing monuments.

Known as the founders of the science of monuments, antiquaries had been routinely publishing monuments since the beginning of the Renaissance. Indeed, they had published at such a pace that publishing, as much as collecting or studying monuments, could be counted amongst the defining features of antiquarianism. There hardly existed a collection of antiquities that was not accompanied by a published version, or a society of antiquaries that had not at some time sponsored the publication of monuments, declared itself into existence by publishing a monument, or even been founded with the specific purpose of publishing monuments. By publishing monuments – by the thousands, in fact – antiquaries were acting on the basis of the commonplace assumption that monuments could be published by way of engraving just as texts could by way of moveable type. Everybody knew, as the nineteenth-century historian of engraving Giuseppe Longhi put it, that 'calcography is for the liberal arts what typography is for literature and science.'[3] Printing and engraving were analogous in that both were icons of modernity – indeed, of the superiority of the moderns over the ancients; both were valued for being instrumental to the advancement of knowledge because they multiplied access to sources; and both were believed to be capable of collapsing time and space. Like printing, engraving was known as the means through which scholars could gain knowledge of the ancient world, as it preserved the memory 'of beautiful Pieces of Painting as well as Sculpture, Architecture &c, the originals of which have been destroyed', but was also the

11

means through which 'all mankind in general' could be acquainted with 'whatever is worthy of observation even in the most distant parts of the globe'.[4]

But, however widely and routinely practised, the publication of monuments revealed substantial divisions within the world of antiquarianism. In the first instance, because eighteenth-century definitions of 'monument' were broad enough to include buildings, sculptures, texts and ordinary objects, there was little consensus on what kind of monuments were most worthy of publication. The reasons for publishing monuments were accordingly wide-ranging and often incompatible. Where some focused on inscriptions or books, others favoured objects. And where some antiquaries published monuments to advertise their collections or boost the value of the originals, others concentrated on public buildings and were moved to publishing by the desire to preserve the memory of artefacts doomed to disappearance. Some hoped to advance the study of art and literature, some that of history and archaeology. More importantly, despite the seeming confidence with which antiquaries published monuments, monuments were simply not subject to unproblematic publication. To be reproduced on the page and contained between the covers of a book, all monuments – texts included – had to undergo some degree of transformation. Antiquaries were faced with the choice of either textualizing monuments – turning monuments from visual or tactile objects into reading material – or reproducing their materiality – even if the monument was a text. The process of reproduction was itself a process of matching technological possibilities to scholarly desiderata, and the contrasting ways that various antiquaries went about that process reveal the conflicting versions of scholarship and aesthetics that informed their representational choices. As the following discussion of Winckelmann's *Monumenti antichi inediti* and the projected facsimile of the Domesday Book under the direction of the London Society of Antiquaries will show, the choice to bypass or reproduce the materiality of monuments raised a host of questions: about scholarship at large; about what was worthy of scholarly investigation and aesthetic appreciation; about the essence of monuments and their value; about their physical boundaries and the best means of their reproduction.

Winckelmann is not often remembered as 'a born antiquary'.[5] Quite the contrary: he is usually lauded for having rescued antiquarianism from its dullness and intellectual cowardice while giving birth to the new discipline of art history. But despite efforts – his own and those of modern scholars – to set him above the underachieving caste of antiquaries, Winckelmann was part of the antiquarian culture of the eighteenth century, which he, like other antiquaries, by turns absorbed and shaped. Before being the author of the first art history written according to the principles of the Enlightenment and the most influential theoretician of neoclassical aesthetics, Winckelmann had been recognized as the most accomplished antiquarian of his time. He was, as the frontispiece of his *History of the Art of Antiquity* (1764) advertised, the Prefect of the Vatican Antiquities under Pope Clement XIII and a fellow of both the London Society of Antiquaries and the Etruscan Academy. He was also the author of works such as the *Description des pierres gravées du feu Baron de Stosch* (1760), a catalogue raisonné of a private collection of gems, and, above all, *Monumenti antichi inediti*, a book in which Winckelmann presented himself in the quintessentially antiquarian guise of publisher of monuments, and which Winckelmann wrote in Italian specifically to conquer a broad international antiquarian audience.[6] *Monumenti antichi inediti* was indeed the work that had 'secured him the esteem of antiquaries' in England[7] and, according to the less charitable Christian Gottlob Heyne, the work that had marked Winckelmann's relapse into the bad habits of antiquarianism.[8]

Despite the fact that as a publisher of monuments Winckelmann advertised his capacity of Prefect of the Roman antiquities and despite the fact that the book grew to include more than 200 plates, Winckelmann quickly dispelled the illusion that his aim in publishing monuments was to inform the world about the latest archaeological finds or, still less, to publish engravings. Perhaps aware of the polysemous nature of the act of publishing monuments, or perhaps conscious of having chosen a title designed to appeal to the antiquarian market, in a dense preface, Winckelmann 'felt compelled' to provide his readers with a definition of his chosen title and with a clear outline of his ambitious agenda, or, as he put it, to account for the 'reasons' that made him undertake the work, the 'monuments' that he published, and, finally, the 'method' he had followed in illustrating the same monuments.[9] This introductory matter left little doubt that, far from setting out to reproduce the material remains of the past, Winckelmann was trying to steer antiquarianism away from monuments and towards texts – indeed, to make monuments indistinguishable from texts.

Winckelmann's rather unconventional explanation of the title 'ancient unpublished monuments' gave readers a first sense of his desire to consider monuments only in so far as they occupied a literary space. If 'unpublished' was to be taken in its broad (and idiosyncratic) sense of possibly already published, although 'not considered before in relation to the subject' (xvi), or 'little known or obscure' (xxiv), 'ancient monuments' was to be understood narrowly as 'statues, marble and terracotta bas-reliefs, gems and paintings' (xvi). But having chosen to focus on the 'subject figured on monuments', in order to keep the book within a reasonable size, Winckelmann further narrowed his definition of monuments to those that represented ancient (Greek) mythology and, even more specifically, 'the most important events in the *Iliad* and *Odyssey*' (xvi). And, while he condescended to discuss a handful of monuments relating to Greek and Roman history, he explicitly declined to consider coins, medals and public monuments commemorating emperors (xix).

His two 'reasons' for publishing thusly defined monuments confirmed his literary bias. First was his desire to belie the incompetence and cowardice of those antiquaries (he mentioned Boissard, Bellori and, especially, Montfaucon) who had either favoured monuments that hardly needed explanation or published monuments because of their beauty and elegance rather than for their 'subject' or 'erudition' (xv) – who had published monuments as objects or artefacts, that is, rather than as texts. The second, and most important, reason was, conversely, that because his daily experience with ancient monuments had taught him that a large number of *texts* could be 'corrected and illustrated' with the aid of monuments, he aspired to prove that monuments were vital to the understanding of ancient literature (xv–xvi). Surpassing all those who had supported the generic 'usefulness' of monuments, Winckelmann argued that without the assistance of antiquaries, philologists were not equipped to make new discoveries, for those few

13

texts that were not of questionable authenticity had been 'squeezed like lemons' to such an extent that they could yield no new information (xvi). And reiterating an opinion that he had already voiced in the *Remarks on the History of Art* (1767), he rather bluntly stated that the primary use of monuments was shedding light on the literature of the time (xvi).[10]

Both Winckelmann's selection of monuments and his stated reasons for publishing them made it clear that publishing a monument did not mean issuing an accurate engraving. Rather it meant explaining its iconography. What made a monument into a monument worth publishing were its literary allusions and what set his collection above other similar repositories were the author's insights into the literary content of monuments and his superior command of the literature of the ancients. Winckelmann's propensity to make monuments into vehicles of texts is even more patent in his chosen 'method'. As he explained in the preface, the two related 'maxims' that had guided his research were not to assume that the subject of ancient monuments was either arbitrary or historical, but, assuming instead that it was mythological, to trace the images chosen by ancient artists 'back to mythology' (xvii).[11] Thus, where others, including himself in an earlier work, had seen merely a young girl pouring water on the tomb of her parents, he now saw 'Electra, daughter of Agamemnon, honouring her dead father' (xvii–xviii). Although he acknowledged that neither maxim was infallible – indeed they were so fallible that he was forced to exclude monuments of historical subject from his selection – giving a taste of what was to follow in the book, Winckelmann dedicated a large portion of the preface to proving that the current historical interpretation of several monuments was erroneous, while maintaining that the only history that made its way into monuments was that which bordered on mythology (xvi–xxii). When he anticipated Keats's pressing and disquieting questions on seeing the enigmatic Grecian Urn: 'What men or gods are these? What maidens loth?/ What mad pursuit? What struggle to escape?/ What pipes and timbrels? What wild ecstasy?', Winckelmann had no doubts: the answer was in the literature and mythology of the ancients. There any unnamed 'bride', 'youth', or 'mysterious priest' would find a name and a story.[12]

Having argued with characteristic inflexibility, that the 'truth' was that 'Homer was the great teacher of ancient artists', and that 'he who wishes to understand the meaning of their images should refer to the ancient poet himself' (xix), in the section of the book dedicated to the illustration of monuments, Winckelmann confidently applied himself to voicing the mute poetry of monuments and to pointing out the correspondences between mythology and figurative arts. Writing about Diana, for instance, Winckelmann recalled that 'both the moon and the sun are said by the poets to hide in the ocean when they disappear from our horizon.' Turning to the monument, he remarked that 'this poetic image is here symbolized by the moon over a venerable bearded head, which represents the father Ocean, where the moon dives when she goes down and extinguishes the light of Fosforus.' (II, 24) Likewise, in the section dedicated to Pallas, having recounted that Pallas 'used to amuse herself playing the flutes and that by playing her cheeks swoll and disfigured her face', Wincklemann went on to say that 'the same story is in part represented on our painting.' (II, 20) Or, having related that in Ovid's account Niobe's children were struck by Apollo's darts while they were riding horses, Winckelmann noted that 'on horseback, indeed, can be seen her children on our marbles.' (II, 119)

More often, rather than simply illustrating the monument at hand, Winckelmann dilated upon the meaning of a myth, or an episode in the Homeric poems, supplementing his tales and arguments with generous quotations and giving the impression that monuments furnished a pretext to revisit favourite stories or air his erudition. About Hebe, for instance, Winckelmann began by identifying her as the 'daughter of Juno and goddess of youth' and by recalling that 'she was elected to the task of offering nectar at the table of the gods, a task previously assigned to Mercury.' Before commenting on the specific representation of Hebe, Winckelmann proceeded to narrate Hebe's vicissitudes at length:

> After some time Hebe was declared unsuited to fulfil this task because she unluckily fell ungracefully and indecently in front of the gods, spilling the nectar. Mortified at being deprived of this honorific position for no real offence, she threw herself at the feet of her mother and the other goddesses asking to be forgiven for her carelessness. But Jupiter had already assigned this task to Ganymede and all Hebe's prayers were useless.

The fact that Hebe was wearing a short dress provided the occasion for Winckelmann to mention a bas-relief and a bronze statue of young servants 'in similarly short dress', known as Camilli, and to explain that Camillus was the Etruscan word for servant; Hebe's dishevelled hair led Winckelmann to refer to female masks of supplicants similarly decorated with long hair. To enable his readers to understand Hebe's story, Winckelmann went on to relate the myth of Ceres and the Bona Dea and to expand in a long digression on the significance of 'a figure with flapping cloth', which Winckelmann interpreted as an allusion to Iris. Iris, Winckelmann suggested,

> is represented with such a cloth perhaps as a hint to the speed with which she, as a messenger of the gods (*iros* meaning messenger), and in particular as deliverer of bad news carries out their orders; and maybe at the same time that cloth flapping as if moved by the wind alludes to her amorous union with Zefirus, from which Love is said to have been born. In this act she seems to have brought the news that Hebe's task was passed onto Ganymede.

Finally, suggesting that the bas-relief shows Vesta interceding with Jupiter on behalf of Hebe, Winckelmann discussed various opinions of the relationship between Vesta and Jupiter as well as the solemn invocation that the ancient peoples of Latium made to Jupiter and Vesta together (II, xvi–xviii).

A perhaps extreme example of Winckelmann's reading of the monuments is provided by the 'Description of the Torso Belvedere', an early piece that he wrote shortly after arriving in Rome for a publication that can be seen as the beginning of *Monumenti*. Looking at what was left of a statue of Hercules, which admittedly appeared as 'nothing more than a shapeless stone', Winckelmann 'saw', in what almost amounts to an hallucination, the poetry of the ancients:

> I see in the robust profile of that body the undomitable strength of him who won over the terrible giants who rebelled against the gods, and whom

he knocked out in the Flegrean Fields ... I cannot contemplate the little
that is left of his shoulder without remembering that on his large and
robust body rested all the weight of the celestial spheres ... Such a chest
must be the one under which the giant Anteus and the three-bodied Gerion
suffocated.[13]

What Winckelmann saw most clearly in the monument were poetry and
mythology, a vision that preceded the promise of publishing an unpublished
monument. Acting on the assumption that monuments were unstable compounds
generated by texts, Winckelmann dedicated himself to reducing the monuments
back to their original state of texts – replacing their missing pieces with the fleshy
possibility of mythology.

As a whole, the book reads more like a treatise on mythology and ancient
literature occasionally illustrated by references to surviving monuments than as a
detailed discussion of individual objects (the format chosen by all his successors
who adopted the title of 'monumenti antichi inediti' for their publications).[14] In
fact, not only are monuments liquidated in most entries with clauses such as
'such indeed appears to be represented in this monument', which signals a desire
to find a confirmation of a theory of mythology in a given monument rather than
to analyse a specific artefact. Hardly ever does Winckelmann focus on a
supposedly previously unpublished monument, most of the entry instead being
taken up by the evocation of artefacts of similar iconography, whether published
or unpublished. It does not come as a surprise that *Monumenti antichi inediti*
was originally entitled 'Explanation of the difficult points of the mythology,
customs and history of the Ancients, taken from unpublished ancient monuments'.[15] Even the table of contents reveals the extent to which Winckelmann's
primary focus was literary. The list of books quoted came first, followed by that
of 'authors corrected and explained' and by the subject index. Last was the
catalogue of the monuments discussed with their respective location. Nowhere,
for all the boasted thoroughness and practicality of the indexes, was there a list
of the engravings.

Indeed, it is perhaps the engravings that reveal most the extent to which
Winckelmann was willing to bypass the objects themselves in favour of their
putative narrative content. The plates were notoriously inaccurate and pathetic-
ally unattractive; they were so mercilessly criticized, even by Winckelmann's
warmest admirers, that in the first edition of Winckelmann's collected works,
Monumenti antichi inediti was described as an elegant book except for the
engravings.[16] The plates also strike the reader as tokenistic. Excluded from the
index, devoid of captions, bound separately from the text, and accessible only via
a text that relied heavily on the discussion of monuments other than those
reproduced in the engravings, the plates appear somewhat accessory. (They were
indeed accessory, if we consider that Winckelmann had planned to sell 200 of the
600 printed copies without plates.)[17] Needless to say, the engravers did not play a
major role in the project. Only one of the 200 or so plates was signed.[18]
Winckelmann did not acknowledge the work of the engraver anywhere in the
book, unlike other antiquaries, his predecessor as keeper of the Vatican antiquities, Pietro Bellori, for one, whose name appeared on the title page together

with that of the engraver Pietro Santi Bartoli, or Jean Jacques Boissard, whose name and effigy appeared together with that of the engraver Theodore de Bry. The engravers are not even mentioned by name in his correspondence. After his falling out with the renowned engraver Giovanni Casanova,[19] who had initially been financially involved in the enterprise, Winckelmann hired a variety of engravers and draughtsmen who were usually referred to by number rather than by name.[20] To avoid, perhaps, naming the engravers, Winckelmann often referred to the process of illustrating in the passive voice: 'the plates are being drawn and engraved again.'[21]

In *Monumenti antichi inediti* the degradation of the engraver went hand in hand with the devaluation of the material and visual aspect of monuments. In the case of objects of remarkable size, shape or material, Winckelmann hastened to make clear that his interest was solely iconographic (II, 80). In contrast with other repositories of published monuments, such as the *Collection of Etruscan, Greek and Roman Antiquities from the Cabinet of the Honble Wm Hamilton* (1766–67), which offered some representations 'in the perspective' and 'in profile ..., where all its parts are measured',[22] in *Monumenti antichi inediti* vases were characteristically reproduced in split engravings with a rough rendering of the object in the upper part and a magnified version of the scene depicted on the bottom. Only occasionally did Winckelmann mention the shape and the material of the monument in question, and when he did, he rarely went beyond notations such as 'terracotta bas-relief', 'mosaic', 'painting'. Measurements were, of course, never included, as, from an iconographic point of view, size and scale did not matter, a huge bas-relief and a gem being perfectly comparable.[23] Winckelmann both devalued the original artefacts through undignified representations and even denied monuments a decorative function by publishing separate erudite explanations of those monuments which were included in the book only to fill empty spaces (ix–xii). Having torn monuments from their material, historical and political context, and consigned them to the timeless regions of poetry and mythology, it is not surprising that the engravings bear hardly any memory of the object. So little effort is made at emphasizing the third dimension or the texture of the object and so little consistency is shown in the choice of representational conventions that it is often very difficult to tell a bas-relief from a painting or a mosaic or, sometimes, a free-standing statue.[24]

Although Winckelmann was not alone in publishing engravings that would only reproduce the iconography of original monuments,[25] these representational choices are a precious index of a specific approach to antiquity, one for which the engravers themselves can hardly be held responsible. As Michel Melot has put it, 'It has often been pointed out that intransigent Neo-Classicism was able to refer to antique art only through the already idealized view of it engraved by academic prints. But the engraver in turn ... saw antique art through the eyes of the theorists of his own time.'[26] The elusively immaterial engravings of *Monumenti antichi inediti* are powerful icons of both Winckelmann's theory of monuments and his theory of scholarship. *Monumenti antichi inediti*'s 'literary engravings' match perfectly Winckelmann's declared intent to advance the study of philology, elucidate ancient literature and prove that monuments are generated by texts and hardly distinguishable from them. Barely speaking to the senses and minimally

17

dependent on the craft of artisans, such engravings more generally fit into what Barbara Maria Stafford has called 'a system of aesthetics that values impalpability'.[27] But knowing that antiquarianism's bad reputation was so closely tied to its misplaced fascination with the inessential materiality of the past – the bricks, the rubbish, the rust and the mould of antiquity – it is hard not to read in Winckelmann's dematerialized monuments and in his negligent attitude to the representation of monuments an effort to nobilitate the study of antiquities. As a book ultimately aimed at proving that antiquarianism had more in common with poetry than with the 'bricks and rubbish' with which it was usually associated, *Monumenti antichi inediti* can be read as the culmination of the tradition of antiquarian studies pioneered earlier in the century in Joseph Addison's *Dialogues upon the Usefulness of Medals* (1726) and Joseph Spence's *Polymetis* (1747), both of which explicitly aimed at salvaging antiquarianism's bad reputation by cleansing monuments from their materiality, freeing them from their compromise with history and power, and, ultimately, making them indistinguishable from the poetry that supposedly originated them. Just as philology itself evolved into respectability, as Carlo Ginzburg has pointed out, through 'the drastic curtailing of what was seen to be relevant' and 'the progressive dematerialization or refinement of texts, a process by which the appeal of the original to our various senses has been purged away', antiquarianism could become respectable by proving its kinship, and subordination, to the more noble study of literature.[28] Indeed, it is by way of contrast to the precedence granted engraving and the reproduction of the materiality of the monuments of the past in another context, the effort of the London Society of Antiquaries to publish a facsimile of the Domesday Book, that Winckelmann's representational policy can be brought into sharpest relief.

In the same years in which, in an effort to turn monuments into texts, Winckelmann published ancient statuary as if monuments were comparable to told tales, the fellows of the London Society of Antiquaries were engaged in the opposite task: they were striving to give adequate visual representation to texts – and, frankly, despairing of ever being able to accomplish their goal. In fact, 1767, the year that saw the publication of Winckelmann's *Monumenti antichi inediti*, was also the year in which the British Parliament allocated funds for the facsimile reproduction of England's most valued medieval document, the Domesday Book.[29] Neatly kept within the pages of the Council minutes of the Society, the diffuse discussion of the various techniques available to produce a facsimile that took place in the rooms of the Society in May 1768 (when Parliament deferred to the Council of the Society to direct the publication of the book) opens a different scenario on the world of publishing monuments from the one offered by *Monumenti antichi inediti*. There, the issue debated was how best to represent the materiality of the monuments of the past; and there, engravers, printers, letter-cutters and paper-makers took centre stage. By providing a unique insight into the culture of the facsimile – an approach to the representation of monuments that, though central to eighteenth-century antiquarianism, has received very little scholarly attention outside the literature on forgery – the record of the negotiations over the production of the facsimile of the Domesday Book further illuminates the relationship between scholarship, aesthetics and the representational choices that shaped antiquarian notions of the past.[30]

It must be said at the outset that by the time the Society of Antiquaries became involved in the publication of *Domesday Book*, the decision to publish the document in facsimile had already been made.[31] In fact a scheme to publish the book by facsimile-cast types was already under way, though it was floundering. The Council of the Society was only called to advise the Treasury on *how* the facsimile should best be produced, whether 'by Types, or by Ingraving'.[32] Moreover, even though printers and engravers were summoned to the apartments of the Society to be interviewed by the Council, and even though, in the final report, the Committee claimed to have 'impartially examined' both printers and engravers,[33] the Council minutes dedicated to the interviews with the several artisans do not contain the advertised equanimous assessment. Instead, having already discussed the issue in an earlier meeting and unanimously decided in favour of the technique of engraving,[34] the fellows agreed upon a set of questions designed to expose the inadequacies of the printing technique to produce a satisfactory facsimile.[35] Hence, whereas printers and type-cutters were questioned, cross-examined (and sometimes scolded), engravers were merely asked to give estimates of the cost and the time required to complete their work. But despite the fact that the minutes do not contain a candid discussion but a set of pretextuous interviews designed to reinforce a preconception – and despite the fact that, in the end, *Domesday Book* was not reproduced in facsimile – the record of the questions that the fellows asked and the answers they received, and, above all, the hostile lectures masquerading as questions that the fellows gave to the various artisans, provide a unique occasion, in which the scholarly and aesthetic needs that the facsimile was to fulfil were explicitly and doggedly articulated.

As the interviews with the several artists abundantly demonstrated, the fellows' most important concern was the unsatisfactory 'degree of accuracy' that could be attained by moveable type. The fact that the shortcomings of their art were obvious to the artisans themselves did not keep the Council of the Society of Antiquaries from relentlessly and impatiently reiterating their rhetorical questions. For instance, when the printer Richardson was asked whether 'he could print a fac-simile Copy of Doomesday Book by Types', he initially answered with a sort of broad mental reservation, that 'He could, provided Types, such as shall be approved of for the purpose, can be formed'. But when asked whether the specimen he had produced was a facsimile, he responded that a true facsimile could not be produced in type on account of 'the Variety of Characters in almost every Page of the Original'. Having firmly elicited the printer's belief that printing could produce only 'A regular, uniform Copy', the committee insisted on asking: 'But Doomesday Book being neither regular nor uniform in the Writing & Characters there used, can a Copy thereof be truly exhibited by Types?' Seemingly oblivious of Richardson's compliant demurral, they pressed on questioning him on the 'Expence, & Time requisite for having Types made to answer all the Variety & Purposes of such a Work'. And when Richardson replied that it was 'So great as not to be ascertained in either Case: 500 Years not being sufficient for making the Types only', the committee nevertheless asked again whether 'supposing Types could be formed, could the Junction and Imbracing of the several Words & Characters, as they stand in the Original, be truly represented?' Richardson's reply that 'Types are incapable of being brought so close together' did not stop the fellows from asking one final time if 'a correct & accurate Copy' could 'be obtained by any kind of Types?' Perhaps the doggedness with which the fellows pressed him to enumerate the shortcomings of his trade, made him summarize what seemed to be the fellows' evident views: 'There will unavoidably be many Faults; no Book that he has yet [seen] printed being without Faults: the Degree of Correctness must depend [in a great measure] upon the Ability, Fidelity, & Exactness of the Person appointed to examine & correct the Work: & Allowance must be made for casual Errors, which it is impossible to guard against.'[36]

Whereas Richardson was made to acknowledge repeatedly the failure of printing to meet the standard of accuracy required by the antiquaries, the next printer to face the fellows, Bowyer, was basically lectured on the virtues of engraving. 'Asked' whether 'ye Errors incidental to Types might not be lessened or prevented, by Engravings made from a traced Copy of the Original?', Bowyer readily agreed that 'a careful Tracing of the Original laid down & Enagraved on Copper Plates, is the only sure, and most effectual Method, of obtaining a faithful Copy, & exact Representation of the Original.'[37] Likewise, those who were responsible for cutting the letters, making the punches, and casting the type, rather than being interviewed, were reprimanded and forced to confess the inadequacy of their trade to the important task of historic preservation. Morgan was rebuked for not observing 'a greater Variety of Character, as well as of Size, for One & the same Letter, than one or two Sorts in the several Pages of the Book', and his specimen dismissed as 'a casual & fortuitous Representation of some Letters & Characters occurring here and there in Domesday Book'.[38] Similarly Cotterell, who had had the temerity to state that it was possible to print a facsimile of the Domesday Book, was quizzed about whether 'he apprehended the right Meaning of the Term *fac-simile*' and subjected to the committee's scalding incredulity when he insisted that he did: 'How then can it be said, that the printed Specimen is an exact Copy & Resemblance of the Original, when most of the Letters & Characters in the one differ so widely from those in the other?'[39]

Perhaps it was the renowned letter-press cutter and founder Caslon who, unable to attend the meeting in person, and without needing to be prompted by the fellows' pressing questions, provided them with the clearest formulation of the hopeless inadequacy of printing to produce a facsimile: 'having ... carefully attended to the Nature of the Work, he deemed it absolutely impracticable to obtain a fac-simile Copy of it by Types; no Sum, nor Time, that could well be limited, being sufficient for such an Undertaking; not even the Number of Years elapsed since the Writing of Doomesday Book.'[40]

To judge by the evidence of their interviews with the printers, the antiquaries went about the business of printing facsimiles with a degree of self-consciousness that belies the commonly accepted notion that they were the unwitting dupes of their own creations. Likewise, when it came to meeting the demands of the fellows, the printers were no less aware of their shortcomings than the inquisitorial fellows themselves. Rather than aspiring forgers, they appeared as honest artisans, realistic about the limits of their art. Both the fellows and the printers, that is, were agreed in treating the question of accuracy as one of degree. Indeed, having opted for the technique of engraving, the fellows harboured no illusion that engravers were able to craft an object that could pass for the original. They set out to inquire into the 'degree of accuracy' and concluded, as they explained in their report to the Treasury, that engraving offered a copy that would only be 'almost as curious as the Original itself',[41] no more and no less than a 'facsimile'. As an imperfect rendering of the original, by definition, in fact, the facsimile expresses only the desire to duplicate an original document, not the fulfilment of that desire. The very etymology of the word (from the Latin 'make similar') intimates the impending failure of the endeavour to produce a perfect duplicate, for all the facsimilists aim to accomplish is approximating by way of asymptote the appearance of the original, in the knowledge that exact duplication is impossible. As Joseph Griegely has put it, 'A facsimile is at best an illusion of iterability: it draws attention to itself as something *factum simile*, as something *much like* an "original", when $x1 \Rightarrow x2$, but $x1 \# x2$. However much two texts are like each other physically or perceptually (whether real or apparent), they are not the same.'[42] Thus, as a necessarily selective version of an original, the facsimile of a text, just like the engraving of a monument, was more a map of scholarly desire – of what was being seen, what was worthy of being preserved, studied or admired, and of what technology could reproduce – than evidence of the facsmilist seeking to smuggle counterfeit copies of original documents or even of the readers' willingness to suspend disbelief.[43]

The fellows' relentless insistence on the inaccuracies of the printed specimen is revealing of what their understanding of 'accuracy' encompassed and what scholarly needs that accuracy was to fulfil. As they put it in their final report, amongst their 'reasons' for rejecting the option of facsimile-cast types were the fact that printing could not adequately reproduce the inequality of the original handwriting, the 'variety of Hands', the personality of the 'different Amanuenses', the 'Abbreviations and Marks', the way letters were 'conjoin'd or tyed together', the 'Size and Shapes of the Letters', the 'form of the Abbreviations', and, finally, the 'different Colours of red and black which appear in many Lines of almost every Page', details that mattered enough to justify their relentless and obstinate questions and the judicial tone assumed during the interview.[44]

Even though the Council did not specify what scholarly need an 'accurate' facsimile was supposed to fulfil, the fact that the accuracy of the specimens was measured to a large extent in their ability to reproduce the handwriting of the document in its fullness is obviously a testimony of the fellows' interest in paleography and, more generally, in the material process by which texts were produced and transmitted – the 'letter' of literature. This field, represented well beyond the exceptional case of *Domesday Book* in the minutes of the Society and in their published transactions, *Archaeologia*, as well as in antiquarian publications in general, was becoming established as worthy of scholarly investigation in its own right and gaining steadily in popularity.[45] Indeed, the publications of the Society abound with communications, especially on epigraphy. In a letter on a Greek inscription that he sent to the Society, Daniel Wray captured the novelty of epigraphy's focus on the process rather than on the result of writing when, at the same time as he confessed his 'mortification' at the thought that the inscription he had come across 'would settle no point of history or chronology, nor illustrate any Grecian custom, civil, or religious; being merely a list of names', he distinguished epigraphy as a discrete and worthy field of inquiry by adding that there was

21

'enough however to excite our curiosity *in the manner of writing*'.[46] Other fellows, more specifically, recounted their struggles with poor copies and voiced their concern for the accurate transmission of 'the manner of writing'.[47] Still other fellows found occasion to express their concern for the accurate transmission of all kinds of documents by sending in their tips on how to produce reliable copies.[48]

There is little doubt, then, that in policing an accurate reproduction of the idiosyncrasies of the handwriting of the Domesday Book, the Council of the Society was speaking in the first instance to a concern often voiced by those fellows who had emphasized the extent to which the very future of the study of the letter of literature was dependent on the production of ever more accurate facsimiles – and extending a policy already operative both in their minutes and in their published transactions, where as a rule, inscriptions and manuscripts were copied in facsimile.[49] But, however important the facsimile was to the advancement of what were to become the separate disciplines of epigraphy, paleography, diplomatics, and, later, the history of the book, it would be wrong to assume that the growing popularity of the facsimile, of which the stir over the reproduction of the Domesday Book was just a single example, was so narrowly focused. As Dean Milles's letter recommending that the Domesday Book be engraved suggested, 'a just and satisfactory representation of the Original' was meant to capture more than the original handwriting. His itemized list of the shortcomings of printing only began with the fact that 'the variety of hands, which occur in it, cannot be faithfully & accurately represented.' It also included the 'number of abbreviating characters being great, various, & peculiarly significative', 'the numerous interlineations' which would be impossible to insert 'in the proper places without lengthening ye Page more than ye paper will allow', the fact that printing could not reproduce 'page for page, & line for line as in the original' and would thus 'totally alter ye form of that book'.[50] Although this version of what a good facsimile was to accomplish might strike the modern reader as unambitious, especially if compared with the impressive achievements of more recent facsimiles, one gets the sense that Milles's list could have gone on for ever. For him, a facsimile worthy of the name was to be able to reproduce the overall visual appearance and make-up of the original, not just give 'an Idea of ye hand of that age'.[51] A facsimile was to preserve all the details of the original, the significance of some of which was not yet even known.[52]

More immediately than speaking the antiquarian scholarly interest in the new field of paleography, the Society's effort to reproduce the largest possible number of the original idiosyncrasies of the Domesday Book signals their commitment to a mode of editing that sought to bypass the mediation of editors in an effort to duplicate the infinite richness of the monuments of the past in order to address the widest possible spectrum of unanticipated – indeed unimaginable – future questions. The facsimile, that is, was the mode of editing of scholars who believed that there was more to an original monument than any single scholar or generation of scholars could hope to comprehend, and who were more interested in safeguarding their possibility of asking ever-new questions of the originals than in investigating any one specific area of the past. Like modern photography, the facsimile was valued as the technology that could catch the original, as it were, unaware and, by unwittingly providing those details on which antiquarian scholarship thrived, allow antiquarians to see beyond what they were meant to see and expand the horizon of their questions.[53]

As, ultimately, a tribute to the inexhaustible value of originals, the facsimile was at the very core of antiquarianism as a new form of scholarship. It memorialized the precious experience of the artefacts of the past and, in many respects, it celebrated an approach to the past the self-conscious novelty of which stemmed from a fresh look at the original monuments as much as from new finds. At the same time, reducing the mediation of editors to a minimun, it aimed at widening access to the originals to ensure that others and future generations could explore ever new facets of monuments. It was also, undoubtedly, a byproduct of the well-known antiquarian anxiety over the vulnerability of ancient monuments. Contrary to the commonly held view that attributed to intellectual cowardice – if not outright incompetence – the antiquaries' penchant for preservation over interpretation, the antiquaries' effort to preserve the original idiosyncrasies of monuments should be ascribed to a sophisticated, if timid, notion of scholarly practice. It was prompted by the novel awareness of the fallibility of scholars and their unwanted manipulation of sources.

Paradoxically, as the taxing interviews with the prospective printers and engravers of *Domesday Book* show, the editorial policy of most use to scholars was one that relied on the mediation of non-scholars, of artists and tradesmen who, as in the case of the engraver Basire, often advertised their own illiteracy. Seeking to procure the *Domesday Book* commission, in fact, Basire had declared that 'tho' he had not engraved the present Specimen, he had no doubt of his being able to execute a fac-simile Copy of Doomesday Book; having engraved several Oriental Characters for Mr Stuart, & others which were well approved of.'[54]

By contrast, the fellows noted that the printers' effort to read and interpret the original handwriting interfered with the accuracy of their work. The type-cutter Morgan was specifically asked whether he could 'read those Characters, & tell wch will serve in the Place of another, & when?', and when he answered that he could 'read the Letters, tho' he does not know the Meaning of several of the Abbreviations', his knowledge was tested immediately on a specific abbreviation.[55] His fallacious answer went uncommented on in the interview, but Dean Milles clearly spelled out the paradox: 'The abbreviating marks particularly will be often omitted & mistaken for each other, wch will totally alter ye meaning of the Record, to which Printers who are unacquainted with the language of Domesday are peculiarly liable, whereas in tracing this work by an engraver, the copy may be accurate tho ye engraver knows not the meaning of the original.'[56] The same ignorance that was turned against the printers as flagrant evidence of their unreliability to produce an accurate facsimile made the engravers most eligible for the same job. Literacy itself was seen as a handicap in the effort to reproduce the materiality of the text.

This exchange allows us to discern yet another layer of the fellows' understanding of 'accuracy'. Far from being confined to a faithful, unmodernized, 'unimproved', word-for-word edition of the original 'text', an accurate copy of a text branched out to include the visual appearance of the original object. What the engravers who advertised their illiteracy could achieve and the printers – or erudite philologists – could not, was the reproduction of a written text as it appeared to the eye. The fellows' concern for the visual appearance of the document is made particularly clear in the final report where, of the eight reasons given for choosing engraving over printing, only one – the seventh – invoked textual accuracy. Otherwise, the report focused on the failure of printing to preserve the visual appearance of the original. Indeed, that the visual dimension of documents was valued by antiquarians independently of verbal accuracy – or even documentary, historical or literary value – is implicit in the telling hendiadys 'exact and facsimile' sometimes used to describe facsimiles.[57] Adding 'exact' where 'facsimile' should have sufficed seemed to indicate that a text was as much for reading as for viewing and therefore its edition asked for the collaboration of a philologist and an artist. Again, the antiquarian sensitivity to the visual aspect of texts can be documented well beyond the exceptional case of *Domesday Book* in the publications of the Society of Antiquaries, such as *Vetusta Monumenta*, where several documents were engraved on separate plates and exhibited for admiration, and in antiquarian publications in general, where 'the continual alternating of many different letter sizes and styles in the texts and titles', as Armando Petrucci has put it, appears to 'emphasize the visual expressiveness of letter signs through the varying of forms'.[58]

Finally, the antiquarian dissatisfaction with the printed specimen was more than scholarly or visual, but aesthetic. Both the Council minutes and the final report indicate the extent to which printers and engravers were cast as proponents of incompatible aesthetics of the facsimile. Asked specifically to account for the unwanted regularity of their specimens, Morgan answered that 'He did observe a great Inequality in the Size, as well as Variety in the form, of the Letters in most Pages of the Book; but those were deemed Blemishes & Imperfections in the Book, & would spoil the intended Beauty & Regularity of the printed Copy; so that he was to omit them in his Plan.'[59] Similarly, Cotterell agreed with Morgan that 'the variety of Handwriting & Character that appeared throughout the Work' was 'a Blemish & not a Beauty, & would therefore spoil it, if copied'.[60] Both Morgan and Cotterell, that is, defended their belief in the superior aesthetic value of a printed copy. In their view, a copy rid of the imperfections and irregularities of the original would be better than the original. By contrast, when the printer Richardson was asked to comment on the work of the type-cutter Morgan, his answer to the question 'By whom were the Types in the printed Specimen cut; & what Rule was follow'd in the executing them' was edited by the secretary of the Society with a revealing aside: 'By Dr. Morton's directions, Mr. Morgan &c selected the fairest & most perfect Letters (as he termed them) from different Parts in the Doomesday Book.'[61] The same effort to distance themselves from an aesthetic sensibility they did not share can be detected in the final report, where the committee related that the specimen produced by moveable type was 'far from a Fac = Simile Copy' for the types had been taken 'from such Letters in Various Pages of Doomesday Book as they thought the best and handsomest'.[62] Thomas Reece, a clergyman with a strong interest in penmanship, put in the clearest terms the fact that the irregularities of the original were not just a source of scholarly interest but also the site of aesthetic appreciation.[63] Suggesting that a handwritten copy 'under the Direction of a skilful Hand' was a better option than either an engraved or a printed one, Reece wrote that 'great care should be taken to preserve the Face of Antiquity that the Original is mark'd with, which, in my Opinion, is its greatest Beauty.'[64]

As the complex neogtiations over the facsimile reproduction of *Domesday Book* only begins to show, there was more to the facsimile than its criminal use as forgery or its commercial exploitation as collectible. In the first instance, the facsimile was the technology that safeguarded the possibility that later scholars, using new tools, might recover meaning in what the current generation could only preserve. Even more importantly, it was the technology that made it possible to represent the aesthetic effects of the handiwork of an earlier age and to appreciate the workings of time. Despite the persistent canard that antiquarianism of this sort represented an absence of aesthetic appreciation – it is, indeed, common to view Winckelmann as that figure who 'helped to rescue ancient art from the province of scholarship and antiquarianism to an area where it could become of living interest as a source of pleasure in its own right'[65] – the predilection for the facsimile was both a scholarly pursuit and a positive aesthetic practice. Indeed, juxtaposed to one another, *Monumenti antichi inediti* and the projected facsimile of the Domesday Book provide mutually revealing accounts of the aesthetic and intellectual complexities of eighteenth-century antiquarian practice. Both Winckelmann's relative unconcern with the materiality and history of monuments in comparison to their universal and timeless character and the Society of Antiquaries' exclusive obsession with the physical effects of time – the accidental, material, individual shape that the past gave to objects – help us to understand the difficulties faced by eighteenth-century antiquaries as they sought to capture the complexities of their historical visions and to reduce them to the portability of a two-dimensional page.

Notes

1 For a reassessment of Winckelmann's death, see Lionel Gossman, 'Death in Trieste', *Journal of European Studies*, vol. 22 (1992), pp. 207–40.

2 See, for instance, Winckelmann to Usteri, 16 July 1763, 6 August 1763, 19 August 1767; to Berendis, 26 July 1765; to Stosch, 28 June 1766, in Winckelmann, *Briefe*, eds Hans Diepolder and Walther Rehm, 4 vols, Berlin: Gruyter, 1952–57, vol. 2, pp. 331, 333 and 308; vol. 3, pp. 112, 182 (hereafter *Briefe*).

3 Giuseppe Longhi, *La calcografia propriamente detta*, Milan, 1830, p. 25.

4 *Sculptura Historico-Technica*, 4th edn, London, J. Marks, 1770, pp. v, 4. See also Joseph Strutt, *A Biographical Dictionary Containing an Historical Account of all the Engravers, from the Earliest Period of the Art of Engraving to the Present Time*, London, printed by J. Davis for Robert Faulder, 1786, vol. I, pp. 1–3; William Faithorne, *The Art of Greaving and Etching*, London: Faithorne, 1662, A2r; John Evelyn, *Sculptura*, second edn, London: J. Payne, 1755;

Francesco Milizia, *Dizionario delle belle arti del disegno estratto in gran parte dalla Enciclopedia metodica*, 2 vols, Bassano, 1797, vol. I, 'Incisione'; Filippo Baldinucci, *Cominciamento e progresso dell'arte dell'intagliare il rame*, 2nd edn, Florence, 1767, p. 1; William S. Baker, *The Origin and Antiquity of Engraving*, Philadelphia, 1872, pp. 48–52; Giovanni Gori Gandellini and Luigi De Angelis, *Notizie istoriche degli intagliatori*, 2nd edn, Siena: Porri, 1806–16, vol. 4, pp. 63–4; *The Rules, Orders and Regulations of the Society of Engravers*, London: Bensley, 1804, pp. 4–6.

5 Walter Pater, 'Winckelmann', *The Renaissance: Studies in Art and Poetry*, Oxford, 1986 (first published 1873), p. 117.

6 See Winckelmann to Genzmar, 10 March 1766 in *Briefe*, vol. 3, p. 169. Joseph Eiselein wrote that *Monumenti antichi inediti* was 'considered by its critics as being written in the Italian style and full of useless erudition', and was known as the work with which Winckelmann intended to

'excell over all contemporary antiquaries' (see note 9 below) (Winckelmann, *Sämtliche Werke*, ed. Joseph Eiselein, 12 vols, Donauoschingen, 1825–29, vol. I, p. cxx).

7 *Gentleman's Magazine*, vol. 54, July 1784, p. 490.

8 Christian Gottlob Heyne, 'Loebschrift auf Winckelmann', Cassel 1778, *Die Kasseler Lobscriften auf Winckelmann*, ed. Arthur Schulz, Berlin: Winckelmann Gesellschaft, 1963, pp. 17–27 (p. 23).

9 Johann Joachim Winckelmann, *Monumenti antichi inediti spiegati ed illustrati da Giovanni Winckelmann Prefetto delle antichità di Roma*, 2 vols, Rome (printed for the author [by Marco Pagliarini], 1767), vol. I, p. xv.

10 In the *Remarks on the History of Art*, he had stated that his moments of 'greatest satisfaction in elucidating works of ancient art' came when they enabled him to 'explain or amend an ancient author'. (Winckelmann, *Anmerkungen über die Geschichte der Kunst der Alterthums*, Dresden, 1767, facsimile edition in *Kunsttheoretische Schriften*, 10 vols, Baden Baden and Strassbourg: Heitz, 1962–71), vol. 6, p. x (English translation *History of Ancient Art*, trans. Henry Lodge, 4 vols, Boston: J. Osgood, 1880, vol. I, p. 126). See also Winckelmann to Marpurg, 8 December 1762; to Usteri, 16 July 1763; to Genzmar, 27 November 1765, in *Briefe*, vol. 2, pp. 276, 331; vol. 3, p. 139.

11 See *Versuch einer Allegorie* (1766), facsimile edition in *Kunsttheoretische Schriften*, op. cit. (note 10), vol. 10; *Anmerkungen*, op. cit. (note 10), pp. vi–vii (English translation, *History of Ancient Art*, vol. I, p. 123).

12 John Keats, 'Ode on a Grecian Urn', *Keats Poetical Works*, ed. H.W. Garrod, Oxford and New York: Oxford University Press, 1987; first published 1956, p. 209.

13 Winckelmann, 'Beschreibung des Torso im Belvedere zu Rom', *Bibliothek der schönen Wissenschaften und der freien Kunste*, 5 (1759), facsimile edition in *Kunsttheoretische Schriften*, op. cit. (note 10), vol. 10, pp. 35–6.

14 See, for instance, Giovanni Guattani, *Monumenti antichi inediti*, 7 vols, Rome, 1784–1805 and *Monumenti inediti pubblicati dall' Instituto di Corrispondenza Archeologica*, 1829–33.

15 Winckelmann to Marpurg, 8 December 1762. See also Winckelmann to Usteri, 16 July 1763; to Genzmar, 27 November 1765, in *Briefe*, vol. 2, pp. 276, 331; vol. 3, p. 139.

16 Eiselein (ed.), *Sämtliche Werke*, op. cit. (note 6), vol. I, p. clxxv.

17 ibid., p. cxix.

18 Plate 180 was signed by N. Mogalli.

19 Winckelmann to Stosch, 15 November 1763, in *Briefe*, vol. 2, p. 355; see also Eiselein (ed.), *Sämtliche Werke*, op. cit. (note 6), vol. I, pp. cxvii–cxix.

20 Winckelmann to Stosch, 8 June, 1765; to Riedesel, in *Briefe*, vol. 3, pp. 101, 126.

21 Winckelmann to Fuessly, 19 June 1765, in *Briefe*, vol. 3, p. 103.

22 Pierre D'Hancarville, *Collection of Etruscan, Greek, and Roman Antiquities from the Cabinet of the Honble Wm Hamilton*, 4 vols, Naples: Morelli, 1766–67, vol. 1, p. 152.

23 Winckelmann's neglect of the object itself is all the more noticeable when the first edition of the *Monumenti* is compared with the second, which included a supplementary volume by the Jesuit Stefano Raffei. Before interpreting the images, Raffei commented on the state of preservation of monuments and on their appearance as objects. He usually located the monument; described its conditions; established whether it had been restored; and noted the material and the dimensions. In addition, Raffei did not fail to alert the reader when the representation – which sometimes reproduced the front, back and profile of the object – could appear as misleading. (*Monumenti antichi inediti*, ed. Paolo Montagnani Mirabili, 2nd edn, 3 vols, Rome: Mordacchini, 1821).

24 As Victor Wiener has pointed out, 'knowing Winckelmann's preoccupation with design, one cannot help but be bewildered by the variety of styles one encounters on every page.' Victor Wiener, 'Eighteenth Century Italian Prints', *Metropolitan Museum of Art Bulletin*, January 1971, pp. 203–25, p. 214.

25 See William M. Ivins, *Prints and Visual Communication*, Cambridge, Mass.: Harvard University Press, 1953, and 'A Note on Engraved Reproductions of Works of Art', in *Studies in Art and Literature for Belle Da Costa*, Princeton: Princeton University Press, 1954, pp. 193–6.

26 Michel Melot, Anthony Griffiths, Richard S. Field and Andre Beguin, *Prints*, New York: Rizzoli, 1981, p. 56.

27 Barbara Maria Stafford, 'Beauty of the Invisible: Winckelmann and the Aesthetics of Imperceptibility', *Zeitschrift für Kunstgeschichte*, vol. 43 (1980), no. 1, pp. 65–78 (p. 74).

28 Carlo Ginzburg, 'Morelli, Freud and Sherlock Holmes: Clues and Scientific Method', *History Workshop Journal*, pp. 3–36, 16.

29 Although the Domesday Book was valued as a precious national monument – 'the most antient and valuable record that exists in the archives of this or any other kingdom', according to John Nichols – its political significance remained controversial. As well as a comprehensive survey of England, the Domesday Book was a stark reminder of England's colonial past – according to Matthew Paris, it marked the moment when 'the manifest oppression of England began'. (John Nichols, *The History and Antiquities of the County of Leicester*, 4 vols, London: J. Nichols, 1795–1815, vol. I, p. xxxiii; Elizabeth M. Hallam, *Domesday Book through Nine Centuries*, London: Thames and Hudson, 1986, p. 7). The publication of a duplicate of the

Domesday Book had long been amongst the desiderata of antiquarians – at least since the beginning of the century – but had been laid aside for lack of funds. See, for instance, Humfrey Wanley, draft of a proposal for the constitution of a Society of Antiquaries, quoted in Joan Evans, *A History of the Society of Antiquaries*, Oxford: Oxford University Press, 1956, p. 40; Thomas Hearne, *A Collection of Curious Discourses*, 2nd edn, 2 vols, London: W. and J. Richardson, 1771, vol. I, pp. lxii–lxiii and *Remarks and Collections of Thomas Hearne*, X, 95, 101, 133, and XI, 140; Society of Antiquaries, Minute Book, 18 December 1755; Philip Carteret Webb, *A Short Account of Some Particulars Concerning Domes-day Book*, London: Society of Antiquaries, 1756; *Archaeologia*, vol. 1 (1770), pp. xxx–xxxiii.

30 Although the facsimile of books, manuscripts and inscriptions was an established and increasingly popular scholarly practice, the scant and dated secondary literature on the subject has treated the facsimile as a variety of forgery – in a few instances the words 'facsimilist' and 'facsimile' have been unheedingly replaced with 'forger' and 'forgery'. Scholars have taken for granted the gullibility of the patrons of early facsimiles and have limited themselves to celebrating their ability to spot modern copies while belittling, at the same time, the facsimilists' efforts to produce convincing duplicates. See A.W. Pollard, Gilbert Grave, R.W. Chapman and W.W. Greg, '"Facsimile" Reprints of Old Books', *Library*, vol. 6 (1926), pp. 305–28; Frank Weitenkampf, 'What is a Facsimile?', *Papers of the Bibliographical Association of America*, vol. 37 (1943), pp. 114–30; A.T. Hazen, 'J. Sturt facsimilist', *Library*, vol. 24 (1944–45), and 'Type-facsimiles', *Modern Philology*, vol. 44 (1947), pp. 209–17; David McKitterick, 'Old Faces and New Acquaintances: Typography and the Association of Ideas', *Papers of the Bibliographical Association of America*, vol. 87 (June 1993), pp. 163–86. For new insights into the role of readers in the history of the facsimiles, see McKitterick, 'Old Faces and New Acquaintances' and John Kerrigan, 'The Editor as Reader: Constructing Renaissance Texts', in *The Practice and Representation of Reading in England*, eds James Raven, Helen Small and Naomi Tadmor, Cambridge: Cambridge University Press, 1996, pp. 102–24. For a thought-provoking collection of essays on copies, see the catalogue of the exhibition of copies *Museo dei musei*, Florence: Condirene, 1988.

31 Of all the records whose publication Parliament had sponsored, the Domesday Book only was expected to be produced in facsimile. The Parliament's decision to publish the book in facsimile sanctioned an established tradition that stretched back almost to the time when the Domesday Book was produced. There is evidence that as early as 1300, 'some domesday certificates were produced with handwriting of a somewhat antique appearance, as though the clerk had tried to imitate the Domesday script.' (Hallam, *Domesday Book Through Nine Centuries*, op. cit. [note 28], p. 59). Despite the recommendation of the Society of Antiquaries to produce a facsimile of the book by engraving, however, the Treasury in the end opted for the cheaper solution of printing the book in a special record type – designed by John Nichols – that would reproduce abbreviations, contractions, superior letters and a few special signs. Having been about ten years in the press, an edition of *Domesday Book* became available for distribution to the members of both houses of Parliament in 1783. The first complete facsimile edition of *Domesday Book* was the photozincographic reproduction made in 1862 under the supervision of Colonel Sir Henry James. For other efforts, see Philip Morant, *The History and Antiquities of the County of Essex*, 2 vols, London: Osborne, 1768, vol. 1, p. xxvi; Treadway Nash, *Collections for the History of Worcestershire*, 2 vols, London: printed for J. White, 1775–99, vol. 2, Appendix; John Nichols, *The History and Antiquities of the County of Leicester*, vol. 1; George Hickes, *Linguarum Vett. Septentrionalium Thesaurus Grammatico-Criticus et Archaeologicus*, 2 vols, Oxford, 1705, vol. 1, p. 144; Owen Manning, *The History and Antiquities of the County of Surrey*, 3 vols, 1804–14 [facsimile executed in 1773]); Francis Grose, *The Antiquities of England and Wales*, vol. 1 (1783), p. 128; Gales, *Registrum Honoris de Richmond*, p. 238. For a detailed account of the history of the printing of *Domesday Book*, see M.M. Condon and Elizabeth M. Hallam, 'Government Printing of the Public Record Office in the Eighteenth Century', *Journal of the Society of Antiquaries*, vol. 7 (6), October 1984, pp. 348–88 (pp. 373–84); Evans, *A History of the Society of Antiquaries*, pp. 125–6; Elizabeth M. Hallam, *Domesday Book through Nine Centuries*; Hilary Jenkinson, *Domesday Rebound*, London: HMSO, 1954; R. Welldon Finn, *An Introduction to Domesday Book*, London: Longmans, 1963; *Domesday Commemoration 1086 A.D.–1886 A.D.*, 2 vols, London: Longman, 1888–91.

32 Society of Antiquaries, Council Book, 12 and 26 May 1768.

33 Society of Antiquaries, Papers, Correspondence, Estimates etc Relating to the Publication of Domesday Book, 1759–1783, Report of the President and Council of the Society of Antiquaries Concerning the Publication of Domesday Book, 30 May 1768.

34 Society of Antiquaries, Minute Book, 5 May 1768.

35 Society of Antiquaries, Council Book, 26 May 1768.

36 ibid.

37 ibid.

38 ibid.

39 ibid.

40 ibid.

41 Society of Antiquaries, Report of the President and Council of the Society of Antiquaries.

42 Joseph Griegely, 'The Textual Event', in *Devils and Angels: Textual Editing and Literary Theory*, ed. Philip Cohen, Charlottesville and London: University Press of Virginia, 1991, pp. 167–94 (p. 174).

43 David McKitterick has argued that 'at the heart of any questions respecting facsimiles lie not only questions respecting their adequacy for other purposes, editorial or otherwise representative, but also the degree to which the reader can be persuaded to suspend disbelief.' (McKitterick, 'Old Faces and New Acquaintances', op. cit. [note 30], p. 164).

44 Society of Antiquaries, Report of the President and Council of the Society of Antiquaries.

45 The subject was, in fact, so popular that David Casley trusted that including 'specimens of the manner of Writing in the different Ages' would 'make the Book more acceptable' and boost the sales of his otherwise unpopular *Catalogue of the Manuscripts in the King's Library*. (David Casley, *A Catalogue of the Manuscripts in the King's Library*, London: printed for the author, 1734, p. iv.)

46 *Archaeologia*, vol. 2 (1773), pp. 216–17; see also Society of Antiquaries, Minute Book, 18 April 1771.

47 See, for example, Society of Antiquaries, Minute Book, 13 December 1759; 24 January 1760; 13 June 1765; 16 March 1769; see also *Archaeologia*, vol. 2 (1773), p. 98.

48 See, for example, Society of Antiquaries, Minute Book, 7 May 1732 and 3 May 1753.

49 Indeed, just as the facsimile imagined by the fellows of the Society of Antiquaries was a response to the eighteenth-century interest in the transmission of texts, to a large extent, the impressive achievement of the latest facsimile of *Domesday* (the Alecto facsimile published in 1986 for the thousandth anniversary of the book) reflects the orientation of more recent scholarship. In tune with the novel interest in the history of the book and the practice of reading, the editors sought to reproduce the marginal additions that the Domesday Book had accrued through the centuries, as well as the 'the weight and character of Great Domesday parchment folios' and the original format by arranging the text in fifty-three separate gatherings in the manner of the original manuscript. The facsimilists even managed to reproduce the 'unsightly patches of oak-gall, probably introduced during the seventeenth or eighteenth centuries' – although since, in the end, the editors decided 'to favour the clarity of the script at the expense of the stains', they reproduced them 'as a dull grey, and rather less prominent than in the manuscript' and only gave 'an example of the actual colour of the stains' in the margins of two pages *(Great Domesday*, London: Alecto Historical Editions, 1986).

50 Society of Antiquaries, Papers, Correspondence, Estimates etc Relating to the Publication of Domesday Book, 1759–83, Dean Milles recommending an engraved copy of the Domesday Book.

51 ibid.

52 The antiquary Joseph Ayloffe gave the clearest expression to this antiquarian article of faith. Discussing 'an ancient picture in Windsor castle', he argued that the original value of the monuments of the past paled in comparison to the insights that the scholars of succeeding generations – and of the antiquarian age in particular – had been able to draw from them: 'however intrinsic the merits of these performances might have been, the satisfaction they afforded at the time of their being compleated was much inferior to the advantages of which such as still remain have since been productive. Their utility to antiquaries, and the light which they have thrown upon many subjects of historical enquiry, have been much greater than could have been originally apprehended.' (Joseph Ayloffe, 'An Historical Description of an Ancient Picture in Windsor Castle', *Archaeologia* vol. 3 [1783], pp. 188–9). The paper was read twice at the Society of Antiquaries, on 29 March 1770 and 7 March 1771.

53 See Walter Benjamin, 'A Small History of Photography', in *One Way Street and Other Writings*, trans. Edmund Jephcott and Kingsley Shorter, London and New York: Verso, 1997 and Angela Cozea, 'Proustian Aesthetics: Photography, Engraving, and Historiography', *Comparative Literature*, vol. 45, no. 3, 1993, pp. 209–29.

54 Society of Antiquaries, Council Book, 26 May 1768.

55 ibid.

56 Society of Antiquaries, Dean Milles recommending an engraved copy of the Domesday Book.

57 Society of Antiquaries, Minute Book, 13 December 1759.

58 Armando Petrucci, *Public Lettering: Script, Power, and Culture*, Chicago and London: University of Chicago Press, 1993, p. 57.

59 Society of Antiquaries, Council Book, 26 May 1768.

60 ibid.

61 ibid.

62 Society of Antiquaries, Report of the President and Council of the Society of Antiquaries.

63 For a discussion of the aesthetics of antiquarianism, see Maria Grazia Lolla, '*Ceci n'est pas un monument: Vetusta Monumenta* and

Antiquarian Aesthetics', in *Producing the Past: Aspects of Antiquarian Culture and Practice 1700–1850*, Aldershot and Brookfield, VT: Ashgate, 1999, pp. 15–34. For some recent examples of the enduring aesthetic appeal of facsimiles – as well as of their value as status symbols – see *Book of Kells*, Luzern: Fine Art Facsimile Publishers of Switzerland, 1990 and the *Kennicott Bible*, which are discussed in Gilbert Adair, 'Making Books', *Connoisseur*, vol. 27 (April 1987), pp. 160–2; Marisa Bulzone, 'A Masterpiece is Recreated', *Graphis*, vol. 47

(March–April 1991), pp. 78–83; Claire Wilson, 'A Hot Manuscript, No Movie Deal', *Art and Antiques*, April 1995, p. 20.

64 Society of Antiquaries, Papers, Correspondence, Estimates etc Relating to the Publication of *Domesday Book*, 1759–83, letter of Thomas Reece; see also Minute Book, 1 February 1770.

65 David Turner, 'Johann Joachim Winckelmann', in *German Men of Letters*, eds Alex Nathan and Brian Keith-Smith, London: Oswald Wolff, 1972, vol. 6, pp. 265–92, 285.

3

Facts or Fragments? Visual histories in the age of mechanical reproduction

Dana Arnold

Let us think of the printing press as the beginning of the age of the mechanical reproduction of visual history. By the opening years of the eighteenth century the proliferation of printed images ran ahead of the increased production of the printed word. The printed image became an essential component of the international currency of intellectual ideas that transcended spoken language boundaries. These images facilitated the transference of ideas about architecture, antiquity and aesthetics in the pan-European arena of artistic and scholarly exchange. There is no doubt that prints were essential to the formulation of a visual repertoire of studies of antique art, architecture and artefacts. Indeed, many of the essays in this volume map out how individual collections of prints were amassed and used, and consider the role these compilations played in shaping attitudes towards antiquity and the evolution and expression of aesthetic theory. Moreover, the relationship of prints to the original object both in terms of the effect on its aura and the print as an interlocutor between the original, the viewer and a three-dimensional reproduction or interpretation of the original is a central concern of some of the chapters in this book. This essay takes the printed images of the temples at Paestum and uses them as a means of exploring how visual histories were constructed in the eighteenth century. In other words, do these images narrate a history that has become invisible in, or at best subsumed into, the tradition of the verbal? Indeed, the authority of the written word endures even today as the histories and theories of art are expressed principally through text rather than image. And it is part of the purpose of this volume as a whole to reposition the role of the print in the making of architectural histories, histories of antiquarianism and the development of aesthetic practices.

An investigation into the relationship of the printed images of the temples at Paestum and the making of histories both prompts and requires an awareness of our concept of history and the ways in which histories can be constructed. Our preoccupation with textuality is a central concern here, as the written word has been privileged over the visual and aural traditions of history. Recently, some attempts have been made to recognize these imbalances and to re-examine our reliance on textual documentation, which is locked into antiquated structures of knowledge which ensure its supremacy.[1] Now oral history has begun to challenge the hegemony of the written word and technological advances in recording the human voice have made spoken history a potent form of cultural investigation by presenting the notion of an eye-witness account which has an aura of authenticity. Printed images can have a similar effect as they both proselytize and democratize their narrative content to give a sense of immediacy and legibility. But are technological advances in the means of mechanical reproduction of the original always necessary for such key changes in our concept of history? One of the problems is the way in which we are conditioned to 'read' an image. Are we then bound up in the conventions and restrictions of the metaphors of our own language? Does an image need to perform linguistically as the practice of 'reading' would imply it has to? After all, images are, in the first instance, non-discursive formations or articulations of a set of specific circumstances. This facilitates the transference of the physical into the conceptual and can represent what cannot be said, because the construction of images is not dependent upon the use of grammar and syntax, which require dependent clauses, serial sentences and such like.[2] A system of non-verbal signs with a distinct set of cultural meanings has been identified by a broad church of cultural theorists and it is not my purpose here to explore these writings.[3] But in terms of the images of art and architectural history in the eighteenth century, these writings prompt us to ask if we can identify comparable hermeneutics to the verbal theory on aesthetics, art history and stylistic supremacy. Moreover, the dominance of the verbal as a way of narrating histories has also been called into question. Language can only constrain the production of history and a new kind of cognition is required, which is independent of these linguistic constraints. Visual histories offer a whole other kind of historical analysis which uses different kinds of perception and knowledge; this both runs parallel to, and intersects with, verbalized perceived norms. Images of antiquity have been mapped against the paradigm of verbal history when, in fact, they also have a history and narrate a history of their own which denies the constraints of sequence and syntax and is free of the teleological constraints of the structures of verbal history. They present, in the Foucauldian sense, an 'archaeology of knowledge' about antiquity.[4] Here the discontinuities identified by Foucault as essential elements of historical narratives are present in the absence of linear, chronological sequence and notions of progress in printed images of antiquity such as those of the temples at Paestum. Indeed, the fact that the currency of visual images was far more widespread in Europe than textual descriptions, and had no verbal language barrier, meant that they were indeed news.

The Grand (de)Tour

The focus of this brief exploration of these questions is the three Doric temples in the ancient Greek city of Poseidonia, now known as Paestum, in southern Italy.[5] The temples provide a cohesive case study not only because of the proliferation and interrelation of the images made of them in the fifty or so years after their 'rediscovery' in the mid-eighteenth century but also because these images were used as 'evidence' by architects and theorists on both sides of the Graeco-Roman controversy. The site of the temples was known from at least the sixteenth century but was only 'rediscovered' in the mid-eighteenth century. A map published by Constantino Gatta in 1732 drew attention to the temples, as a consequence of which they gradually became part of the Grand Tour, or rather – usually – a detour from the more well-trodden route between Sicily and Naples.

The temples at Paestum were known in the eighteenth century as the Basilica (plate 1), the Temple of Ceres (plate 2) and the Temple of Neptune (plate 3),[6] and alongside the temples on the Acropolis in Athens and at Agrigentum in Sicily, they represented the most outstanding extant examples of Greek Doric architecture. The temples at Paestum – particularly as regards their aesthetic character – provoked some quite vigorous responses from visitors: not least because of the apparently crude nature of their baseless Doric order and the open-textured, almost spongy, red stone from which they were constructed. Paestum was only for the truly intrepid because access was difficult and the journey to the site and the local accommodation was uncomfortable. On his visit in 1761 James Adam remarked 'no milk for one's tea, no butter to one's bread ... we send to water at 4 miles distance and in short there is plenty of nothing but fleas which exist in a quantity not to be ignored.'[7] Perhaps the lack of home comforts and lack of proper access to the site influenced Adam's opinion when he said that 'The famous antiquities so much talked of of late as wonders, but which curiosity apart, don't merit half the time and trouble they have cost me. They are an early, inelegant, unenriched Doric and scarcely provide two good views, so much for Paestum.'[8] Richard Payne Knight, who visited the site in 1767, was more generous in his final appraisal. Payne Knight was struck by the temples' distinctive aesthetic and remarked 'When one examines the parts near, they appear rude, massive and heavy, but seen at a proper distance, the general effect is grand simple and even elegant.'[9] Some twenty years later Goethe expressed a similar view:

> The first impression could only arouse surprise. I found myself in an entirely alien world. For as centuries shaped themselves from the grave to the pleasantry, so they shape making at the same time, nay they create it. Now our eyes and with them our whole being are attracted and decisively determined by slender architecture so that these obstruse, conical closely set masses of columns appear irksome, nay terrible. However, soon I pulled myself together, remembered the history of art, thought of the age whose spirit considered such an architectural style appropriate, presented to myself the severe style of sculpture, and in less than half an hour I felt attracted, nay praised my genius for permitting me to see these well preserved fragments.[10]

The remote location of the temples meant they were less well visited than their Sicilian or Greek counterparts and their striking aesthetic could certainly challenge the sensibilities of some visitors. But the temples became the best-known examples of Greek architecture in the latter part of the eighteenth century through their appearance in engravings and *veduta* paintings.[11] Between 1764 and 1784 eight works were published on Paestum – four times as many as appeared on the temples at Agrigentum or on the Acropolis. The visual hegemony of the temples was ensured by Count Gazola, an engineer from Parma and the commander of the

1 The Basilica, Paestum. Photo: the author.

2 The Temple of Ceres, Paestum. Photo: the author.

3 The Temple of Neptune, Paestum. Photo: the author.

Royal Artillery of the Kingdom of Sicily and Naples.[12] In the early 1750s Gazola commissioned drawings of the temples which he sent to be engraved by Bartolozzi, who had set up a workshop in Rome in 1750. The drawings were not published as a volume as Gazola intended and did not appear until 1784, as part of Paolantonio Paoli's *Rovine della Citta di Pesto*, although it appears the plates were ready by 1755 as Gazola may well have collected them on a visit to Rome in that year. But as Suzanne Lang has demonstrated, Gazola's images of the temples became the standard views of them for the following fifty years.[13] The most commonly used images were interior views of the Temples of Ceres and Neptune and a general view of all three temples. The similarities between the images are compelling and they appear either as identical plates in different publications or the same view in reverse where an image had been copied from an engraving. These views, based on Gazola's drawings, provided a core of plates, complemented by reconstructions, sections and details of the temples, for the many volumes on Paestum which appeared in the third quarter of the eighteenth century. Each of these volumes provided more of an assemblage of images of different sizes, produced by different hands at different times, than a systematic survey of the ruins. The publications included Dumont's *Les Ruines de Paestum* which appeared in 1764; Filippo Morghen's *Sei Vedute delle Rovine di Pesto* of 1765; John Berkenhout's descriptively titled *The Ruins of Paestum or Poseidonia, a City in Magna Grecia in the Kingdom of Naples Containing a Description on and Views of the Remaining Antiquities with the Ancient and Modern History Inscriptions etc and Some Observations on the Ancient Doric*, published in 1767; and Thomas Major's *The Ruins of Paestum, otherwise Poseidonia in Magna Grecia* of 1768. These publications – especially Thomas Major's – in turn influenced later archaeologists and historians, for instance, the Abbé St Non, who published his *Voyage Pittoresque de Naples et de Sicile* in 1783 and Delagardette's *Les Ruines de Paestum ou Poseidonia, Ancienne Ville de la Grande Grèce*, which appeared a few years later. And Gazola's images continued to influence early nineteenth-century writers, including William Wilkins, whose *Magna Grecia* was published in 1807. Moreover, the drawings formed the basis of *veduta* paintings of the temples, as seen in the work of Louis Ducros, who never visited Paestum, and Antonio Jolli.[14] The connectivity, through Gazola, between this range of visual images of the temples is demonstrated in the following sequence – Thomas Major's view of the interior of the Temple of Neptune in his *Ruins of Paestum*, 1768 (plate 4) uses the same source as that which had appeared three years earlier in Filippo Morghen's *Sei Vedute*. An interior view of the same temple from a different vantage point appears in both Morghen (plate 5) and in a *veduta* painting by Antonio Jolli, now in the Palazzo Reale, Caserta. Jolli, whose son Raphael worked for Bartolozzi in Rome where Gazola's views were engraved, produced the plates for Morghen's volume and may well be the source for many of Major's images.[15]

The remoteness of the temples may to some extent explain why Gazola's images were used in preference to fresh on-site studies. Although serious scholars of the antique, including Robert Mylne, Stephen Riou, Le Roy, James Adam and Sir John Soane, visited, measured and recorded the temples, they often used Gazola's views as their guide. I have already considered the relationship between

Internal View of the Hexastyle Ipetral Temple, taken from the South
Vue du dedans du Temple Hexastyle Ipetre, prise du coté du Sud.

Publish'd Jan. 1768.

Th. Major sculp.

4   View of the interior of the Temple of Neptune, in Thomas Major, *Ruins of Paestum*, 1768. Engraving. Courtesy of the Trustees of Sir John Soane's Museum.

5   View of the interior of the Temple of Neptune, in Filippo Morghen, *Sei Vedute delle Rovine de Pesto*, 1765. Engraving. Private collection.

the resonance of the approval of Gazola's images of Paestum as standard views against the dissonance of verbal responses of visitors to the site.[16] And the interrelationship of the images of Paestum has been clearly mapped out elsewhere.[17] Here I am exploring the role played by Gazola's images of Paestum together with other contemporary studies, which appealed to those on either side of the Graeco-Roman controversy, in the construction of architectural histories in the eighteenth century. The aesthetic practices evident in these various visual representations stand distinct from the constraints of verbal taxonomies. This reveals a pan-European currency of printed images of antiquity which relied on a common visual language, which in turn reveals how mass-produced studies of the antique were used as facts or fragments of knowledge which became histories. The common thread between the publications on Paestum, alongside Gazola, was that most of these texts comprised an assemblage of different images produced at different times by different artists or engravers.[18] This kind of publication was not unusual in the eighteenth century, nor were the different kinds of graphic notation used in the plates in any way out of the ordinary. Therefore, Paestum is discussed here as a specific case study of more general trends concerning eighteenth-century attitudes towards aesthetics, language and history. In this way the printed images of the temples collate their space–time location and represent their geographically and temporally remote subjects as information which met the needs of the passion both for picturesque images and of scientific observation. These images offered at once the excitement of vicarious travel – and as we have seen access to the temples was difficult – and a means by which the spectacular fragments of the past could be absorbed into the historical consciousness of the present.

My discussion focuses on two specific examples of different kinds of visual history – Thomas Major's orthogonal reconstruction of the Temple of Neptune together with his detailed study of the order (plates 6 and 7) and Piranesi's 'pictorial' view of the same (plate 10). These representations, when considered in the context of the nature of the images of Paestum, facilitate the exploration of two central themes of this essay: firstly the idea of history and the creation of its narratives, either visual or verbal; and secondly the idea of the author of these narrations, as negotiated through Walter Benjamin's idea of the collector.[19] Although Benjamin's concern was with the modernity of nineteenth-century Paris, his investigation of the relationship between the past and the present, and the construction of histories through the collection of fragments, can be used to explore the dialectical relationship between the printed images of Paestum and their subject – the temples themselves. Moreover, Benjamin's preoccupation with the impact of mechanical reproduction and the subsequent democratization of images has direct relevance to the spread of knowledge about the temples at Paestum through prints as a means of collating the past.[20]

The Graeco-Roman controversy and history as system

The Graeco-Roman controversy, which featured prominently in architectural debate in the latter part of the eighteenth century, had its basis in theoretical and visual disputes (mainly expressed in prints) rather than in actual buildings. Arguments for the supremacy of Greek over Roman challenged the cultural pre-eminence of modern Italy, which was based, in part at least, on ancient Roman art and architecture being seen as the pinnacle of Western achievement. In this way archaeology became a part of the modern Rome. And this cemented the relationship between archaeology and artistic activity in the flurry of prints and *veduta* paintings which took antiquity as their subject. Alongside this a literary tradition flourished where meticulously compiled indices of inscriptions underscored the importance of verbal evidence to the mapping and understanding of the past. The pan-European concern about the relationship of past to present is important, as it focuses both on how to dismantle and then how to reconfigure Roman dominance, as presented in, for instance, the architectural treatises of Alberti, Palladio and Serlio.[21] Assertions that Roman architecture was a debased and overdecorated form of Greek architecture and therefore represented a decline was a central plank in the evolving notion of chronology and progress in western culture. These ideas were most ably expressed in the writings of Johann Joachim Winckelmann who introduced a systematic, chronological study of art history.[22] The ruins of antiquity were seen as coherent survivors of the classical age that could at once determine and augment the human condition. The 'invention' of ancient Greece was an essential element of this Eurocentric concept of an ideal or classical tradition which had relevance for modern times. In his *Reflections on the Painting and Sculpture of the Greeks*, 1755, translated into English in 1765,[23] Winckelmann states '[there] is but one way for the moderns to become great, and perhaps unequalled ... by imitating the ancients ... It is not only nature which the votaries of the Greeks find in their works, but still more, something superior to nature; ideal beauties, brain-born images.'[24] Paestum featured in this survey of the arts of ancient Greece and was seen as part of the stylistic progression towards the perfection of Periclean Athens. But Winckelmann relied on textual descriptions of objects to write his verbal history which has remained the standard chronology for art history. Winckelmann's ideas also draw heavily on mid-eighteenth-century theories of language, which was itself seen as having developed its resources to allow a clear knowledge of things but excesses in style and rhetoric led to its degeneration.[25] This locates Winckelmann's analysis, or 'system of history' as he preferred to call it, firmly in the verbal tradition. Moreover, the methods of representing this ideal were based on an archetypal image rather than on a literal imitation of nature. And it is here that we can locate one of the central problematics of the aesthetic practices of antiquarianism. The orderly (masculine) forms of the classical ideal were intended to discipline and cultivate taste by imposing themselves on the phantasmagorical (to use Benjamin's term) fragments of antiquity, as evident in the newly discovered monuments of ancient Greece.

The predilection for the Greek was countered by the 'invention of the Etruscans' – an older civilisation than that of the Greeks – by those who championed Rome. This provided an earlier source for the architecture of Rome and repositioned cultural supremacy back on Italian soil. The temples at Paestum provided a stepping stone between Etruscan and Roman architecture, and their presence in Italy enhanced their attraction and their usefulness to this cause. The Graeco-Roman controversy was essentially an aesthetic argument with its basis in verbal histories where both sides of the argument claimed the temples at Paestum as part of the developmental processes of their architecture. One of the principal apologists for Roman supremacy was G.B. Piranesi. His *Della Magnificenza ed Architettura de' Romani* (1761) offered a firm rebuke to the Hellenism which the architectural theorist Marc-Antoine Laugier expressed in his *Essai sur L'Architecture*, printed a few years earlier.[26] In addition to his lavishly illustrated surveys of Roman architecture, Piranesi also produced a series of plates of the temples at Paestum entitled *Differentes Vues de Quelques Restes de Trois Grands Edifices qui Subsistent encore dans le Milieu de L'Ancienne Ville de Pesto autrement Posidonia*, published two months after his death, in 1778, by his son Francesco (plate 10). Like Gazola's images, these plates show the temples as ruins, albeit with the status of monuments. The visual fragments – the ruins of the temples – recorded in images of Paestum could become an invented cultural memory of ancient Greece or Rome where the past was used as a means of validating the present. Even though the primitive nature of the baseless Doric was problematic – if not shocking – to the defenders of both Greek and Roman supremacy, it became part of the aesthetic repertoire used in the creation of modern identities for European cultures.

History or the invention of memory

The enlightenment idea of history embraced at once the visual and the verbal subject, so images played an important part in the construction of historical knowledge. Optical demonstration and visualization were essential processes in the search to uncover the pure historical condition of humankind. This is seen, for instance, in the superlative position held by history painting in the academic hierarchy of subjects, where painters of only the highest calibre depicted the past.[27] In terms of an artist's academic training and the influence this had on public taste, the past – history – was privileged over representations of the landscape or even portraiture. If history was conceived as a visual subject, how could it be related verbally? And what were the consequences of this?

The discovery and ordering of the past played an important part in the life of modern Europe and even became a symbol of modernity. To this end archaeology and the archaeological survey were used to excite the imagination and to proselytize ideas and to re-tell history. Here it is important to consider the intellectual climate in which these histories were constructed, where reason played a pivotal role in the development of historical and linguistic thought and knowledge. And in this context the Aristotelian notion of the relationship between reason, memory and imagination is important in the construction of histories and as a keystone of aesthetic discourse in the eighteenth century.[28] If we accept the Aristotelian notion that reason precedes verbalized ideas, and imagination operates as a visual expression or sensation with memory sitting between reason and imagination, this sequence then begins to reveal something of the role of the status of the image in eighteenth-century architectural debate. In other words, we need a visual recollection of the object to provoke a response. This recollection can also be verbal, but in this case, following Aristotle's sequence, a reliance on the verbal implies the dilution of reason. Aristotle's ideas about imitation or 'mimesis' refer principally to literary aesthetics. But in the eighteenth century the interplay between the verbal and the visual and this questioning of the role of reason was current. For instance, Sir Joshua Reynolds asked to what extent the visual activity of painting could be taught through words.[29] But it is clear that the making of history, whether verbal or visual, required the imitation or representation of objects and events and the practice falls into two main categories: pictorial imitation or literary imitation. But both methods strive to provide an assemblage of 'facts'. We are familiar with textual 'facts' – descriptions of events or actions. But what constituted a visual 'fact' or fragment of knowledge? And were these facts ready for the manipulation of the historian in the same way as verbal ones and have they the same kind of originality?[30]

If we compare the sample of written reactions made by visitors to Paestum discussed earlier in this essay with the array of images of the temples, we see very different kinds of responses. And the language – the taxonomic systems of categorization and description – at the disposal of the authors of these textual accounts often lacks the precision achievable in a visual image. Indeed, Goethe had to 'remember the [linear] history of art' before he could rationalize the aesthetic of the temples. Moreover, it is important to remember that the images of the temples at Paestum offer no narration of progression and sequence which would be a hallmark of verbal histories.[31] We are left then with the question of what kinds of history, if any, the images of Paestum narrate. Does the answer to this lie to some extent in the way in which images were recorded – that is to say, in the case of the temples at Paestum, the mass-produced printed image and the conventions of architectural drawing used, which are, after all, the 'language' of the image.

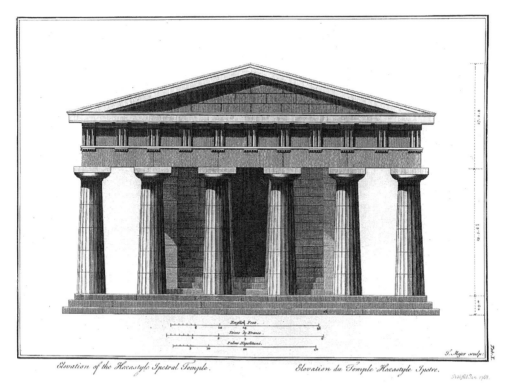

Elevation of the Hexastyle Ipetral Temple.

Elevation du Temple Hexastyle Ipetre.

6 Orthogonal elevation of the Temple of Neptune, in Thomas Major, *Ruins of Paestum*, 1768. Engraving. Courtesy of the Trustees of Sir John Soane's Museum.

Architectural drawing or the visual language of architecture uses various kinds of graphic conventions, which range from the pictorial, drawing inspiration from stage sets and *veduta* painting, to a discrete system of signs which represented three-dimensional architectural forms. The latter system of architectural drawings, using perspective views, orthogonal elevation, details and working drawings, was not merely imitative. Instead buildings were disembodied and dissected, order was imposed on chaos – marks on paper evoked the built fabric. Thomas Major's studies of the Temple of Neptune and its Doric order demonstrate this technique (plates 6 and 7). Here the ruined edifice is reconstructed in orthogonal elevation and is presented outside of its physical context as there is no surrounding landscape and the stone has no texture or patina of age. This method of representation relies on imagination as the construction of this artificial composition is the creation of something other than the object under scrutiny. The abstraction of detail which became a hallmark of 'scientific' or archaeological survey drawings became a system of standardization akin to the dictionaries and encyclopedias which proliferated in the eighteenth century. This produced a legible language of signs which could be subjugated to verbal argument and could, if desired, follow linguistic systems.

This method of recording harnessed the visual image into a system of text-based description. Major's image of the Temple of Neptune is at once an artificial construction and an imitation of the temple which uses 'mimesis' and other rhetorical devices to create a set of pictorial conventions which re-perform the past.

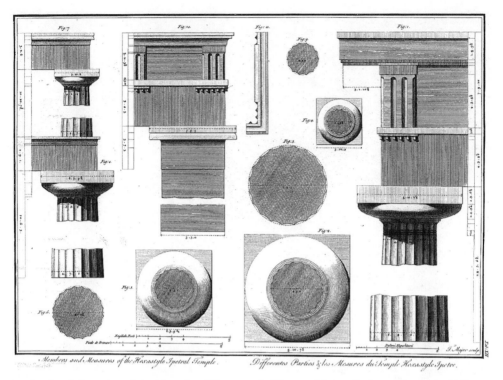

Members and Measures of the Hexastyle Ipetral Temple.   *Différentes Parties & les Mesures du Temple Hexastyle Ipetre.*

7   Study of the order of the Temple of Neptune, in Thomas Major, *Ruins of Paestum*, 1768. Engraving. Courtesy of the Trustees of Sir John Soane's Museum.

Like the camera, with its zoom lens, Major's studies focus in and re-present the original in such a way as to make it conform to the cognitive thought processes involved in its memorialization. The temple front is reconstructed and its component parts are dissected and dismembered, presented instead as elements which help to comprise a vocabulary of classical architecture. The parts and the whole of the temple are measured and these dimensions are expressed three times – in English, French and Piedmontese feet, so emphasizing the pan-European currency and status of these images. And this facilitates the re-use of the various elements of this aesthetic by eighteenth-century architects, as the printed reconstruction of, for instance, the distinctive baseless Doric order of the Temple of Neptune – enables its physical reconstruction, or reperformance, in buildings like the Mausoleum at the Dulwich Picture Gallery (plate 8). In this way the printed images of Paestum encouraged an invented cultural memory which reconfigured the relationship between past and present as the past – Paestum's architecture – could be found in the present – Dulwich. But this is only one kind of history that can be presented in visual terms. Yet the orthogonal reconstruction, together with studies of the architectural members of a building, became an established route or pathway of seeing and perceiving the architecture of the past. The rationalizing system of representing architecture was part of a reductive process based on *logos* – the philosophical method for revealing the truth through linguistic means. This mode of graphic notation and narration of history had been pioneered in the

41

8   The Mausoleum of Noel Desenfans by Sir John Soane at Dulwich Picture Gallery, 1811–1814. Watercolour. Courtesy of the Trustees of Sir John Soane's Museum.

Renaissance and can be seen at full strength in the Vicentine architect Andrea Palladio's *I Quattro Libri dell'Architettura* (1570). The books rely on innovative techniques in architectural drawing to present plans, elevations, sections and details of their subjects, both ancient and modern, which are complemented by textual descriptions of the buildings. And it is here that the resonance between the verbal and the visual can be seen at first hand – with the predominantly visual character of the *Quattro Libri* providing the most legible feature, so ensuring its Europe-wide use as a source book for design and guidebook well in advance of any adequate translations of Palladio's text.[32] Book 4, on antique architecture, where Palladio attempts to reconstruct the buildings of ancient Rome, demonstrates at once the potency of the technique of representing the architecture of the ancient world and the way in which it is made to conform to a set of predetermined conventions governed by abstract notions of geometry which were *seen* to pertain to classical architecture. These values are translated into Palladio's own buildings which appear in Books 2 and 3. His villas, of which *La Rotonda* is perhaps the best

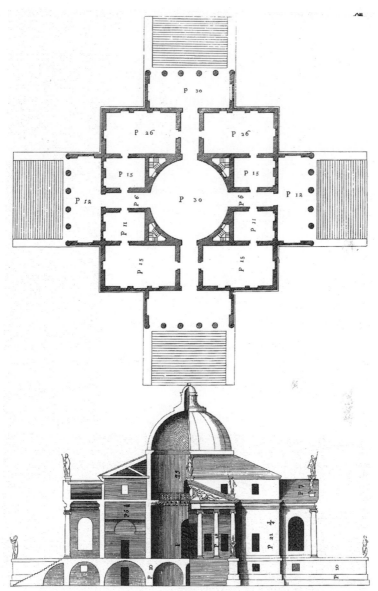

9   Andrea Palladio, The Villa Rotonda, Vicenza, in Andrea Palladio,
I Quattro Libri dell'Architettura, 1570. Engraving. Private collection.

known (plate 9), were essays in the rationalizing use of antique architecture, and
became an almost obligatory part of the Grand Tour.

The order or perfect form of the circle or square had, then, been used since
Palladio's time, at least, to impose order on images of ruins to promote a rational,
linear, geometric, and ultimately male, world, based on pre-existing verbal laws.
Here, in Major's images, we see the rationalizing, 'masculine' forces of analysis,
based on verbal histories, transform the unruly 'feminine' ruined state of the
temples which may well have greater appeal to the imagination. These extractable

43

10   View of the exterior of the Temple of Neptune, in G.B. Piranesi, *Différentes Vues ... de Pesto*, 1778. Engraving. Courtesy of the Trustees of Sir John Soane's Museum.

signs, linguistic procedures for pictorial clarification, created a universal science of recording and expression of a common ideal. This logocentric system distinguishes between the imitated and the imitation, and fitted into the cartesian, rationalist philosophy which found its best expression in the formulaic use of antique architecture in styles often called Palladian and neoclassical, but which, in fact, bore little relation to the actuality of antiquity. This visual tradition of architectural history established theoretical hegemonies and aesthetic practices based on 'tangible reality'. But what of the imagination?

The eighteenth-century discovery of the subconscious and the power and potential of the imagination revealed a world outside that of physical experience. What system could be used to reduce them to a simplistic set of linguistic principles? Or is the psychological experience expressed in non-verbal values where the invisible was made visible? Piranesi's views of the temples offer evidence for this, as they are at once an image of the actuality of the ruins themselves and a carefully constructed reperformance of the temples which, unlike Major's studies, places the temples firmly in the past (plate 10). The scale and size of the temples in relation to the size of the print is important here as they fill the frame and the inclusion of human figures who are dwarfed by the massive bulk of the buildings underscores the awesome appearance of the temples. Compared to Major's views – or rather his reconstructions – there is a very different way of seeing, which guides the mind to a different kind of cognition of the images. Major's reconstruction of the Temple of Neptune presents an image devoid of context and comparative scale. Moreover, his studies of the reconstructed architectural details of the temple on subsequent pages of his publication re-present the temple – or parts of it – in a range of contrasting scales, so privileging various kinds of information about it and prompting an alternative kind of cognition, response or understanding of it. Piranesi's images re-present a different kind of past, which draws attention to the surface texture of the temples and their ruined state, and emphasizes their imposing and emotive aesthetic. Although Piranesi stood in opposition to theorists like Laugier, the narrative technique of his images of Paestum is evocative of the latter's representation of the primitive in architecture, and of the first principles of design as being based on mother nature and having a feminine quality.

These diverse ways of seeing and types of psychological response to both the temples and the images of them do not seem unusual from our viewpoint today. The hypothesis that emotion could be expressed outside of verbal systems had currency in the eighteenth century as aesthetic philosophers moved away from the Albertian position that a picture is a window on the world and developed more speculative theories about the nature of vision. For instance, Bishop Berkeley's *An Essay Towards a New Theory of Vision* (1709) suggests that sight, and the processes of mimesis or recording that follow on from it, are part of a subjective gaze of an ethereal field. This signalled a profound shift in conceptions of vision and the act of viewing as the power and potency of non-verbal expression was recognized. But at the same time this recognition prompted the wish to neuter these images into an established cartesian, rationalist linguistic system of signs which separated the physiological from the psychological. The relationship between vision and cognition had currency in the eighteenth century. But can we call this visual history a form of cognition? The links between the visual and human imagination have been stressed throughout this essay. Moreover, prints were used as a means of expressing knowledge which ran parallel to, and intersected with, other ways of communicating ideas. They were at once 'exterior aids but also interior transformations of consciousness'.[33] Moreover, it has been argued that the authority or the aura of the original has gone in the act of mechanical reproduction.[34] But does the reproduced or printed image have special status? Associations are, after all, culturally determined and in the eighteenth century, if not before, a print would carry weight as it was a published document.[35] The special status of prints and their concomitant authority was recognized at the very beginning of the eighteenth century by Roger de Piles in his *Of the Usefulness and Use of Prints* (1699).[36] Piles expressed admiration for prints as displays of skill in their own right but also as bearers of information, mental aids and for their receptiveness to diverse systems of classification. Importantly for us, de Piles also recognizes the ability of prints to

> represent absent and distant things, as if they were before our eyes ... we see countries, towns, and all the considerable places that we have read of in history, or have seen in our travels [and that these may replace travel for those] who have no strength, leisure or convenience to travel.[37]

But all of this was based on the democratic nature of prints. Their ability to proselytize knowledge was doubtless important. And prints had the potential to represent 'all the visible productions of art and nature' to a wide range of publics who could afford them. But there is a paradox here. The democratizing processes of the printing press also created a different kind of rarefied object in both material and intellectual terms. Prints came to represent what was not visible. As John Locke wrote in his *Essay Concerning Human Understanding*,[38] 'the materials of all our knowledge, are suggested and furnished to the mind only by sensation and reflection. When the understanding is once stored [the mind] has the power to repeat, compare, and unite them . . . and so can make . . . new and complex ideas.'[39]

The fusion of artistic and 'archaeological' activity, that is to say the different conventions of recording architecture, come together in the realm of prints. Prints become 'facts' or fragments of knowledge – syntax and subject matter of a visual history – which both shatter the tradition from which the image came as the image is dislocated from its original context, and create the need for a new context. There is no such thing as an authentic print – reproducibility is part of the work, and the lack of authenticity in prints is important as it constructs a new history, or archaeology of knowledge, as the act of reproduction emancipates art from its dependence on ritual. This process of democratization removes the work of art from what Benjamin identifies as the cult value of the original to the exhibition value and refers to the practice of displaying objects, here also representative of knowledge, which become part of a new cultural tradition.[40] This had its roots in the sometimes random assemblage of the cabinet of curiosities. Prints played an important part in such collections and were traded regularly so collections were fluid and the configuration of a group of prints continually changed. Perhaps this is partly to do with the social class of the print collector, who was looking to move up the social ladder using an increasingly impressive array of possessions. But it was not a process of amassing as was the case with other objects. The practice of regrouping bodies of printed material also found expression in assemblages of prints which made up a publication on a certain theme – in this case the temples at Paestum. In this way prints acquire a different status and meaning as the 'author', that is to say the collector or publisher, of their sequence or interrelationship could change and so present a diverse range of histories.

Benjamin's ideas about history, memory and modernity also help us to see how these prints operated as facts or fragments of knowledge.[41] Although he was concerned with the nineteenth century – his modernity – the recognition that antiquity resided within modernity, and functioned as a stimulus to unconscious thought, can also be applied to earlier periods. Whilst these lost thoughts and fantasies come to the fore they reveal the *prehistory* (in Benjamin's terms) of modernity. For us this shows how these images, as fragments of a lost language, might serve to place memory-accounts in contemporary configurations of knowledge. These configurations are in our case the assemblages of prints which remain fluid – an ever-changing discourse – as collections changed according to the taste of individual collectors. Our understanding of the linguistic processes and aesthetic practices involved in the production, dissemination and collation of the images of Paestum is an essential part of our understanding of visual histories. Moreover, Benjamin's collector (or rag picker – a phrase he also uses) is not a curator who wishes to place objects in false contexts, as the past lies beyond the reach of the intellect and can only be regained through flashes or fragments which emanate from the material object or image of that object. Collecting, then, becomes a way of transmitting experience through objects.

The cultural 'ownership' of the temples at Paestum is diverse and complex, as they appear and reappear in various ways at various points in time. They can be copied and recreated in landscape gardens or quoted in architectural forms. And prints of them are objects in their own right. Moreover, the means of expression is appropriate for the subject as architecture is experienced principally by sight – that is, the act of perception which is a visual rather than a verbal phenomenon. The culture of collecting not only represents the exhibition value of prints and the growth of a socially mobile intellectual class, but also demonstrates how this practice was aligned to the methods of scientific investigation which involved the collating and ordering of knowledge through the use of system. Many of the essays in this collection examine how the remains of the past were recorded and configured into a range of intellectual systems, and how antiquity was interrogated as a means of exploring contemporary intellectual concerns. The juxtaposition of these contemporary concerns with recent theories of ways of seeing and the reproducibility and legibility of images remains a central theme in this volume, and it is the intention that the essays form a discourse around these ideas. If we accept that our ideas can be expressed and retained visually, then our starting point for this consideration of the interrelationship between architecture, antiquarianism and aesthetic practices, the images of Paestum, take on a new dimension. They are not merely aestheticized history which requires narrative but comprise another kind of history and knowledge which exists in the realm of the senses.

Notes

1 See especially F. Haskell, *History and its Images*, New Haven and London: Yale University Press, 1993 and A. Potts, *Flesh and the Ideal: Winckelmann and the Origins of Art History*, New Haven and London: Yale University Press, 1994.

2 See B. Stafford, *Body Criticism: imaging the unseen in enlightenment art and medicine*, Boston, Mass.: MIT, 1991, especially chap. 1.

3 There is a substantial body of literature on this topic: see, for instance, Jacques Derrida, *Of Grammatology*, Baltimore: Johns Hopkins, 1976, and Paul de Man, *The Resistance to Theory*, Manchester: MUP, 1986 and *Blindness and Insight*, Minneapolis: University of Minnesota, 1983, which critiques Derrida.

4 M. Foucault, *The Archaeology of Knowledge*, trans. A.M. Sheridan Smith, London: Tavistock, 1972, especially chap. 1.

5 The temples are fully discussed together with the various identifications made of them, in A.W. Lawrence, *Greek Architecture*, Harmondsworth: Pelican History of Art, 1973.

6 In the interests of clarity, I use these names throughout this article although various names and descriptions were used in the range of publications I discuss.

7 Diary note dated 21 November 1761, as quoted in J. Fleming, *Robert Adam and his Circle*, pp.

293 ff.

8 ibid.

9 Richard Payne Knight, MS Sicilian Diary, f 3. This was rediscovered in Weimar: the Goethe Schiller Institute, in 1980 and published as C. Stumpf (ed.), *Richard Payne Knight: Expedition into Sicily, 1777*, London: British Museum Publications, 1986.

10 Goethe, *Italienische Riese* 1, 23 March 1787. The remarks of Payne Knight and Goethe may have a closer connection than an expression of a similar response. Goethe owned a copy of Richard Payne Knight's diary of his Sicilian tour (now the only known example, see note 9) and used it as a kind of guidebook for his travels about Italy.

11 See J. Serra (ed.), *Paestum and the Doric Revival 1750–1830*, Florence: Centro di institution, 1986; a fuller version of this exhibition catalogue was published simultaneously in Italian.

12 See D. Arnold, 'Count Gazola and the Temples at Paestum: An influential Grand Tour Guide', *Apollo*, August 1992, vol. 136, no. 366, pp. 95–9.

13 S. Lang, 'Early Publications of the Temples at Paestum', *Journal of the Warburg and Courtauld Institutes*, vol. 13, 1950, pp. 48–64.

14 Ducros's images of Paestum are discussed in *Images of the Grand Tour: Louis Ducros 1748–1810*, Musée Cantonale, Geneva: Editions Tricorne, 1985.

15 See Lang, op. cit. (note 13), and Arnold, op. cit. (note 12), for a full discussion of the complex connections between Gazola's images and the assemblages of prints of Paestum.

16 Arnold, op. cit. (note 12).

17 Lang, op. cit. (note 13).

18 See ibid.

19 W. Benjamin, *The Arcades Project*, trans. H. Eiland and K. McLaughlin, Boston, Mass.: Harvard University Press, 2001.

20 W. Benjamin, 'The Work of Art in the Age of Mechanical Reproduction', in *Illuminations*, ed. Hannah Arendt, trans. Harry Zohn, London, 1973.

21 The re-use of Roman architectural motifs and their role in the creation of an invented cultural memory are discussed in D. Arnold, *The Georgian Country House: Architecture, Landscape and Society,* Stroud: Sutton Publishing, 1998, chap. 6, especially pp. 100–16.

22 For a discussion of Winckelmann's system, see Potts, op. cit. (note 1), and Maria Grazia Lolla's essay in this volume.

23 J.J. Winckelmann, *Gedanken über die Nachahmung der griechischen Werke in der Malerei und Bildhauerkunst, 1755,* trans. H. Fuseli as *Reflections on the Painting and Sculpture of the Greeks*, London, 1765. Reprinted by Menston: Scolar Press, 1972.

24 As quoted in Robert Eisner, *Travelers to an Antique Land*, Ann Arbor: University of Michigan Press, 1991, p 76.

25 Winckelmann's approach to writing history is discussed in Potts, op cit. (note 1), especially pp. 33 ff.

26 Marc-Antoine Laugier (later known as l'Abbé Laugier), *Essai sur L'Architecture*, 1753, republished in English with additions in 1755 and 1756. The translation by Wolfgang and Anni Hermann, *Marc-Antoine Laugier, An Essay on Architecture*, Los Angeles: Hennessey and Ingalls Inc., 1977, is based on the 1753 version.

27 See, for instance, Haskell, op. cit. (note 1).

28 Aristotle, *Poetics I*, 25. This is essentially an account of Greek tragedy, which demonstrates how plot, character and spectacle combine to provoke emotional responses. It introduces the concepts of 'mimesis' ('imitation'), 'hamartia' ('error') and 'katharsis', which continue to inform thinking about literature and aesthetics. Aristotle's ideas about the relationship between thought and representation and the rejection of Platonic systems of aesthetic thinking were also expressed in *Metaphysics*: see especially book V.

29 See M. Postle, *Sir Joshua Reynolds and History Painting*, Cambridge: CUP, 1995.

30 For a discussion of the relationship between the historian and 'facts', see E.H. Carr, *What is History?*, Harmondsworth: Penguin, 1961.

31 The problematics of this kind of contrived notion of historical sequence are discussed by de Man, op. cit. (note 3), especially p. 67.

32 Various translations of *I Quattro Libri dell'Architettura* appeared in the eighteenth century in Britain. These included Giacomo Leoni's unreliable 1715–16 edition (translated from a French version) and Isaac Ware's more accurate translation which appeared in 1738 with the help of Lord Burlington, who provided financial support and the translated text.

33 See W. Ong, *Orality and Literature: The technologising of the world*, London and New York: Routledge, 1982.

34 See Benjamin, *Illuminations*, op. cit. (note 20).

35 On this point, see C. Talbot, 'Prints and the Definitive Image', in G. Tyson and S. Wagonheim (eds), *Print Culture in the Renaissance: Essays on the advent of printing in Europe*, Newark, Delaware: University of Delaware Press, 1986.

36 Roger de Piles, 'De l'utilité des estampes, et de leur usage', in *Abrégé de la vie des peintres, avec des réflexions sur leurs ouvrages*, Paris, 1699, translated as 'Of the Usefulness and Use of Prints', in *The Art of Painting, with the Lives and Characters … of the Most Eminent Painters*, 3rd edn, London, 1754.

37 De Piles, op. cit. (note 36), pp. 56, 58.

38 John Locke, *An Essay Concerning Human Understanding*, London, 1706. Abridged and edited by J.W. Yolton, London and Melbourne, 1976.

39 Locke, op. cit. (note 38), p. 45.

40 See Benjamin, 'The Work of Art in the Age of Mechanical Reproduction', op. cit. (note 20).

41 Benjamin, *The Arcades Project*, op. cit. (note 19).

4

The Sources and Fortunes of Piranesi's Archaeological Illustrations

Susan M. Dixon

Giovanni Battista Piranesi's prints have long been regarded as instrumental in constructing aesthetic preferences in mid-eighteenth- and nineteenth-century European art. Well known are his contributions to the neoclassical style, via Adam and Fontaine and Percier, and to Eyptomania, via his chimneypiece designs.[1] Equally influential was his mode of representing architectural monuments. Piranesi's sublime conceptions preceded the creations of French luminères, such as Boulée and Ledoux, and his picturesque or proto-Romantic depictions of ancient Rome have been credited with fueling the subsequent fashion for the ruin.[2] There is much about Piranesi's work, however, that was given little attention by his contemporaries and near contemporaries. This essay will focus on a less successful aesthetic, that of his mode of illustrating his archaeological publications. In these, he combined various types and scales of representation on one sheet. There can be dizzying juxtaposition of unlike imagery: a stark geometric section next to a palpable view, or an over-sized detail – perhaps sketchily drawn – next to a bird's-eye view – perhaps rendered with richly textured shadows (plates 11–13). The individual images are distinguished often in dramatic ways by being set against a white void or more commonly within a trompe-l'oeil framing device. These devices include a curling piece of parchment nailed or roped into place, and sometimes a bracketed stone plaque. They can be layered one upon another, sometimes obscuring one image in favour of another. These illustrations appear first in great number in Piranesi's *L'Antichità Romane* of 1756, and then throughout the early 1760s in his seven shorter archaeological texts and the polemical *Della Magnificenza*.[3] They are confusing, as was noted by some critics in his day.[4] They might be regarded as akin to contemporary webpages in their eclectic presentation, differing in that the separate frames are immovable, and the scale alters with a glance of the eye rather than the click of a mouse.[5]

Giovanni Battista Piranesi was prolific in his production of prints.[6] The multi-informational image, as I will term the type of print described above, is not the one that connoisseurs regard as quintessential Piranesi. This description is usually reserved for his atmospheric *vedute* or his macabre *carceri*. However, they are quintessentially Piranesian in that this artist alone exploited this mode of

11 G.B. Piranesi, Illustrations of the Outlet Building of the Emissarium of Lago Albano, plate 7 from *Descizione e Disegno dell'Emissaro del Lago Albano*. By permission of the Division of Rare and Manuscript Collections, Cornell University Library, Ithaca, NY.

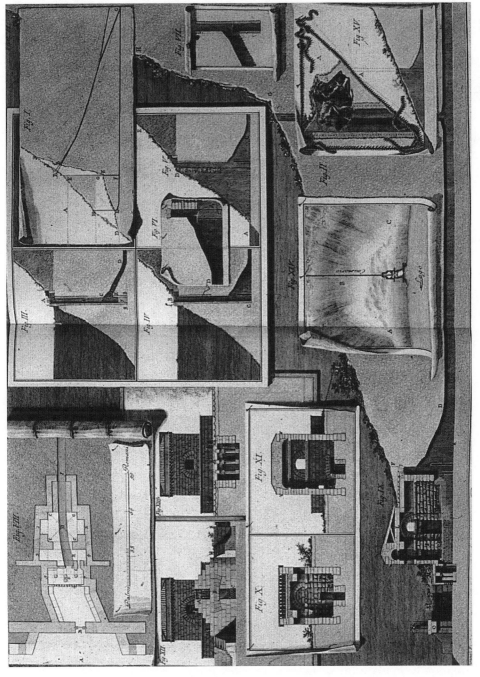

12 G.B. Piranesi, Various illustrations of the Emissarium of Lago Albano, plate 2 from *Descizione e Disegno dell'Emissaro del Lago Albano*. By permission of the Division of Rare and Manuscript Collections, Cornell University Library, Ithaca, NY.

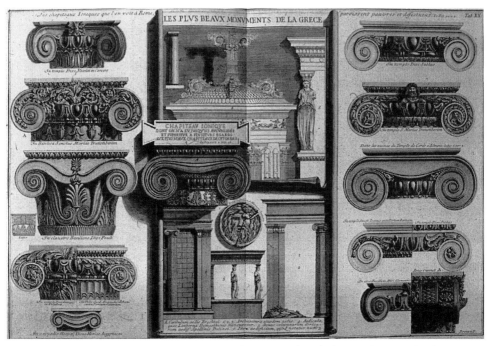

13 G.B. Piranesi, Various Roman Ionic Capitals compared with the Greek example of Le Roy, plate 20 from *Della Magnificenza*. By permission of the Division of Rare and Manuscript Collections, Cornell University Library, Ithaca, NY.

representation to great extreme. There are only a handful of artists who imitated it.

In this article, I will explore first the precedents of such images: mainly, the cartographic and antiquarian traditions. The second part of the article will elaborate on the images of one of Piranesi's most successful emulators: Jean-Laurent-Pierre Hoüel. Nearly one-sixth of the 264 illustrations in Hoüel's *Voyage pittoresque des isles de Sicile, de Malte, et de Lipari*, a two-volume work issued in 1782 and 1787, are multi-informational in the manner of Piranesi. I will argue that this particular mode of illustration appealed to Hoüel because it enhanced his goal of assessing all types of information, in order to offer his reader a living cultural history of the islands off the south-western coast of Italy.[7]

Sources

The cartographic tradition provides the most substantial visual precedents for the presentation of various types of images within separate framing devices. As early as the beginning of the sixteenth century, a separate key containing verbal information to explain the imagery in the base map was a standard feature. That information was integral to the understanding of the map, and could not easily be divorced from it. The key was usually placed in a separate frame, on trompe-l'oeil stone plaques or as if engraved into illusionistic leather strapwork most often associated with Mannerist printed page design, which was represented as securely affixed to the base map. These framing devices facilitated the connection between the seemingly incompatible but mutually dependent verbal and visual information. This can be seen in Etienne Du Pérac's mid-sixteenth-century maps of Rome and Giambattista Falda's of the last quarter of the seventeenth century.[8] Soon after its initial appearance, the framing device was used as well to shelter supplementary visual information. For example, the artists of the sixteenth-century fresco map series in the Galleria delle carte geografiche in the Vatican Palace displayed plans and views of important cities on trompe-l'oeil sheets illusionistically pinned to the base regional map.[9] The plans and views are of a scale much larger than that of the map represented as underneath them.

Piranesi was keenly interested in mapping. He aided in the publication of the Nolli map of 1748. In response to a Papal commission to survey Rome to help create demarcations of the city's traditional fourteen rioni, or districts, the architect Giambattista Nolli produced a representation of the city innovative not only for its topographic accuracy, but also for its method of representation: an ichnographic plan in which the poched areas immediately signal built space and the white, open space. Piranesi created the *vedute* over which the map is illusionistically placed, reversing the expectation that the *vedute* should be in the attached frame by having Nolli's map appear as if it was on a piece of parchment curled to reveal the composite views of major ancient and modern buildings of Rome underneath it. The artist was also very likely involved in hanging the fragmented map of ancient Rome known as the *Forma Urbis* in the Capitoline Museum;[10] the map was one of Pope Benedict XIV's prized acquisitions.[11] Furthermore, Piranesi created various maps for his *L'Antichità Romane* of 1756 and *Il Campo Marzio* of 1762, which utilize the framing device to display all kinds of supplemental information.

Some antiquarians and archaeologists of late seventeenth and early eighteenth century employed this illustrative technique in their publications of the built monuments of ancient civilizations, including of ancient Rome. Maria Grazia Lolla has recently noted that such use of the trompe-l'oeil sheets 'celebrated paper as the ultimate technology of preservation' in a field of study in which the destruction of many of the artefacts and monuments was sometimes imminent.[12] Within the frames, all matter of things could be presented: plans and sections of underground chambers; architectural decorative and structural details; and visual sources for reconstructions, such as medals. To list just a few, Pietro Santi di Bartoli, Carlo Fontana and Johann Fischer von Erlach used the multi-informational image in their *Gli antichi sepolchri ovvero mausolei romani et etruschi* of 1697, *Discorso sopra l'antico Monte Citatorio* of 1704, and *Entwurff einer historischen Architektur* of 1721, respectively. In his own work, Piranesi relied heavily on Bartoli's research on ancient Roman tombs; he borrowed wholesale one of Fontana's illustrations, and he copied some of Fischer von Erlach's imagery.[13] Surely Piranesi learned the usefulness of this kind of pictorial invention from these and other scholars.

The noted architect Filippo Juvarra, whom Piranesi admired, used the trompe-l'oeil framing device cleverly in his presentation drawings, especially early in his career. In his creative architectural projects for the competitions held by Rome's art academy, the Accademia di San Luca, plans, elevations, sections, and perspectival drawing, sometimes of different scale, appear on same sheet. Consider the prize-winning design for a royal palace he submitted for the Concorsi Clementino of 1705.[14] If not the inventor of such combinations, Juvarra was surely the popularizer of this means of presenting various types of information about a building project. Pietro Paolo Coccetti and Carlo Marchionni, among others, submitted drawings for the competitions sponsored by the Accademia di San Luca, which exemplify this fashion.[15]

The architectural discourse of the day, too, must have had some impact on Piranesi's choice of the multi-informational image, albeit in a reactionary way. Aware of the trend in Roman architectural drawing Jacques-François Blondel, the president of the Académie royale d'architecture, stated emphatically that it was distasteful to include geometric and perspective drawings on the same page.[16] Blondel's comments were made during lectures he delivered to architectural students at the Academy, which were later published. It was taken to heart by some engineers and archaeologists of the day, including Julien David Le Roy. In his *Les Ruines des plus beaux monuments de la Grèce*, first published in 1757, Le Roy asserted the supremacy of ancient Greek over Roman architectural design. Le Roy had provided many more geometric drawings – plans, sections and elevations – of the Greek temples than he had perspective views. Views were included in *Les Ruines* but these were relegated to separate sheets and even to a separate part of the publication. The text sparked a polemic between mainly French and Italian thinkers in which national cultural pride was at stake. In his *Della Magnificenza* of 1761, Piranesi unleashed one of his strongest polemical responses to this text. Piranesi acerbically countered Le Roy's arguments by producing evidence of the wonderfully imaginative creations of the ancient Roman designers. He redrew what Le Roy had deemed the 'most beautiful' capital created by Greek architects, and surrounded it with nearly a dozen of what Piranesi believed were much more sumptuous Roman capitals.[17] He made use of the trompe-l'oeil framing device, creating an assemblage that looks as if he snipped pages from Le Roy's publication and pasted them in the centre of his own presentation (plate 11). To heighten his criticism of Le Roy, Piranesi poked fun at the Frenchman's manner of illustration. He brought attention to the shallowness of Le Roy's renderings by adding strong shadows to the capital in question, as well as to the roof ornament of the Choratic Monument of Lysicrates, which is represented in elevation with other famous examples of Athenian architecture. The disembodied shadow of the roof ornament, in particular, seems to underscore the lack of substance to Le Roy's original illustrations.

Of his multi-informational images, Piranesi wrote: 'I have portrayed ... the ruins, representing more than their exterior facades, but also their plans, their interiors, distinguishing their parts in section and profile and indicating their materials and the manner of their construction – according to what I could derive in the course of many years of exact observation, excavation and research.'[18] In effect, his images provided a whole body of information which took him years to accumulate. Piranesi manipulated that information, making selections and re-arranging the artefacts when necessary. He wrote: 'I have proposed to publish those [artefacts] that I feel merit more than the others to be illustrated, those remains that are useful in recovering' the historical monuments.[19] He was aware of the criticism that his notion of historical reconstruction might be considered too fanciful, too much the product of his imagination, and he defended his use of 'reasonable conjecture' in the process.[20] Piranesi's larger goal was to gather and sort through all this diverse information, and with the help of his imagination, to devise a reconstruction of the ancient Rome and its culture. The *Ichnographia* of the *Campo Marzio* is only a partial realization of that goal.[21] It could be argued that the multi-informational image was Piranesi's tool in the process of obtaining a reasonable historical reconstruction.

Some of the intellectual discourse of the day on questions of epistemology contained language that parallels that found in Piranesi's description of his archaeological methods of reconstruction. Ludovico Muratori, noted theologian and historian at the Papal court in Piranesi's day, explored the subject of the functions and malfunctions of the brain in a polemical text on witchcraft entitled *Della forza della fantasia umana* of 1745.[22] Citing many ancient and modern philosophers, Muratori stated what were very traditional ideas about memory. Like Aristotle, he distinguished the intellect or mind as that which treats the immaterial or the spiritual, from fantasy or imagination as that which deals with the material, those things understood by the senses. The sense impressions received – 'ideas, images, species or traces of things seen, heard, smelt, tasted or touched' – are retained by the memory, which he likened to an actual storehouse, and to a gallery.[23] In this analogy, Muratori illustrates his adherence to a very ancient memory tradition. He elaborated on the traditional by maintaining that memory could not exist without the help of fantasy; the mind has the capacity to commit images and ideas to memory only because fantasy received and acted upon the impressions conveyed from the senses. To him, fantasy was not initially an active force, but one that was reactive to the sensations that it encountered, an operation on sense impressions. It was not a process solely of accumulation, but also of selection. Fantasy helped 'combine, divide, abstract ... and judge the impressions it received', for eventually that information expressed itself not as a wealth of images, but as a single image or a 'compendium' in the mind's eye.[24] Muratori supplied a visual analogy for the operation of fantasy; the topographical map of a city is a 'portrait' of this aspect of human fantasy. The process of creating a map, he inferred, is akin to the process through which fantasy makes sense out of the sundry perceptions of the city. Although the map is inferior to what is represented, it had taken all the impressions of the city, and distilled or encapsulated them into a single image, a 'compendium' that was an expression of those impressions.[25] In light of Muratori's description, Piranesi's multi-informational images appear not as products of the workings of fantasy on a wealth of informational sources (this could be reserved for his *Ichnographia*), but rather as representations of the process of the workings of fantasy or imagination on that information. They assembled in one place, on one sheet, different visual facts, which when juxtaposed allowed for the potential operations – 'combining, dividing, abstracting, ... and judging' – for Piranesi's eventual synthesis into a single image, a reconstructed vision of ancient Rome.

The multi-informational image as a presentation tool, however, was not taken up by the generation of archaeologists after Piranesi. The methods and the goals of the newly developing science of archaeology underwent a sea change in the next century. From Carlo Fea, excavator of the Roman Forum in the late eighteenth century to Rudolfo Lanciani, the renowned nineteenth-century archaeologist of Rome, nearly all chose what was to their mind a less invasive method of procedure and a more precise if narrower analysis of the artefacts and their find spots.[26] More important to this study, they utilized a manner of representation very different from Piranesi's. The drawings are, in the main, geometric, with plans being highly favoured. They are tentatively and at times incompletely rendered, illustrating for the most part only that which was determined from the tangible evidence. They employ new graphic conventions such as dashed lines and poched walls to distinguish what existed at the time of excavation from what was thought to have existed in the past, and the use of colour or varied line weight to suggest different 'layers' of a building. Piranesi's renderings of the past, although layered, are not a palimpsest in the same way; the components are always full-bodied, often awash with shadow and hence located in a place that is real and a time that is specific. Piranesi's presentation of history, however, is of a prolonged, sustained and sustainable history rather than the single fleeting moment of that presented by Lanciani's drawings, for example. And with the multi-informational image, Piranesi acknowledges the nooks and crannies among the incomplete remains, and they are teeming with potential new knowledge.[27]

Fortunes

As far as I know, the only purpose to which the multi-informational image was put after Piranesi was to illustrate some of the *voyages pittoresques*, travel literature that became very popular in the late eighteenth century. For example, a few of the many artists employed to create the illustrations for Abbé de Saint-Non's *Voyage pittoresque: ou, description des royaumes de Naples et de Sicile* (1781–86) utilized this mode of representation.[28] The second part of this essay will focus on the most bold of Piranesi's imitators, Jean-Laurent-Pierre Houël, author and illustrator of a publication about his travels from 1776 to 1779 in Sicily, Malta and the isles of Lipari. The text *Voyage pittoresque des isles de Sicile, de Malte, et de Lipari, ou l'on traite des Antiquités qui s'y trouvent encore des principaux Phénomènes que la Nature y offre; du Costumes de Habitans, & quelques usages*, was issued in two tomes in 1782 and 1787.

The *voyage pittoresque* is difficult to categorize as a literary genre. It is distinct from travel writing of the Grand Tour in that the subject is a region then considered exotic, and (nearly) uncommented upon by foreigners. They are not strictly histories, although the history of the region is often recounted in them. Nor do they present only the cultural objects that a visitor would find in a region, and thus they do not belong to the guidebook tradition. While the authors often made extensive notes of the ancient architectural works visited, the texts they produced were not archaeological like those of Le Roy's or Stuart and Revett's, full of carefully measured and delineated geometric drawings.[29] Instead, they provided a broad spectrum of information, such as regional geography, political institutions, economic practices and social customs. The contents of the *voyage pittoresque* have been credited with inspiring all manners of Enlightened thinking induced by the mind-broadening coming-to-terms, however wrongheaded, with the otherness in the foreign.[30]

Some of Hoüel's first comments in the preface of his *Voyage pittoresque* stress the archaeological aspect of the book; he wrote that he has represented a certain number of ancient amphitheatres, temples, tombs and the like, found in the region.[31] But it is much more than a presentation of the extant ancient monuments, as the title infers, and the lengthy and unsystematic text makes very clear. It is an odd mix of geographical, geological, ethnographic, economic, commercial, as well as archaeological information about the places that he visited. It is, in fact, organized so that the reader follows Hoüel's movements throughout the area, from his departure from Marseilles to his springboard point at Naples, through parts of northern Sicily, to the Lipari Islands, and then back to western and southern Sicily. Probably the best known passages are the lengthy sections on the ever-changing appearance and workings of the volcanoes, particularly Mount Aetna, and the basalt rock formations created by volcanic eruptions.[32] Scattered throughout the text are comments regarding the varied costumes of certain villagers, and the festivities they engaged in on certain holidays.[33] There are accounts of the villagers' practice of making rope, forming soap, mining salt and salting fish. Native and imported plant life is recorded in the illustrations, and agricultural methods of the region are described.[34] Also, the author recorded encounters with particularly charming villagers and hospitable regional princes.[35] Throughout, one glimpses Hoüel's attitudes towards culture as a product of history, and towards history as accessible from its present culture. He read the past as preserved in the present: for example, contemporary fishing techniques were little altered from those practised by the ancients; costumes and institutions retained ancient forms. Imported plants record a history of colonization and of trading routes. He was at times interested in oral history, even of very recent events. Accounts of the visit of foreign dignitaries in their provinces, as recalled by villagers, are recorded with great elaboration, although also with scepticism in some cases.[36] Hoüel attempted to describe the total aspects of culture, shaped by the ecology of an area, a task that required knowledge of the symbiotic relationship of past and present circumstances of the region.

Barbara Stafford, one of the few scholars to study Hoüel's *Voyage pittoresque*, has limited her discussion to his interest in natural science, in particular the effects of the volcanic action at Aetna.[37] She marks the late eighteenth-century sea change in attitudes towards nature – perhaps put too simply here – from the employ of a subjective to an objective gaze, and the ensuing drive to invent the means to represent these new attitudes in the literary and visual arts. Hoüel is undoubtedly a transition figure in this sea change. Stafford has chosen only certain illustrations of the natural wonders of these islands in which she feels Hoüel leans towards denying his role in the presentation, particularly in his absorbing far- and close-range views. In some cases, however, the text and imagery convey Hoüel's highly involved – and in this sense picturesque – shaping of what he encountered on the Mediterranean islands.

Hoüel's *Voyage pittoresque* was the product of not one, but two trips to the region, a phenomenon highly unusual for the time. Having studied painting, engraving and architecture in France, he made his first journey to Italy, from 1769 to 1772, to conduct a type of grand tour for his artistic improvement.[38] Regarded as a highly talented painter of landscapes – he had a keen aptitude for rendering the landscape wholistically, i.e., the seamless relation of sky to land, or sky to sea – Hoüel travelled to Sicily in the company of the Marquis d'Havricourt and rendered 'the effects of nature perfectly'.[39] When he returned to the region a second time in 1776, his intent was to compile a *voyage pittoresque* on Sicily and the adjacent islands to rival the newly published and very popular ones by Patrick Brydone and the Baron de Riesedel then being circulated in translation in Paris.[40] He was operating with a stipend from the Directeur Général des Bâtiments du Roi, the Comte d'Angiviller, although monies from that source dissipated long before his excursion was up and Hoüel had to find other ways to finance his publication: selling some of his drawings to Catherine the Great, for example.[41] What is important for us to know is that he returned home with about 1,000 drawings, these in addition to the drawings from the first trip, and compiled the illustrations that were then engraved for his publication in France. These included: measured drawings of architecture and sometimes of artefacts, mainly of black crayon with a grey sepia wash; views in gouache; and various rough sketches.[42] It has been noted that in creating the illustrations, Hoüel became analytical, 'erasing the emotion of his first impressions' of the subject after consulting his original sketches and after referencing various texts, both ancient and contemporary, on finer points of knowledge.[43] However, while emotion may have been eradicated from some illustrations of *Voyage pittoresque*, Hoüel's manipulation of the material is present, especially in his multi-informational images.[44]

The format used so lavishly by Piranesi was a pictorial means to present varied types of information and the artist's engagement with, and synthesis of, that information, and so must have seemed suitable for Hoüel's purposes. Nearly 50 of the 264 illustrations of *Voyage pittoresque* are multi-informational in format. And as in Piranesi's archaeological publications, Hoüel's text is driven by the images. He stated: 'I support my illustrations (*dessins*) with what I have written, and I verify my writing with what I have illustrated.'[45] As my interest is in his mode of illustration and its effectiveness for his purposes, I will curtail my discussion to five prints which are Piranesian in their use of multiple framing devices. The first depicts the archaeological remains of a Greek amphitheatre at ancient Tyndaris on the island of Sicily (plate 14).[46] This theatre, probably Greek in origin and heavily remodelled by the Romans, had been built at the edge of Tyndaris's decumanus. Because the city occupied a plateau at the summit of a hill overlooking the northern coast of Sicily, the amphitheatre clung to the slope of that hill. Hoüel represented it in four different images on the one sheet. A rendered section is located in the lower right-hand corner. The scale bar is drawn as if it were underground in relation to the amphitheatre section. A plan of the same scale lies to the section's left; it, too, is rendered with shadows. It is presented as if on a surface sheet whose right-hand edge appears as a rip in the paper and whose lower edge appears to be formed by the horizon of the amphitheatre's section. The ripped paper is obscured towards the top of the page by a trompe-l'oeil sheet, draped over a dowel and suspended on tasselled ropes originating beyond the edge of the print.

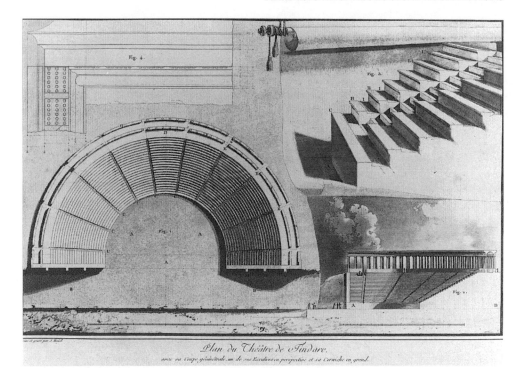

Plan du Théâtre de Tyndare.
avec une Coupe géométrale au de ses Escaliers en perspective et sa Corniche en grand.

14   J.L.P. Hoüel, Plan of the Theatre at Tyndaris, plate 58 from *Voyage pittoresque*, vol. 1. By permission of the Research Collections of The New York Public Library, New York.

This draped sheet holds a perspectival section of the theatre seats and stairs, in a scale decidedly larger than that of the theatre and section. The sheet's bottom edge appears to curl to reveal the amphitheatre section below. In the upper left-hand corner is a very sketchy plan of a cornice, an architectural fragment from the building, rendered as if suspended in the void on the sheet above the amphitheatre plan. In all, the print exhibits three different scales, three different types of rendering, and three different implied surfaces on which the artist has placed those renderings. The effect is indeed Piranesian. At his most complex, Piranesi employed nine trompe-l'oeil layers on a base sheet, with fourteen different images in at least four different scales (plate 12).

Because of the different nature of their researches, Hoüel's subject matter sometimes differs vastly from that of Piranesi. Consider Hoüel's image which informs the viewer of the manner by which Sicilian fishermen catch tuna and prepare it for market (plate 15).[47] Tuna fishing was one of the major economic activities on the island and had been for many centuries; Hoüel concluded that the manner of fishing had not been altered substantially over the years. In a low vista from the shoreline, one can see two makeshift racks on which are suspended sheets of paper. On one sheet is a rendered section of the fishermen's netting techniques, represented in a very small scale. A second sheet holds a view of the boat full of fishermen outfitted for the catch; below this is a third sheet on which are several sketchy diagrams. One of these diagrams is of a tuna body, designating where the fishermen make cuts to create the best fillets; another is of two tools

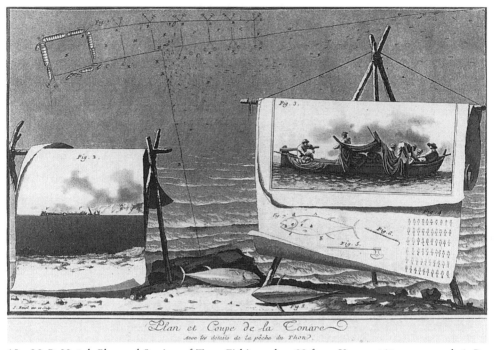

15   J.L.P. Hoüel, Plan and Section of Tuna Fishing, plate 28 from *Voyage pittoresque*, vol. 1. By permission of the Research Collections of The New York Public Library, New York.

used in the filleting process; and the third, curious diagram, shows how the fish would be arranged on the beach as part of the preparation process. Realistically represented tuna also appear as if beached on the shore, one positioned so as to show the viewer its underside and hence the meat of its fillet. Again there is the mixing of types of representation, size and scale among the image as well as degrees of realism, and the trompe-l'oeil sheet is used to help distinguish the various images. Hoüel has added visual interest by having the surface of the sea, a large area given the low vantage point, provide the base sheet upon which the other images are layered. Floating in this area is the plan of a typical positioning of boats and nets during a catch. Throughout the publication, with only few exceptions, a view acts as the backdrop for Hoüel's trompe-l'oeil framing devices. As far as I can ascertain, only in one case does Piranesi conceive of a view as the sole backdrop for successive layers of images, in his illustration of the outlet building to the emissary of the Lago Albano in the environs of Rome (plate 12). Piranesi defies the pictorial aspect of his *vedute* by pinning two sheets, one housing a section and the other, an interior view, to an exterior view of the structure. Piranesi's multi-informational image is bold in calling attention to his method of representation; Hoüel's composition, however, is more successful in retaining a picturesque quality, despite the disruption of the view.

In a variety of ways, Hoüel utilized this mode of illustration to his own pictorial ends. In two cases, he includes the plans of various structures within the traditional *vedute*. The first is the temple of Aesculpius in the plains of ancient Agrigentum (plate 16).[48] Located on the southwest coast of Sicily and occupying a

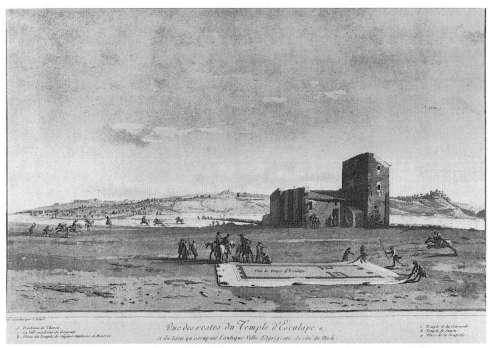

16   J.L.P. Houël, View of the ruins of the Temple of Aesculpius, plate 215 from *Voyage pittoresque*, vol. 4. By permission of the Research Collections of The New York Public Library, New York.

stunning site high above the sea, Agrigentum was the site of many beautiful temples in ancient times. Houël here depicted a destroyed temple in the flattened coastal area beneath the colony city proper, and between two rivers which wend their way to the sea. He rendered the temple plan as an image within a conventional *veduta* of the site, by laying it out in perspective, on a sheet – here not a trompe-l'oeil sheet of paper, but a cloth sheet, perhaps a fishing sail or tarpaulin, or a stretch of linen. That sheet lies on the ground as if it is being dried or bleached in the southern Mediterranean sun, stretched and weighted down by small boulders borne by various stock-figure gentlemen in the landscape. Short of providing a reconstruction, the artist makes as tangible as possible the presence of the lost temple in the landscape, and at the same time, he undermines that presence with the artificiality of the gentlemen's actions. This way of inserting an image within an image, here a geometrical drawing within a view is, as far as I know, Houël's invention. Piranesi in many cases tacked a plan rendered on a trompe-l'oeil sheet onto a *veduta*, but never did he represent that plan as if it adhered to the perspectival rules of the *veduta*.

In a *capriccio*, a composition of ancient fragments randomly chosen and arranged, Houël compiled some of the architectural remains of the temple of Agrigentum, and included among them geometric drawings of some of those fragments, rendered on trompe-l'oeil sheets (plate 17). *Capricci* were common-place in Piranesi's publications, and he created many a version as illustrations for his archaeological texts.[49] The inclusion of a geometrical drawing in a *capriccio*,

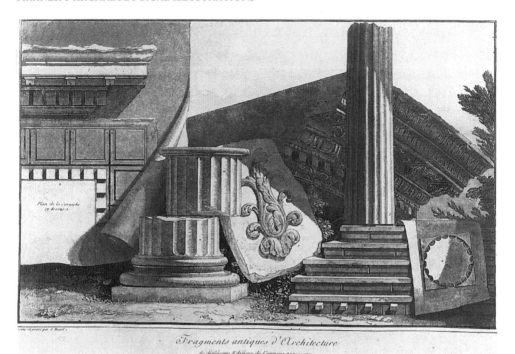

17   J.L.P. Hoüel, Fragmented Architectural Remains, from Agrigentum, plate 232 from *Voyage pittoresque*, vol. 4. By permission of the Research Collections of The New York Public Library, New York.

as one can see in Hoüel's print, however, is rare in Piranesi's publications. The only Piranesian example that has so far come to light is less visually harmonious than Hoüel's. Piranesi rendered the plan of a tomb chamber in a vineyard near Porta San Sebastione as if on a fragmented stone plaque that was placed upright on a shelf along with various objects from the tomb.[50]

Arguably the most innovative of Hoüel's images use the bird's-eye plan, for example his rendering of an underground Roman bath located in ancient Katane, modern-day Catania, one of the first Greek colonies to submit to the Romans during the Punic Wars (plate 18).[51] There were many baths in this city, which is located at the foot of Mount Aetna, and this example lay beneath the temple of Bacchus. This one, even today, retains some of the original Roman stucco decoration, and Hoüel has captured this in the print. Hoüel remarked that he chose the bird's-eye plan because it was good for conveying information about how one might enter an underground chamber. To this image, Hoüel adds a trompe-l'oeil sheet on which is drawn a schematic plan of an adjacent structure.[52]

The last four multi-informational prints discussed (plates 15–18), with their incorporation of geometric or schematic drawings into a view, underscore Hoüel's interaction with the natural environment and the artefactual evidence for the effective, subjective and imaginative presentation of the little-known region to his readers. While they owe much to Piranesi's archaeological illustrations, Hoüel's images were not concerned exclusively with that which no longer existed, as were

18   J.L.P. Hoüel, Plan and bird's-eye view of the Bath of the Temple of Bacchus, plate 147 from *Voyage pittoresque*, vol. 3. By permission of the Research Collections of The New York Public Library, New York.

Piranesi's. Instead, Hoüel nearly always grounded his framing devices within a convincing view, and thus conveyed a sense of an exotic but very real place full of hidden knowledge now revealed to the reader.

Piranesi's and Hoüel's publications are very different in content. In his archaeological publications, Piranesi focused on the monuments of ancient Roman civilizations, and Hoüel, in his *Voyage pittoresque*, on the many aspects of contemporary as well as historical southern Italy. Hoüel did not share Piranesi's desire to reconstruct and bring to life a world completely lost, but rather he inserted himself as an observer of a world still vibrant but apart from his own. While Piranesi's illustrations are a means to an end, his way of assimilating a mass of information, creating a jumbled hectic work in seemingly perpetual progress, Hoüel, ever conscious of his readers who were following in his footsteps, used the same type of illustration to remind them of his role in processing and ordering knowledge about the curious world he has encountered. With these illustrations, he has let them know what they should understand when they see Sicilian fishermen casting nets from their boats, what they should make of a seemingly empty landscape, and how they can gain access to an ancient underground chamber. The creator of the multi-informational image – perhaps more than most images – always shows his authoritive hand.

The multi-informational image never became a popular means of illustration. The practitioners of archaeology soon rejected it as they embraced what they believed were more rational and objective goals and methods. Aside from Hoüel, very few other illustrators of *voyages pittoresques* employed it. Even Hoüel had a limited use for the multi-informational format; some of his illustrations are breathtaking landscape views taken from such long-range, or conversely, such constricted vantage points that the presence of the artist seems to dissolve. While Hoüel was in Malta and Sicily, he met a number of illustrious fellow voyagers, such as the poet Roland de La Platière and the topographer Louis Mayer. After he returned to France, other notables, such as Goethe, made their tours of the region. It may have been that in such a climate, Hoüel found his voice a little less authoritive and the multi-informational image a little less desirable an instrument.

Notes

1 Damie Stillman, 'Robert Adam and Piranesi', in *Essays in the History of Architecture presented to Rudolf Wittkower*, ed. D. Fraser et al., London: Phaidon, 1967, pp. 197–206; John Wilton-Ely, *Piranesi as Architect and Designer*, New Haven and London: Yale University Press, 1993, pp. 121–63; Jean-Marcel Humbert, Michael Pantazzi and Christiane Ziegler, *Egytomania: Egypt in Western Art, 1730–1930*, Ottawa: National Gallery of Canada, 1994, pp. 38–45, 66–74.

2 Various articles in Georges Brunel (ed.), *Piranèse et les français: colloque tenu à la Villa Medicis 12–14 mai 1976*, Rome: Edizione dell'Elefante, 1978; catalogue entries in idem, *Piranèse et les français, 1740–90*, Rome, 1976; and Robin Middleton, 'Giovanni Battista Piranesi (1720–

1778): review of recent literature', *Journal of the Society of Architectural Historians*, vol. 41, no. 4, December 1982, pp. 340–3.

3 The seven publications are as follows. *Le Rovine del Castello dell'Acqua Giulia*, Rome: Generoso Salomoni, 1761, considered the history and function of the ruinous monument known as the Castello, the building whose function was to monitor the distribution of the waters from the Acqua Giulia through ancient Rome. *Il Campo Marzio dell'antica Roma*, Rome, 1762, aimed at a reconstruction of the area of ancient Rome for which it was titled. The four publications dealing with subjects of monuments from the Laziale region include *Descrizione e Disegno dell'Emissario del Lago Albano*, approved in

April 1762 and issued by the next year, which dealt with the extensive drainage system leading from the Lago Albano to the Laziale countryside. In *Di due spelonche ornate dagli antichi*, also approved in 1762 and issued later, Piranesi depicted two caves on the banks of the Lago Albano thought to have served the ancients as sanctuaries and bathing cabanas. *Antichità di Albano e di Castel Gandolfo*, published in 1764 and *Antichità di Cora*, also 1764, considered various ancient monuments. Lastly, *Lapides Capitolini*, Rome, 1761, featured one fold-out illustration of the fragmented ancient plaques known as the *Fasti Consolari* and the *Fasti Trionfali*. *Della Magnificenza* was issued in 1761.

4 A major critic was Francesco Milizia (1720–1798).

5 There is a software program entitled *Piranesi*, although it does not exploit this aspect of the webpage. See Richard Spöhrer, 'Piranesi: the software application that could change your life', *World Architecture*, vol. 67, June 1998, p. 30.

6 See Wilton-Ely, *The Complete Etchings of Piranesi*, 2 vols, San Francisco: Alan Wolfsy, 1993; 1,018 plates are reproduced here.

7 I thank Prof. Middleton for drawing my attention to the affinity between Hoüel's and Piranesi's methods of representation. In this essay, I will not establish a direct connection between Hoüel and Piranesi. As far as I know, the two did not ever meet. It could easily be argued that Hoüel might have had direct visual access to Piranesi's archaeological prints; Piranesi's prints were accessible in France at the time (although his archaeological prints were less popular with collectors), and Hoüel made two extended trips to Italy, as we will see. Middleton, p. 341, in reference to an entry in the exhibition catalogue *Piranèse et les français, 1740–90*, states, 'Hoüel's archaeological representations [here referring to his views] might be judged independent of Piranesi's but the refined and elegiac style that François Hutin and L.F.J. Saly cultivated at the *Académie de France* [in Rome] in the 1740s, however different it might be from that of Piranesi, is an integral part of any investigation of the relationship between these artists. ...' Hutin's and Saly's roles as intermediaries between Piranesi and Hoüel remain to be explored.

8 For a chronological presentation of maps of Rome, see Amato P. Frutaz, *Le piante di Roma*, 3 vols, Rome: Istituto di studi romano, 1962. Du Pérac's map, with verbal information in the key, is represented in vol. 2, pl. CCXXVII; Falda's map, with both verbal and visual information in the attached imagery is in vol. 3, pl. CLVIII.

9 Roberto Almagia, *Le pitture murali della galleria delle carte geografiche*, vol. 3 (of 4): *Monumenta cartographica vaticana*, Vatican City: Biblioteca apostolica vaticana, 1952, and Lucio Gambi, *The Gallery of Maps in the Vatican*, trans. P. Tucker, New York: George Braziller, 1997, for example,

pls 14 and 21 for map of Etruria and bird's-eye view of Florence, respectively. The creators of these frescoes include the cosmographer Egnazio Danti, the brothers Mattäus and Paul Bril and Girolamo Muziano.

10 See Stefano Borsi (ed.), *Roma di Benedetto XIV: la pianta di Giovan Battista Nolli, 1748*, Roma: Officina, 1993; Allan Ceen, 'Introduction', *Pianta Grande di Roma of G.B. Nolli in facsimile*, Highmount, NY: J.H. Aronson, 1984; and Jürgen Zanker, 'Die Nuova Pianta di Roma von Giovanni Battista Nolli, 1748', *Wallraf-Richartz Jahrbuch*, vol. 35, Cologne 1973, pp. 309–42. Also see John Pinto, 'Origins and Development of the Ichnographic City Plan', *Journal of the Society of Architectural Historians*, vol. 25, 1976, pp. 35–50.

11 Ceen, 'Introduction', op. cit. (note 10), p. III; and Ludwig Pastor, *History of the Popes*, vol. 25, pp. 175–6. The fragments had originally belonged to the Farnese family, but in the eighteenth century much of their collection of antiquities devolved to the Spanish Borbone. Benedict XIV obtained the fragments from Charles III of Naples at the end of 1741. Piranesi rendered some of these fragments in many of his archaeological publications.

12 Maria Grazia Lolla, 'Ceci n'est pas un monument: Vetusta Monumenta and antiquarian aesthetics', in *Producing the Past: Aspects of Antiquarian Culture and Practice, 1700–1850*, eds Martin Myrone and Lucy Peltz, Aldershot and Brookfield, VT: Ashgate, 1999, p. 20. She also posits that this device, as seen in English antiquarian publications, underscores the idea that illustrations are '"just" representations of the objects depicted (as per Magritte's pipe) ... self-consciously constructed as triggers to the imagination and aids to the memory'. It is interesting to note that the multi-informational image was also used in late sixteenth- through eighteenth-century publications devoted to natural history topics.

13 Wilton-Ely has noted the affinity between Santi Bartoli's and Piranesi's images in his 'Piranesi and the role of archaeological illustration', in *Piranesi e la cultura antiquaria: gli antecedenti e il contesto*, Rome: Multigrafica, 1983, pp. 317–21. One of Fontana's large fold-out illustrations appears in *Il Campo Marzio*, op. cit. (note 3), pl. 21. Piranesi copied Fischer von Erlach's vase designs in a drawing now in the Pierpont Morgan Library in New York City; see Felice Stample, *Giovanni Battista Piranesi: drawings in the Pierpont Morgan Library*, New York: Dover Publications, 1978, pp. xxii–xxiii for bibliography, and pl. 17.

14 Paolo Marconi, Angela Cipriani and Enrico Valeriani, *I disegni di architettura dell'Archivio Storico dell'Accademia di San Luca*, 2 vols, Rome: De Luca, 1974, vol. 2, pls 140–2.

15 ibid., vol. 2, pls 275, 322, 324–7, 416, among

others.

16 Jean-Marie Perouse de Montclos, *Les Prix de Rome: Concours de l'Académie royale d'architecture au XVIIIe siècle*, Paris: Berger-Levrault, 1984, p. 28, citing Blondel, 'De l'utilité de joindre à l'étude de l'architecture celle des sciences et des arts qui leur sont relatifs', in *Cours d'architecture, ou Traitè de la décoration, distribution et construction des bâtiments … contenant les leçons données en 1750 et les années suivantes*, 6 vols, Paris: Desaint, 1771, p. 24.

17 On Piranesi's stance in the Greco-Romano controversy, see Rudolf Wittkower, 'Piranesi's "Parere sull'Architettura"', *Journal of the Warburg and Courtauld Institutes*, vol. 2, 1938, pp. 147–58, and Wilton-Ely, *Giovanni Battista Piranesi: the Polemical Works*, Farnsborough: Gregg International, 1972.

18 *Antichità Romane*, 4 vols, Rome: Angelo Rotili, 1756, vol. 1, introduction.

19 *Antichità di Albano e di Castel Gandolfo*, 1761, chap. 1. In reference to fragments from a temple, he wrote: '… nella raccolta che ho proposto di pubblicare di quelle antichità, fra l'Albane, che, secondo me, più meritano d'essere poste in vista, non dovevo io traslasciare di porvi, per gli primi, que' residui che mi é risuscito di rinvenire del … tempio …'.

20 *Il Campo Marzio*, op. cit. (note 3), dedication. 'Ma per obbedirvi in guisa da dar insieme prova della mia accuratezza e diligenza nell'adempi quest'impegno … essendomi lusingato, col far ciò, di non trovar veruno che si disse a credere, aver io piuttosto operato a capriccio, che con sodo fondamento, o con ragionevole congettura …'. He continues, in the most famous part of this passage, that whoever should condemn him should first observe the architecture of the villas of Lazio, of Hadrian's Villa and the tombs and baths outside the Porta Capena, which are highly inventive.

21 The *Ichnographia* is reproduced in Wilton-Ely, *The Complete Etchings*, op. cit. (note 6), vol. 2, p. 625, fig. 571.

22 The publication, *Della forza della fantasia umana*, Venice: Giambattista Pasquali, 1745, was one side of a polemic regarding the nature of what motivated witchcraft, a malfunction of the brain or the influence of the demonic. See Luciano Parinetto, *Magia e ragione: una polemica sulle streghe in Italian intorno al 1750*, Florence, 1974, pp. 38–46.

23 Muratori, *Della forza*, op. cit. (note 22), pp. 10, 18 and 29. The mind received 'idee, imagini, specie o vestigi della cosa o veduta o udita o odorata, o guastata o toccata …' and stored them 'nel magazzino del Fantasia … [E]ssere questa Fantasia un maraviglioso lavoro … perchè solamente un'Ente tale ho potuto formare nel breve giro del capo umano una galeria doviziosa di tante idee e idee con si bell'ordine

ivi disposte …'.

24 ibid., p. 6, 'Noi con questo nome [Mente] intendiamo la facoltà o potenza, che ha l'anima nostra di pensare, cioè di apprendere le idee delle cose, di combinarle, di dividerle, di astraere, di guidicare, di formare assioni universale, di razioncinare, di fare altre simili azioni, delle quali e solamente capace un'ente ed agente reale spirituale, ed e incapace la materia …'. For the reference to the resulting 'compendio', see ibid., pp. 20 and 25.

25 ibid., p. 26. 'Le carte geografiche e topografiche sono un ritratto di questa parte dell'umana fantasia, ma troppo inferiori all'originale …'.

26 Histories of the discipline of Classical Roman archaeology begin with the mid-nineteenth-century scholars, such as Giuseppe Fiorelli and Rudolfo Lanciani, who take into account the immediate site context for archaeological evidence. See Glyn E. Daniel, *A Short History of Archaeology*, London: Thames and Hudson, 1981, and I. Morris, 'History of Archaeology: Classical Archaeology', in *The Oxford Companion to Archaeology*, eds B. Fagan et al., New York and Oxford: Oxford University Press, 1996, pp. 288–90.

27 See, for example, the illustrations in Rudolfo Lanciani, *The Ruins and Excavations of Ancient Rome*, rpt. 1897, Salem, NH: Ayer Co., 1988. For an account of the beginnings of this new type of archaeological illustration as concurrent with new attitudes in archaeological excavation, see Christopher C. Parslow, *Rediscovering Antiquity: Karl Weber and the Excavation of Herculaneum, Pompeii, and Stabiae*, Cambridge: Cambridge University Press, 1998. See also Ronald T. Riley, *The Pope's Archaeologist: the life and times of Carlo Fea*, Rome: Quasar, 2000.

28 Abbé Jean Claude Richard de Saint-Non, *Voyage pittoresque; ou, description des royaumes de Naples et de Sicile*, 4 vols, Paris: Clousier, 1781–86. Also, see Atanasio Mozzillo and G. Vallet (eds), *Settecento Siciliano, traduzione del Voyage en Sicile di Dominique Vivant Denon, illustrata da 130 tavole tratte dal Voyage pittoresque, ou description des royaumes de Naples et de Sicile di Richard di Sant-Non*, trans. L. Mascoli, Palermo and Naples: Società Editrici della Storia di Napoli e delle Sicile, 1979.

29 James Stuart and Nicholas Revett, *The antiquities of Athens, measured and delineated*, 4 vols, London: J. Taylor, 1762–1816. This book is akin to Le Roy's in that it contains in the main geometric drawings, some highly detailed.

30 René Pomeau, 'Voyages et luminères dans la littérature française du XVIIIe siècle', *Studies on Voltaire and the Eighteenth Century*, vol. 57, 1967, pp. 1269–89. The Université de Paris/Sorbonne houses the Centre de Recherche sur la Littérature des Voyages, established in 1984, which is dedicated to the study of *voyages pittoresques* as well as all types of travel

literature.

31 Hoüel, *Voyage pittoresque*, Paris: Imprimerie de Monsieur, 1782, vol. 1, p. vi. He states that he has included ten amphitheatres, six theatres, twenty-six temples, three triumphal monuments, two palaces, and various villas, bridges, aqueducts, tombs and 'unique buildings'.

32 ibid., 1784, vol. 2, pp. 62–78 and 94–127.

33 ibid., vol. 1, pp. 72–5 on the Feast of St Rosalie; and ibid., 1787, vol. 3, p. 151 on the Feast of the Harvest, among other citations. Also notable is ibid., vol. 3, p. 165–8 on baptismal and marriage rituals and costumes of those of Albanian descent.

34 ibid., vol. 1, p. 37 on anchovy salting; p. 37 on harvesting carts; pp. 53 and 69 on types of plants, including bananas; p. 83 on rope making; vol. 2, p. 85 on soap making, among other citations.

35 ibid., vol. 4, pp. 6–8.

36 ibid.

37 Barbara Stafford, *Voyage into Substance: Art, Science, Nature: Illustrated Travel Accounts, 1760–1840*, Cambridge, Mass.: MIT Press, 1984, p. 254, among other places. Stafford suggests that despite the term *pittoresque* in Hoüel's title, the artist was at times not attending to nature as if it were the object of his picturesque vision ('an enfeebling of the material object'), but rather was attempting to record nature, particularly the volcanic landscape in Sicily, unmediated by his subjectivity.

38 On Hoüel's training, Madeleine Pinault, *Hoüel: Voyage en Sicile, 1776–79*, exhib. cat., Paris: Editions Herscher, 1990, p. 9. The only monograph to date on the artist is Maurice Vloberg, *Jean Hoüel, Peintre et Graveur, 1735–1813*, Paris: Jean Naert, 1930.

39 Hoüel was recommended to Mariette by the Duc du Choiseul, a one-time patron, and the Marquis de Marigny. The comments assessing Hoüel's talents are Mariette's; they are published in his *Abedecario* and cited in Pinault, op. cit. (note 38), p. 9.

40 Patrick Brydone, *A Tour through Sicily and Malta*, London, 1773, and Baron de Riesedel, *Reise durch Sicilien und Gross Griechland*, Zurich, 1771, were both available in French

translation before 1776. Hoüel mentions them in his preface.

41 Pinault, op. cit. (note 38), pp. 13–15. A total of five hundred gouaches and drawings were sold to Catherine II of Russia, and are now part of the Hermitage collection in Leningrad.

42 ibid., pp. 15–16.

43 ibid., p. 12. See also Leonard Sciascia, 'Hoüel in Sicilia', in *Jean Hoüel, Viaggio pittoresco alle isole eolie*, Messina: Pungitopo Editore, 1988, pp. 5–7.

44 Chloe Chard, *Pleasure and guilt on the Grand Tour: travel writing and imaginative geography, 1600–1830*, Manchester and New York: Manchester University Press, 1999, pp. 9–10, argues effectively 'that travel writing is closely concerned with the traveller-narrator's own rhetorical strategies', and demonstrates that as one of the characteristics of travel writing, the authors, with their claims to be concerned with ordering knowledge, are aware of how they are manipulating language. In this case, Hoüel was aware of how he manipulated his images.

45 Pinault, op. cit. (note 38), p. 12. Hoüel wrote in the preface of *Voyage pittoresque*, op. cit. (note 31), vol. 1: 'J'affirme mes dessins par mes écrits, et je confirme mes écrits par mes dessins.'

46 Hoüel, op. cit. (note 30), vol. 1, pp. 104–5, for discussion of theatre.

47 ibid., p. 47, for discussion of fishing.

48 ibid., vol. 4, p. 17, for discussion of the so-called temple of Aesculpius.

49 This print is illustrated in Wilton-Ely, *The Complete Etchings*, op. cit. (note 6), vol. 1, p. 561, fig. 507, depicting *Antichità Romane*, vol. 4, pl. 38.

50 Dixon, 'Piranesi and Francesco Bianchini's "L'istoria universale": *capricci* in the service of pre-scientific archaeology', *Art History*, vol. 22, no. 2, June 1999, pp. 184–213.

51 Hoüel, op. cit. (note 31), vol. 3, pp. 6–8, for discussion of this temple and bath.

52 Piranesi reserved the bird's-eye view for his reconstructions. Three of these can be found in *Campo Marzio*, op. cit. (note 3). They are reproduced in Wilton-Ely, *The Complete Etchings*, op. cit. (note 6), vol. 2, p. 615, pl. 560; pp. 666–7, pls 611 and 612.

5

Antiquity and Improvement in the National Landscape: the Bucks' views of antiquities 1726–42

Andrew Kennedy

Samuel and Nathaniel Buck's views of antiquities (1726–42) and their principal series of views of towns (1728–53) were arguably the most important topographical print series produced in Britain in the early eighteenth century in terms of their scale and scope. Ralph Hyde's invaluable research has uncovered the support given to the Bucks by antiquarians in relation to both these projects, although his main concern is with the towns series.[1] In this article, I want to focus on the antiquities series, in order to investigate the relationship between antiquarianism and improvement in the Bucks' work.[2] I will attempt to show that the Bucks' audience could have seen medieval antiquities and contemporary improvements (economic and cultural) as contrary, but essentially complementary terms. Situating the interest in medieval antiquities within this framework may also help to explain why several prominent adherents of the modern style associated with improvement – albeit that this was based on Roman antiquity – would subscribe to a series of publications on medieval antiquities in addition to their patronage of Romano-British antiquarian studies.

Hyde has described how the assistance and patronage of antiquarians, particularly that of William Stukeley and the Society of Antiquaries, were instrumental in allowing the Yorkshireman Samuel Buck to establish a healthy business in London based principally on the production of views of towns and medieval antiquities. In January 1724 Buck issued a handbill containing his proposals for publishing the first (Yorkshire) set of antiquities,[3] and in April 1724 he brought several related drawings to show to the Society of Antiquaries.[4] In the first group of thirty-three subscribers in the British Library copy of the 1724 handbill[5] appear the names of the antiquarians William Stukeley, the Society's Secretary, Roger Gale, the Society's Vice-President, and Ralph Thoresby – a principal patron of Samuel Buck in Yorkshire.[6] Another subscriber was John Talman, the first Director of the Society of Antiquaries, responsible for overseeing the publication of its engravings and looking after its collection of books, drawings and prints.[7] From the final engraved list of names which appears on the title plate of the first collection of antiquities, dated May

1726,[8] it appears that at least fifteen fellows of the Society subscribed – the majority of the active members.[9]

As Hyde notes, 'when it comes to the national, rather than local, recording of antiquities, it seems to be William Stukeley who deserves the credit.'[10] Certainly, the use of prints was of particular importance to Stukeley at this time in the representation of antiquities in the British landscape. In his *Itinerarium Curiosum Centuria I* (1724) and *Centuria II* (published posthumously in 1776), the plates, executed by John Vandergucht,[11] after Stukeley's drawings, show a succession of diverse subject matter, by no means restricted to antiquities, such as Reading Abbey, the town of Newbury and the Earl of Hertford's seat at Marlborough. Indeed, Stukeley's project is potentially of an encyclopedic nature, encompassing man-made objects of all ages, as well as natural curiosities that feature in the British landscape. Improvement becomes part of the context for antiquities, and vice versa. Moreover, the way in which the information is presented recreates the traveller's personal, empirical experience of these phenomena in the course of traversing the national territory.[12] In his Preface to *Centuria I* (1724), Stukeley professes to have 'avoided prejudice. ... taking things in the natural order and manner they presented themselves. ...'. This is close to Daniel Defoe's depiction of Britain in the Preface to his *Tour* of that decade, as a 'flowing variety of materials; [in which] all the particulars are fruitful of instructing and diverting objects'.[13] In each case, the traveller's experience of journeying through Britain, secure in the knowledge that every aspect, old and new, will furnish material of general import to the whole, is the subject of celebration. For Stukeley, however, engravings offered an opportunity to classify and order more easily this promiscuous variety, by virtue of the amount of information they could contain. In the Preface to *Centuria I*, Stukeley writes

> The prints, besides their use in illustrating the discourses, are ranged in such a manner as to become an index of inquiries for those that travel, for a British Antiquary ... It is evident how proper engravings are to preserve the memory of things, and how much better an idea they convey to the mind than written descriptions, which often not at all, often not sufficiently, explain them. ...

While the engravings in the *Itinerarium Curiosum*, in terms both of their numbers and their scope, are a long way from fulfilling the purpose of 'an index of inquiries' for tourists and antiquaries at large in the national landscape, this seems to have been the objective of the Bucks and their supporters in undertaking the ambitious and comprehensive series of towns (81 views) and antiquities (420 views). The antiquities were published in seventeen annual sets, beginning in 1726. Each set comprises subjects from between one and four counties and usually contains twenty-four plates. In total, there are 420 subjects, taken from every county in England and Wales except Radnorshire. Martin Myrone has remarked that both the antiquarian and the antiquarian engraver were perceived to lack discrimination in their choice and treatment of objects, the former being concerned 'to amass rather than order', and the latter being concerned to minutely describe the items amassed.[14] Nevertheless, some order is imposed on the chaos of objects through the Bucks' project, albeit of a limited character: Defoe's 'flowing variety of materials' is evoked here by a taxonomic system that is basic, yet capacious.

The sets, being large and issued on an annual basis, were priced at two guineas, in contrast to the more affordable format, common in the 1770s and 1780s, of monthly numbers, containing one or more fine (albeit small) topographical engravings that were typically priced at one shilling each.[15] The Bucks' scheme ensured that their clientele would have to be either dedicated to antiquarian study, or wealthy, or both. There are 132 names among the subscribers listed on the title page of the first collection, numerically a modest total, but among them figure archbishops, three bishops and thirty-seven peers. Most of the remainder of the subscribers to this collection appear to be from among the upper gentry, including a number of Members of Parliament.[16] Thus, as Robert Sayer later commented, a 'more respectable list of Subscribers is rarely seen than favoured their first publication.'[17]

Samuel Buck was certainly able to benefit in this regard from Stukeley's contacts among the aristocracy. Among the first subscribers to this Yorkshire set[18] were the Earl of Hertford, proposed by Stukeley for membership of the Society of Antiquaries in January 1723 and elected President in 1724;[19] the Earl of Winchelsea, Stukeley's friend, pupil and patron, who was proposed by Stukeley at the same time as the Earl of Hertford and became a Vice-President in 1725;[20] and Viscount Tyrconnel, a powerful figure in Lincolnshire, who was eventually elected as a Fellow in 1740.[21] In the second, slightly later group of subscribers appears the Duke of Montague, a Fellow of the Society from 1725, and certainly Stukeley's patron from 1741–42, if not earlier.[22]

The representation of medieval remains in the Bucks' series seems inseparable from the celebration of property and hence of improvement. Evidently, landowners could be persuaded to subscribe for a set if it included a view of an antiquity with a dedication that clearly identified the building as their property. Twelve of the twenty-four plates in the first collection are accordingly dedicated to a nobleman or an archbishop, one to a knight and two to gentlemen. Of these fifteen individuals, only two were known for their antiquarian interests, and significantly, in these two cases, the ruins depicted were not on their estates.[23] Moreover, in the case of abbeys and priories, the inscriptions usually give the value of their lands at the time of dissolution.[24] This lends a touch of antiquarian erudition, but at the same time acts as an indication of the wealth that accrued to landowners with the dissolution of the monasteries. This is to say nothing of the kinds of vicarious proprietorship that may be invoked by the conventions of the view.

Furthermore, a number of so-called views of antiquities are, in many or all respects, views of seats. The proportion of views showing inhabited houses rises to about twenty per cent of the total number of views from the fifth set (1730) onwards. Some of the houses depicted, as in the example of Belvoir Castle discussed below (plate 19) are not wholly or even partly medieval in origin. Tim Clayton cites a number of cases, including that of Kip and Knyff's *Britannia Illustrata* (1707), to show that landowners were often persuaded to pay for the cost of drawing and engraving their houses in order to ensure their inclusion in a print publication.[25]

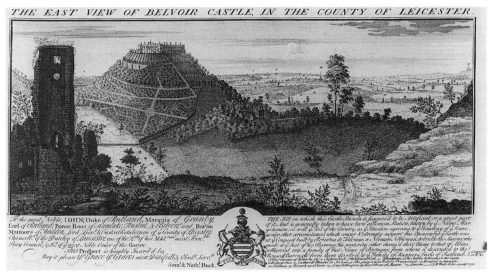

19   Samuel and Nathaniel Buck, *The East View of Belvoir Castle*, 1730. Engraving on copper, 14.3 × 24.7 cm. Published in the Bucks' sixth set of antiquities, 1731.

Invariably, in these views of houses by the Bucks, the antiquarian and lineal information about the sites and their successive owners contained in the images and captions creates associations which assist in legitimizing and glamorizing contemporary power. This is conspicuously the case with *The East View of Belvoir Castle* (dated 1730, published in 1731; plate 19). Owned by John Manners, third Duke of Rutland (1696–1779), who had been a subscriber since the first set and to whom the plate is dedicated, the Castle is shown overlooking the surrounding terrain from its medieval motte,[26] which the caption suggests is Roman.[27] The house is evidently not medieval (it had been rebuilt between 1655 and 1668, after having been slighted in the Civil War),[28] but its name, its dramatic site and its inclusion in a series ostensibly devoted to antiquities emphasize both the seat's historical credentials and its present-day importance.[29] Indeed, the function of antiquity in this image is clearly to support the representation of modern improvement. The unimpressive-looking medieval 'remains of Wolstrop [Woolsthorpe] Ch.[urch]' on the hill in the left foreground only serve to frame the view of Belvoir Castle and its gardens, emphasizing the seat's dominating contemporary role in the landscape. Moreover, while the Castle is seen more or less in perspective view, the gardens – 'still improving by ye Duke of Rutland the present noble Owner', as the caption to the succeeding *West View* notes – are represented in bird's-eye view, almost in plan, a not uncommon mode of depiction at this time, which draws the viewer's attention yet more closely to the seat's extent and magnificence.

It will be noted that the image under discussion is in the wide-angle prospect format, the elevated viewpoint of the improver, adopted, as in military and economic surveys, in order to map, itemize, classify and facilitate imaginative and physical control over the features of a large piece of terrain. Yet the medieval antiquities shown in the views are usually depicted by the Bucks in relative close-up in order to enable inspection of their architectural details and state of preservation. The focal adjustment

71

20   Samuel Buck, *The North East View of Louth Park Abbey near Louth, in the County of Lincoln*, 1726. Engraving on copper, 14.3 × 24.5 cm. Published in the Bucks' second set of antiquities, 1727.

made when the viewer transfers their attention from foreground to middle ground/ distance, or vice versa, especially in the earlier views, therefore enacts a potentially disturbing disjunction between antiquity and improvement. One might say that although each element depends for its meaning upon the other, improvement always threatens to disrupt this delicate balance. Thus, in one plate in the second collection, *The North East View of Louth Park Abbey, near Louth, in the County of Lincoln* (dated 1726, published 1727; plate 20), the relationship between past and present receives rather a brutal visual formulation. The medieval remains, though apparently the principal subject, could also be seen as furnishing merely a decaying, gap-toothed foreground to the view of Louth, which, the caption informs us, is 'a well Built, Rich, Populous, & Pleasant Market Town'.

This sort of relationship between antiquarian studies and the concerns of the present is also perceptible when one examines the circumstances in which this second collection of antiquities, covering Lincolnshire and Nottinghamshire, and published in May 1727, was produced. The number of named subscribers on the title page rises by over fifty per cent, from 132 for the first set to 200 for the second. This set functioned in part as a homage to the Gentlemen's Society of Spalding, in Lincolnshire, an antiquarian body founded in 1709–10, the membership of which overlapped to some extent with that of the London Society of Antiquaries.[30] One plate is inscribed to the Spalding Society as a body. Two other plates are dedicated to individuals who were members of both societies: Maurice Johnson and William Stukeley.[31] The Spalding Society's antiquarian activities expanded markedly between 1724 and 1729.[32] In May 1726, the month that Samuel Buck's Yorkshire set was published, Stukeley gave up the secretaryship of the Society of Antiquaries of London, following ructions therein, and took up residence in Grantham, Lincolnshire.[33] Samuel Buck was admitted to membership of the Spalding Society in 1729, as, at some point, was his brother Nathaniel.[34]

72

Several factors had contributed to the efflorescence of antiquarian activity in Lincolnshire. Since the early seventeenth century, values of agricultural land had been increasing as the fens were drained and agricultural methods improved.[35] Towards the end of the seventeenth century, City of London merchants, seeking both profitable investment and increased social prestige, began to move in among the traditional Tory squirearchy. Thus, for instance, the dedicatee of Samuel Buck's *The South Prospect of Tupholme Priory, near Lincoln* is Robert Vyner, 'owner of this Priory', and Whig Member of Parliament for Lincolnshire, who was from a family of London goldsmiths that had acquired land in the county.[36] Spalding, the chief market town of the improving fen district of South Holland, had become by the early eighteenth century a desirable place of residence for minor gentry, clergy and professional men, for merchants trading in corn and coal through its port on the River Welland, and for surveyors and drainage engineers.[37] The Gentlemen's Society of Spalding drew upon this concentration of leisured and professional men and, evidently, upon opportunities for the study of Roman, Anglo-Saxon and medieval remains created by the digging associated with improvements such as turnpike roads.[38]

Given the connection suggested between antiquarianism and economic – not just cultural – improvement, it would seem relevant to set out the evidence that those with a background in trade could take an interest in the Bucks' views of antiquities.[39] For example, the brothers Sir John and Sir Joseph Eyles, both wealthy and powerful City merchants, who had been directors of the East India Company and of the Bank of England, lent their support to the first set. Sir John served as Lord Mayor of London in 1726–27. Sir Joseph, who had been Sheriff of London in 1724–25, became a regular subscriber to the sets of antiquities.[40] James Ansdell and Samuel Powell, whose names appear in the list of subscribers for the set of Lancashire, Cheshire and Derbyshire antiquities (third set, published 1728), are described as merchants in the Liverpool Poll Book of 1734.[41] Another name in the same list of subscribers – that of William Blakey – is associated with the establishment in France of the kind of precision iron and steel manufacturing and processing that was associated with British, including Liverpudlian, watch-making.[42] And among the subscribers to the third set, as well as to the later ones, is 'The Library at Manchester'. This would have been the free public library attached to Chetham school, which seems to have been a resource for the more self-improving of Manchester's inhabitants.[43] A visitor in *c.*1716 deplored the fact that a library in a town of tradespeople should dream of adding valuable manu-scripts to its collection.[44] It is also worth pointing out that for the 1737 set of antiquities subscriptions rose by sixty per cent, from 239 to 384. It is no coincidence that this set covered Sussex, Surrey, Middlesex and Hertfordshire and included four Thames-side views. Virtually all of the increase in subscriptions was due to new subscribers below the ranks of baronet and knight, many of whom, surely, would have been wealthy London citizens.[45]

All this is not to disguise the fact that for much of the history of the series, the aristocracy and upper gentry dominated the subscribers' lists. This is evident if one compares the list of subscribers for the set of Kent antiquities (1736) with one of the rare extant lists of subscribers for a set of the Bucks' towns – six views of towns in Kent, Surrey and Sussex (1738).[46] Of the 286 subscribers for the town prospects, 53, or 18.5 per cent, are peers, bishops, knights and baronets, but these ranks comprise 91 of the 239 subscribers to the set of Kent antiquities (1736) – 38 per cent, or roughly double the proportion. What should be remembered, however, is that antiquarian-minded aristocrats and landed gentry – and the smaller gentry and professionals in their orbit, who formed the bulk of active antiquaries at this time – were also quite likely to be commercially minded and responsive to modernity. William Stukeley, as we have seen, was attentive to new landscape features as well as old. In the Preface to his *Itinerarium Curiosum Centuria I* (1724), he specifically linked the study of engravings to 'the pleasure of observing the various changes in the face of nature, of countries, and the like, through the current of time and vicissitude of things'. Here he is in agreement with the tradesman's champion, Defoe, who saw it as an essential task of the topographer to describe such change. In the Preface to his *Tour Thro' the Whole Island of Great Britain* (1724–26), Defoe wrote:

> great towns decay, and small towns rise; new towns, new palaces, new seats are built every day; great rivers and good harbours dry up, and grow useless; again, ... ports and harbours are made where none were before, and the like. Several towns, which antiquity speaks of as considerable, are now lost and swallow'd up by the sea ... and others, which antiquity knew nothing of, are now grown considerable.

The Buck engraving entitled *The North West View of Portchester Castle, in Hampshire* (dated 1733, published in 1734; plate 21) could be read as representing geographical and economic change in a manner akin to Defoe's. Beyond the delapidated castle, the houses of Portsmouth and Gosport are visible at a distance, with the Solent and Isle of Wight beyond. The placing of these objects serves to illustrate the description in the caption below: the sea has over time 'left ye. town' and 'ye Inhabitants, who depended on Trade and Navigation, remov'd to ye. Mouth of this great Haven; and on Portsey Island built Portsmouth'. Yet the way in which the castle is seen situated between two waterways dotted with ships, and the sign of continuing usage provided by the church inside its walls, suggests that the protection the castle afforded in its day was crucial to the development of trade and settlement.

In addressing this relationship between ancient and modern, it is of particular interest that prominent adherents of that most enlightened and 'improving' style, based on the architecture of antiquity, were subscribers to a series containing mainly medieval subject matter. For example, the Earl of Burlington supported the Bucks' project. The Earl had been a patron of the map-maker John Warburton and a subscriber to Ralph Thoresby's *Ducatus Leodiensis* (1715). Both Thoresby and Warburton had encouraged Samuel Buck in his forays into antiquarian print-making in Yorkshire.[47] Moreover, Burlington was elected a Fellow of the Society of Antiquaries in 1724.[48] He figures among the earliest recorded group of subscribers to the Yorkshire set of antiquities,[49] and the second plate in that collection, showing Bolton Abbey, part-house, part-ruin, on his Londesborough estate in Yorkshire, is dedicated to him. The antiquary Sir Andrew Fountaine, then regarded as one of the triumvirs of taste (with Burlington and the ninth Earl

74

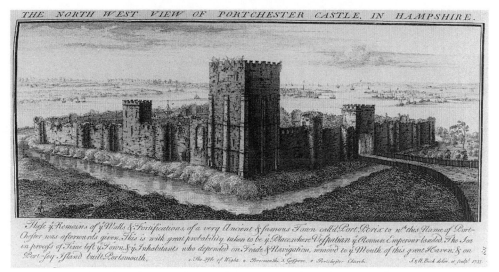

21   Samuel and Nathaniel Buck, *The North West View of Portchester Castle, in Hampshire*,
1733. Engraving on copper, 14.4 × 34.7 cm. Published in the Bucks' ninth set of antiquities, 1734.

of Pembroke), was also one of this early group of subscribers.[50] Richard Arundell,
a member of Burlington's circle and Surveyor of the King's Works between 1726
and 1737, appears among the second-earliest recorded group of subscribers,[51] as
does Thomas Robinson of Rokeby in North Yorkshire, a noted amateur architect
and an ardent disciple of Burlington.[52] All these men subscribed until the end of
the series. Another in the second group of subscribers was William Aislabie
(*c.*1699–1781). He was the son of John Aislabie of Studley Royal in Yorkshire
(1670–1742), a friend of Burlington, who built a new house at Studley after 1716,
and carried out major garden works there.[53]

As we have already seen in the case of Belvoir Castle (plate 19), in the early
eighteenth century the medieval and classical styles of building were increasingly
seen in meaningful juxtaposition at country seats,[54] those emblems of modern
cultural and economic improvement.[55] Moreover, when James Tyrrell built a
'gothic' temple at Shotover Park, near Oxford, in 1716–17, he identified ancient
Saxon liberty with the liberty of landowners.[56] Both sides of the political spectrum
– the Tories and the Whig Opposition – might have attempted to give their
particular slants to medieval architecture or 'gothic' in the two succeeding
decades, but the contending groups all basically identified the 'gothic' with
historic national freedoms, and the related virtues of the natural and the rustic. It
was, indeed, the Tory and Jacobite Lord Bathurst who ordered the building of
probably the first fictitious 'gothic' ruin in the 1720s or early 1730s, situated in the
all'antica setting of his park at Cirencester.[57] This structure came to be known as
Alfred's Hall, after the king who was widely seen as instrumental in establishing
English (and therefore British) liberties.[58]

Both the medieval and classical architecture are in evidence in the Bucks' plate
entitled *The West View of Wetherall-Priory, in the County of Cumberland*, 1733
(published on 26 March 1739; plate 22). Although the main subject of the
engraving, the priory gatehouse, was owned by Jerome Tullie (to whom the

75

22   Samuel and Nathaniel Buck, *The West View of Wetherall-Priory, in the County of Cumberland*, 1733. Engraving on copper, 14.4 × 34.9 cm. Published in the Bucks' fourteenth set of antiquities, 26 March 1739.

engraving is dedicated), the building is depicted in relation to the gardens of Corby Castle, laid out from *c.* 1730[59] by their owner, Thomas Howard. A view such as this seems to be related to contemporary practice by Yorkshire grandees, who favoured the classical architectural style of the age of improvement (John Aislabie and Thomas Robinson, both mentioned above, for example). Medieval ruins may be seen in explicit relation to a house or garden, forming an element in the vista from it or to it, although they are seldom fully integrated into a garden setting. This was the case at Aislabie's Studley Royal, with Fountains Abbey, and at Thomas Robinson's Rokeby Hall, with the medieval Mortham Tower.[60] The viewpoint in the Buck engraving is low and close to the priory, so that, in contrast to the earlier view of Belvoir Castle (plate 19) and the two case studies just mentioned, the owner's house and gardens do not obviously dominate – indeed, the antiquity is evidently cast here as the main subject, rather than as a foreground for the seat. Nevertheless, there are classical elements in the view, even though the house partly depicted here, Corby Castle, does not recall the architecture of the ancient world in the same way as Studley Royal and Rokeby Hall. Thus, the grandiloquent forms of the cascade on the left provide one evident counterpoint to the ruin and suggest the influence of Italian gardens seen on the Grand Tour.[61] There is also a Tuscan tempietto visible on the extreme right. The contrast between the plain forms of this small classical temple and the smooth, grassy walk that leads to it with the medieval ruin in the foreground and its rough environs is an understated one, but important nevertheless.

It has recently been argued that Romano-British architecture, rather than medieval antiquarianism, represents modernizing British imperial ambitions, expressed partly through the need to be affiliated with the culture of the Roman Empire.[62] However, the Bucks' subscribers tend to contradict the notion that medieval antiquarian studies were simply left out in the cold even at this time of intense interest in the ancient world. Scholars interested in both Roman and medieval antiquities, including Stukeley and his fellow members of the Society of Roman Knights, the Earls of Hertford and Winchelsea, who engaged in Romano-British field-work with him in 1723,[63] as well as Roger Gale and the arch-Gothicizer Browne Willis[64] together with Lord Burlington and his circle, subscribed at one time or another to the Bucks' views of antiquities. All this, together with the evidence from landscape gardens, actual and represented, suggests that for antiquaries and their landed patrons, there was not the unbridgeable chasm between the medieval and the classical that some historians have asked us to suppose. Indeed, in the Bucks' plate of Wetherall Priory (plate 22), both these elements have their place in the landscape and therefore become signs of the nation – the one standing for its historic, natural identity, the other for its present, polished state. The inclusion of this image in an encyclopedic survey of the nation which celebrates each of these aspects is thus entirely appropriate.

Notes

All images are reproduced by kind permission of the Guildhall Library, Corporation of London.

1 On the Bucks' principal towns series and earlier town views, see Ralph Hyde, *Gilded Scenes and Shining Prospects: Prospects and Panoramas of British Towns 1575–1900*, New Haven: Yale Center for British Art, exhib. cat., 1985, pp. 22–3, 26–7, 100–27, and Ralph Hyde, *A Prospect of Britain: The Town Panoramas of Samuel and Nathaniel Buck*, London: Pavillion Books, 1994.

2 The relationship between antiquity and improvement in regard to *both* series is explored in the first chapter of my PhD thesis, 'British topographical print series in their social and economic context, *c*.1720–1840', University of London, Courtauld Institute, 1998.

3 Samuel Buck, *Proposals for Publishing by Subscription a Collection of twenty four Perspective Views of Ruins of Abbeys, Castles and Religious Foundations; in the County of York*, London, 8 January 1724, British Library Lansdowne MS. 895, f. 135.

4 Minute Books in the collection of Society of Antiquaries, vol. I, f. 118, 22 April 1724.

5 Buck, ... *Perspective Views of Ruins of Abbeys ... County of York*, op. cit. (note 3). These names (83 of them) are arranged in three groups, in a clear chronological sequence.

6 He died in 1725, before the set could be published (see DNB). On the production of Samuel Buck's earliest published town prospects, and Thoresby's part in this, see Hyde, *A Prospect of Britain*, op. cit. (note 1), pp. 7–18, and *Gilded Scenes*, op. cit. (note 1), pp. 101–7.

7 On John Talman, see, for example, Joan Evans, *A History of the Society of Antiquaries*, Oxford: Oxford University Press, 1956, p. 77. On the duties of the Director, see ibid., p. 59.

8 Each set is prefixed by an engraved title page which also contains a list of subscribers.

9 See *A List of the Members of the Society of Antiquaries of London, from their revival in 1717 to June 19, 1796, arranged in Chronological and Alphabetical Order*, London, 1798. The attendances at the Society's Annual General Meetings on 18 January 1725 and 19 January 1726 were sixteen and twenty-five, respectively. See entries in Minutes, cited in Evans, op cit. (note 7), pp. 75–6.

10 Hyde, *A Prospect of Britain*, op. cit. (note 1), p. 18.

11 Vandergucht engraved Samuel Buck's prospect of York in 1721 (on this and the two related prospects see Hyde, *Gilded Prospects*, op. cit. [note 1], pp. 101–3, and *A Prospect of Britain*, op. cit. [note 1], pp. 10–13).

12 Stukeley's approach is, for instance, considered in relation to both contextual archaeology and to garden tourism in David Haycock, '"A small journey into the country": William Stukeley and the formal landscapes of Stonehenge and Avebury', in *Producing the Past: Aspects of Antiquarian Culture and Practice 1700–1850*, eds Martin Myrone and Lucy Peltz, Aldershot and Brookfield, VT: Ashgate, 1999, pp. 67–82. On Stukeley and gardens, see also David Coffin, *The English Garden: Meditation and Memorial*, Princeton, NJ: Princeton University Press, 1994, pp. 117–8, 136–7 and *passim*.

13 Daniel Defoe, *A Tour Through the Whole Island of Great Britain*, (1724–6), 2 vols, London, 1962.

14 Martin Myrone, 'Graphic Antiquarianism in Eighteenth-Century Britain', in Myrone and Peltz, op cit. (note 12), p. 45.

15 See, for example, George Kearsley's *Virtuosi's Museum*, with engravings after Paul Sandby, published between 1778 and 1781. This series is discussed in chap. 2 of my thesis, op. cit. (note

2), and, for example, in David Morris, *Thomas Hearne and his Landscape*, London: Reaktion, 1989, p. 32; and Patrick Conner, *Michael Angelo Rooker*, London: Batsford, 1984, pp. 32–4.

16 Three subscribers, it should be said (whether as private individuals acting for family/ friends/ acquaintances or whether as booksellers is not clear), each subscribed for six sets, thus potentially adding a further 15 names to the total of 132.

17 Robert Sayer, Preface to his edition of *Bucks' Antiquities and Towns*, 3 vols, London, 1774, vol. I, p.v.

18 See British Library handbill, op. cit. in note 3 above.

19 Minutes of the Society of Antiquaries, vol. I, f. 75, 9 January 1723 and f. 102, 22 January 1724.

20 ibid., f. 136, 18 January 1725. For his relationship with Stukeley, see Stuart Piggott, *William Stukeley: an Eighteenth Century Antiquary*, 2nd edn, London: Thames and Hudson, 1985, *passim*.

21 See *A List ...*, op. cit. (note 9).

22 On Montague's relationship with Stukeley, see Piggott, op cit. (note 20), pp. 118–20, 123–5. Piggott thinks that Montague's patronage of Stukeley only began in 1741–2, but two facts suggest that the seeds of this relationship were sown rather earlier: firstly, Montague's early membership of the Society of Antiquaries (see *A List ...*, op. cit. [note 9], also Evans, op. cit. [note 7], pp. 55, 81); secondly, the dedication to him of the plate of Sawley Abbey, dated 1724, in Samuel Buck's set of views of Yorkshire antiquities (1726).

23 I refer to the plate of Sawley Abbey, dedicated to the Duke of Montague (see note 22), and the plate of Whitby Abbey, dedicated to the Earl of Hertford (see note 19).

24 As recorded by Speed in R. Dodsworth and W. Dugdale, *Monasticon Anglicanum*, 3 vols, London, 1655–73.

25 Tim Clayton, 'Publishing Houses: Prints of Country Seats', in Dana Arnold (ed.), *The Georgian Country House: Architecture, Landscape and Society*, Stroud: Sutton Publishing, 1998, pp. 45–9.

26 See Nikolaus Pevsner, *The Buildings of England: Leicestershire and Rutland*, Harmondsworth: Penguin, 2nd edn, 1984, p. 96.

27 See, for example, Philip Ayres, *Classical Culture and the Idea of Rome in Eighteenth Century England*, Cambridge: Cambridge University Press, 1997, pp. 109–11, on the concern of Francis Drake to associate the Earl of Burlington's seat at Londesborough with the Romano-British past. Although I argue below that an interest in the medieval period could co-exist with an interest in the Roman or classical, it is, of course, true that in many (most) contexts the classical would have enjoyed significantly more prestige than medieval architecture.

28 Pevsner, op cit. (note 26).

29 Defoe, visiting the area a few years previously, observed that the Duke had 'a very noble estate, equal to the demesnes of some sovereign princes' (Defoe, op. cit. [note 13], vol. 2, p. 103).

30 See Dorothy Owen (ed.), *The Minute-Books of the Spalding Gentlemen's Society, 1712–1755*, published as *Lincoln Record Society*, vol. 73, Fakenham, 1981; and *Bibliotheca Topographica Britannica*, vol. 3, 1790, no. 20 (1784), 'Containing An Account of the Gentlemen's Society at Spalding: being an introduction to the Reliquiae Galeanae'.

31 Compare *A List ...* op. cit. (note 9) with the lists of Spalding Society members in *Bibliotheca Topographica Britannica*, op. cit. (note 30), appendix, pp. viii–xxxviii.

32 Owen, op. cit. (note 30), p. vii.

33 See Evans, op. cit. (note 7), pp. 75–6, and Piggott, op. cit. (note 20), pp. 44, 55–6, 75–7.

34 *Bibliotheca Topographica Britannica*, op. cit. (note 30), appendix, p.xvi.

35 See J.W.F. Hill, *Georgian Lincoln*, Cambridge: Cambridge University Press, 1966, pp. 110–11, and Owen, op. cit. (note 30), p. vii.

36 See Hill, op. cit. (note 35), pp. 25–7, 111 and Romney Sedgwick (ed.), *The History of Parliament: The House of Commons 1715–54*, 2 vols, London: Stationery Office Books, 1970, vol. 2, p. 501.

37 See Owen, op. cit. (note 30), pp. vii–viii.

38 ibid., pp. xiii–xiv.

39 On the audience for antiquities in the later eighteenth century, see Stephen Bending's essay, 'Every Man His Own Antiquary: Francis Grose and polite antiquities' in this volume.

40 See Sedgwick, op. cit. (note 36), vol. 2, pp. 21–2.

41 Poll Book for Liverpool election of 29 April 1734, p. 3.

42 See F.A. Bailey and T.C. Barker, 'The Seventeenth-Century Origins of Watchmaking in South-West Lancashire', p. 7 and p. 15, n. 37, in J.R. Harris (ed.), *Liverpool and Merseyside: Essays in the Economic and Social History of the Port and its Hinterland*, London: Frank Cass, 1969, pp. 1–15.

43 See Anon., *Chetham's Hospital and Library*, Manchester, 1956.

44 ibid., p. 17.

45 The highpoint was reached the following year, 1738, with a total of 398 subscribers for the set of antiquities of Norfolk, Suffolk and Essex (wealthy counties in terms of both agriculture and trade). What is remarkable is that the set for 1739, which depicted antiquities in remote and rugged Cumberland and Westmorland, attracted 383 subscribers, almost as many as subscribed to the 1737 set, with its metropolitan angle. Much attention in several of the views of castles – for instance, Cockermouth, Dacre and Highhead Castles – is given to the atmospheric depiction

of the rocky outcrops on which they stand. This kind of emphasis would later be described as picturesque, and suggests that the interests of the metropolitan print audience were even at this date not merely focused on antiquarianism or the latest economic and cultural improvements. See Timothy Clayton, *The English Print: 1688–1802*, New Haven and London: Yale University Press, 1997, pp. 158–61: by focusing on prints and print promotion rather than literary sources, Clayton has shown that an imagery and language of the kind previously associated by historians with picturesque tourism of the 1760s onwards was developing as early as the 1740s. Also, for example, Coffin, op. cit. (note 12), p. 37, quotes Bishop Herring, who toured the Welsh mountains in 1738 and was 'agreeably terrified' by them.

46 See Samuel and Nathaniel Buck, *Proposals for Publishing by Subscription, Six Perspective Views [of Canterbury, Rochester, Chichester, Guildford, Maidstone and Chatham]*, London, 1737, British Museum Prints and Drawings vol. S. 6. 39 (f. 6).

47 See Hyde, op. cit., loc. cit. (in note 6).

48 Minutes of the Society of Antiquaries, vol. I, f. 106, 5 February 1724.

49 See Buck, op. cit. (note 3).

50 See ibid., and John Harris, *The Palladians*, London, 1981, p. 37.

51 See Buck, op. cit. (note 3), and Howard Colvin, *The History of the King's Works*, vol. 5 (1660–1782), London: HMSO, 1976, p. 74 *et passim*.

52 See Buck, op. cit. in note 3 above. Robinson built his own house, Rokeby Hall, in the Palladian style, *c.* 1735: see Giles Worsley, 'Rokeby Park, Yorkshire-I', *Country Life*, 19 March 1987, pp. 74–9. Robinson also became a Fellow of the Society of Antiquaries in 1735 (see *A List ...*, op. cit. [note 9]).

53 See, for example, Mavis Batey and David Lambert, *The English Garden Tour: A View into the Past*, London, 1990, p. 163. William Aislabie continued the garden improvements after his father's death in 1742. He subscribed to the Bucks' series of antiquities until 1732. John Aislabie then subscribed between 1733 and 1739.

54 A common starting point is 1709, when Vanbrugh unsuccessfully pleaded for the preservation of the ruins of Woodstock Manor, in the grounds of Blenheim, on both historical-patriotic and aesthetic grounds. See John Dixon Hunt and Peter Willis (eds), *The Genius of the Place: The English Landscape Garden 1620–1820*, Cambridge, Mass., and London, 1988, pp. 119–21; also David Green, 'Blenheim: The Palace and Gardens under Vanbrugh, Hawksmoor and Wise', in J. Bond and K. Tiller, *Blenheim, Landscape for a Palace*, Gloucester and Oxford: Sutton and Oxford University Department for External Studies, 1997, pp. 67–79.

55 As has been pointed out, 'it is not unusual to find references to classically designed houses [in eighteenth-century Britain] as simply "modern".' See Dana Arnold, 'The Country House: Form, Function and Meaning', in Arnold (ed.), op. cit. [note 25], p. 12.

56 For a succinct account of the relationship between the Gothic and politics in the early eighteenth century, see Chris Brooks, *The Gothic Revival*, London: Phaidon, 1999, esp. pp. 51–62. The Saxon and the Gothic were usually conflated in this period.

57 See, for example, Coffin, op. cit. (note 12), pp. 33–5, 112. Another example of early Tory (and Jacobite) garden Gothic is Stainborough Castle (1730), built in the grounds of Wentworth Castle (a Palladian house) for the Earl of Strafford. See Michael Charlesworth, 'Elevation and Succession: the Representation of Jacobite and Hanoverian Politics in the Landscape Gardens of Wentworth Castle and Wentworth Woodhouse', in *New Arcadians Journal*, no. 31–2, 1991, pp. 7–65, esp. 18–29.

58 Alfred also famously appears in the Temple of British Worthies, built in the garden at Stowe, the seat of the Whig Oppositionist Lord Cobham. The classical design, by the Palladian architect William Kent, was initially intended to be realized in the garden of Kent's patron Lord Burlington at Chiswick. See, for example, Coffin, op. cit. (note 12), p. 158.

59 See John Harris, *The Artist and the Country House*, 2nd edn, London: Sotheby, Parke, Bernet, 1985, p. 166, commentary on pl. 169, which is a reproduction of the Buck engraving. See also Gordon Nares, 'Corby Castle, Cumberland-I', *Country Life*, 7 January 1954, pp. 32–5.

60 On the roles of the medieval structures mentioned, see Batey and Lambert, op. cit. (note 53), pp. 163–7, and Worsley, op. cit. (note 52), pp. 78–9; respectively, also Ian Ousby, *The Englishman's England: Taste, Travel and the Rise of Tourism*, Cambridge: Cambridge University Press, 1990, pp. 110–16, on Fountains Abbey.

61 See list of cascades in Continental and British gardens in Richard Hewlings, 'Chiswick House and Gardens: Appearance and Meaning', in Toby Barnard and Jane Clark (eds), *Lord Burlington: Architecture, Art and Life*, London: Hambledon, 1995, p. 46.

62 See Ayres, op. cit. (note 27), esp. pp. 84–114.

63 ibid., pp. 89, 91.

64 On Willis's Gothicism, see Evans, op. cit. (note 7), pp. 55–6, 98–9, 129. She quotes from a pamphlet by Andrew Ducarel on Willis published in 1760: 'During the Course of his long Life he had visited every Cathedral in England and Wales, except Carlisle: which journeys he used to call his Pilgrimages.' (p. 129)

6

Data, Documentation and Display in Eighteenth-Century Investigations of Exeter Cathedral

Sam Smiles

This article examines a development in the eighteenth century's understanding of medieval architecture, when the emergence of empirical observation can be witnessed taking shape as a new investigative methodology. The accurate recording and interpretation of visual evidence characterized one of the most important innovations in antiquarian method, bidding by these means to offer a secure stock of material data as a counter-weight to hearsay and traditional written accounts. While we may take for granted that an historic building is marked by the traces of its transformations, and that rigorous examination is required to make the stones give up their secrets, the emergence of that idea is itself the product of a particular time. Specifically, learning to look at medieval buildings, seeing them as repositories of historical data from which inferences can be drawn, is part of a development in antiquarian scholarship from the middle years of the eighteenth century onwards.[1]

In what follows, I have chosen to pay particular attention to the recuperation of Exeter cathedral's building history, which offers a clear example of this development. There are three reasons for this. First, the cathedral possesses an extraordinarily rich source of medieval records and, as such, is extremely well supplied with first-hand textual accounts of the fabric. Second, from 1747 to 1784 the cathedral's officiating clergy included two successive Deans, Charles Lyttleton and Jeremiah Milles, who were keen antiquarians and would serve as President of the Society of Antiquaries (Lyttleton from 1765 to 1768; Milles from 1769 to 1784).[2] Third, the Society of Antiquaries published Lyttleton's account of the cathedral in its own pioneering study of the building, published in 1797 with a further commentary, allowing some comparisons to be made about the growth of empirical methods between the 1750s and the 1790s. This conjunction of detailed archival records with eighteenth-century scholars able to make proper use of them, places the examination of Exeter cathedral's building history at the heart of the antiquarian endeavour. The balance struck there between textual and material evidence helps to illuminate how the methodology of medievalist research changed during the eighteenth century.

Exeter cathedral's archives are well known today for their extensive coverage of the construction history of the fabric. As Audrey Erskine has pointed out, no other cathedral church in Europe built before 1350 has more extensive surviving records from the medieval period. Over some seventy years, from *c.* 1270 to the 1340s, the Norman cathedral, constructed originally from about 1114 to the 1170s, was remodelled to become the essentially Decorated structure we see today. The fabric accounts list the various masters employed on the work, the materials purchased and the rate of completion of the new building. The most ample sequence of fabric accounts dates from 1279 to 1353, with a slightly less full series from 1371 to 1467, and it is these early records that have provided modern scholarship with the means to clarify the building sequence at Exeter.[3] The accepted view of architectural development at Exeter was recently advanced by research conducted on the building during its latest phase of conservation, from 1975 to the present. The essays collected in the British Archaeological Association's volume on Exeter cathedral, published in 1991, constitute a detailed and authoritive summary of these findings.[4] A skeleton history of the cathedral, based on today's consensus view, can therefore be set against those earlier understandings of the cathedral with which this present article is concerned. Modern scholarship agrees that a Saxon monastery existed in the late seventh century, to the west of the present cathedral. In the early tenth century Athelstan raised a Saxon minster in place of the monastery and donated a large number of valuable relics to it. This building was damaged by Danish raiders in 1003 and rebuilt by Canute in 1016. In 1050 Leofric was installed as the first Bishop of Exeter by Edward the Confessor, thus re-establishing the old Saxon minster as a cathedral. In 1114 a new building was begun, east of the Saxon church, by Bishop Warelwast, dedicated in 1133 and completed by the end of the twelfth century. The present North and South towers are the most visible remains of this structure, together with some footings and fragments of decoration (plate 23). This Norman building was in turn replaced by the present structure, in a programme initiated by Bishop Bronescombe in 1275. Beginning at the east end, the Lady Chapel and retro choir were completed first under Bishop Quinil, followed by the Presbytery (1301–2) and Choir (1303–7), under Bishop Bitton (plate 24). Between the 1310s and the 1340s, during the time of Bishop Stapledon and Bishop Grandisson, the nave was completed and the image screen on the west front begun (plate 25). Many of the window tracery designs, together with the pulpitum, reredos and Bishop's throne can be attributed to Thomas de Witney, working at Exeter between 1312 and 1329. Three major medieval reconsiderations complicate this picture: the Great East Window was initially glazed in 1303–4 by Master Walter the Glazier, but was substantially redesigned and reglazed by Robert Lyen between 1389 and 1391; the Chapter House was begun in 1224, but its upper part was rebuilt in the 1460s; the image screen on the west front was heightened, with an extra tier of figures added *c.* 1460–80.

Today, as with comparable buildings, we have a sense of Exeter cathedral in its historical formation, marked by evolution and dissolution, repair and decay. This understanding of history tends to render the structure transparent, substituting for its ponderous authority an awareness of its historical reinvention and fragility. Over nearly 1,000 years, the cathedral has been subjected to new architectural imperatives, changes in liturgical practice, iconoclasm, warfare and at least four major programmes of restoration.[5] Yet this sense of the historicity of the cathedral is itself indicative of modern consciousness; we are sensitive to

81

23   North Tower, Exeter Cathedral. Photo: David Griffiths.

change and accustomed to detecting its workings. Equally, we operate with a terminology and an understanding of architectural development that binds buildings to historical periods and cultural contexts. This article is concerned with the beginnings of such understanding, when the medieval legacy still lacked terminological precision, or a developed knowledge of stylistic sequences, and the comparative dating such research made possible was still in its infancy. In this regard, then, the patterns detectable in the historiography of the cathedral make sense as a minute sub-set of much larger shifts in historical consciousness from the sixteenth to the nineteenth century. Close examination of antiquarian debates over the building history of the cathedral allows us to trace in them the growth of a new articulation of history, a more rigorous attention to documentary evidence and a suspicion of conjectural accounts. Most interestingly of all, the willingness

24   Interior of Lady Chapel, Exeter Cathedral. Photo: David Griffiths.

of antiquarian scholars to make deductive inferences from the fabric itself points
to the development of a new archaeological methodology.

To get some measure of this achievement, it is helpful to review understandings of the cathedral's history prior to Lyttleton's and Milles's research. The
task facing earlier chroniclers was fraught with difficulties. For John Leland,
pursuing his inquiries in the late 1530s, local report and hearsay were probably all
he had to go on, although he had made a point of visiting the cathedral library and
may conceivably have had some access to the documentary records it contained.[6]
He reported that the cathedral was begun by 'Peter the first' (i.e., Bishop Peter
Quinil [1280–91]), that Bishop Stapledon (1308–26) vaulted the presbytery and
also commissioned the High Altar; that John de Grandisson (1327–69) enlarged

83

the western end of the church, adding two bays and vaulting the body of the nave; and that Bishop Lacy and also, perhaps, Bishop Neville built the Chapter House.[7] But the brief remarks on the cathedral in his *Itinerary* are marked by hesitancy and contradiction, the product, one presumes, of competing local traditions concerning the cathedral's history. Leland records, for example, that Bishop Stapledon commissioned the High Altar's 'Riche Silver Table in the midle of it', but continues: 'Yet sum saye Bishop Lacye made this Silver Table; but ther is no likelyhod yn it.'[8] The Chapter House he first ascribes entirely to Bishop Neville, but then adds: 'Syns I heard that Edmund Lacy began the Chapiter House, and Neville performid it.' What strikes a modern reader is the variance of the accounts. Walter Stapledon is correctly identified with the presbytery vault and the High Altar, yet some of Leland's informants wished to posit Bishop Edmund Lacy (1420–55) as the originator of the altar's retable, a whole century later.[9] Similarly, the entire building programme of the Chapter House, not just the rebuilding of its upper part, is given to the fifteenth century, whether under Lacy or in combination with George Neville (1456–65). The haze surrounding these ascriptions to Bishop Lacy is notable, given that work of the 1450s might still have been remembered some eighty years later, when Leland visited Exeter. Leland's inquiries nevertheless constitute the first attempt to outline the history of the cathedral and for that reason they were a legitimate point of reference for eighteenth-century antiquaries, familiar with Hearne's first published edition of the *Itinerary*, which appeared in 1710.

Leland's difficulties in finding reliable evidence also dogged the first major account of the fabric, published by John Hooker in 1584. Hooker was Chamberlain of the City of Exeter and understood the value of the city's own archives in preparing his history of Exeter, but the cathedral authorities refused him access to their own muniments and he had to write the cathedral's history using other sources.[10] Notwithstanding these difficulties, his account is fuller than Leland's and incorporates more detail. He attributes the enlargement of the cathedral to Bishop Warelwast in about 1112, when the foundations of the choir were laid. The completion of the chancel and choir is given to Bishop Quinil, as also the beginning of the nave in 1284. To Bishop Grandisson are ascribed the western extension of the nave and the roof. For the Chapter House, Hooker reverses Leland's order, with Bishop Neville beginning the work in 1456 and Bishop Lacy completing it during his episcopate.[11]

The inclusion of definite dates and a better understanding of episcopal succession give Hooker's account an authority that all who followed him tended to accept. Crucially, Hooker's speculations about the Saxon origins of the cathedral had a long-lasting influence. In his account, King Athelstan's foundation is identified with the present Lady Chapel (plate 24) on a number of occasions. On first introducing the Saxon cathedral Hooker describes it as 'at the first [was] but small, and that Part which is now called The Ladie Chapel ...'[12] Later in his account, Athelstan's monastic house in Exeter, established in 932, is described as 'that Part of the Cathedral Church now called the Lady Chapel'.[13] Thus, for Hooker, when Warelwast began to enlarge the cathedral in 1112, he was extending the fabric westwards from a Saxon cathedral 'which at that time was no bigger than that Part which is now the Lady Chappel'.[14] Yet it was obvious to

Hooker, as it would be to any visitor, that the building was stylistically uniform on the interior, despite the four centuries separating Athelstan's foundation in 932 from Grandisson's death in 1369. It is telling that, given this evidence, rather than reconsider the supposed Saxon origins of the Lady Chapel, Hooker simply points out that uniformity as a notable feature:

> And this one Thing is to be noted, that albeit there were about Four Hundred Years distant from the first Foundation and Building thereof, until the ending and finishing of the same, yet it is so uniformly and decently compact and builded in one Mould, as though it had been done at one Instant.[15]

Nothing could express more eloquently Hooker's difficulties in being denied access to the cathedral records than this refusal to trust the evidence of his own eyes.

Hooker's authority dominated seventeenth-century accounts of the cathedral and echoes or paraphrases of his conclusions can be found in Francis Godwin's *De Praesulibus Angliae Commentarius* (1616), Peter Heylyn's *An Help to English History* (1641) and Richard Izacke's *Remarkable Antiquities of the City of Exeter* (1677).[16] Godwin's account was later to be censured as a missed opportunity to improve on Hooker. Appointed sub-Dean at Exeter in 1587, he had access to the cathedral archives, whose use had recently been denied to Hooker, but he appears to have made no use of them.[17] Izacke, similarly, was later deemed culpable of laziness, given that his office of Chamberlain of Exeter, from 1653 to 1683, gave him access to the city's archives, which should therefore have enabled him to write with more authority.[18] Given these failures to undertake new research on the cathedral's history, it is little surprise to find Hooker's belief in the Lady Chapel as a Saxon structure instantiated in its very appearance. The cathedral underwent changes of use during the Commonwealth and its library room in the cloisters was demolished in 1655. The library itself was housed in St John's Hospital while the city Chamber debated what to do with it. To save this resource from destruction, an Exeter physician, Robert Vilvaine, undertook to re-house the collection at his own expense in the Lady Chapel. Accordingly, in December 1657 the Lady Chapel was fitted up as a library, with a wooden entrance in the Corinthian style bearing inscriptions recording its installation and also the date of the Lady Chapel itself, 'ab Athelstano Rege olim fundatam'.[19] For the next 150 years, until the removal of the library early in the nineteenth century, the Lady Chapel's supposed Saxon origins remained inscribed over its entrance.

It is this received opinion and reliance on tradition that the new antiquarianism of the eighteenth century would challenge. Charles Lyttleton's researches at Exeter are revealing of antiquarianism at mid-century in its development towards a more rigorous approach to medieval antiquities. As we shall see, the investigations at Exeter between the 1740s and the 1790s drew on the talents and opinions of many of those most closely associated with the development of antiquarian scholarship. The new awareness of the cathedral's history, produced by Lyttleton and others, is thus a product of, but also a contribution to, national developments in antiquarian method.

The timing of Lyttleton's appointment as Dean of Exeter in 1748 was certainly propitious. The Society of Antiquaries had become more prominent in English intellectual life, receiving their own charter in 1751 and moving to new premises in Chancery Lane in 1753. Lyttleton himself had become a Fellow of the Society in 1746, two years before he was installed at Exeter. His background was privileged; he was the son of Sir Thomas Lyttleton, the fourth baronet, and was related to the Grenville family, a connection that helped to secure his position as Chaplain to George II in 1747 and his promotion from Dean of Exeter to Bishop of Carlisle in 1762.[20] Educated at Eton and Oxford, he was called to the Bar at the Middle Temple in 1738 and ordained in 1742, taking up the rich living of Alvechurch, Worcestershire, close to the family home. He was elected Fellow of the Royal Society in the same year. As well as his account of Exeter cathedral, seven of his papers were selected for the first three volumes of *Archaeologia* and he provided an account of Worcester cathedral for Valentine Green's *Worcester* (1764). He was sufficiently esteemed as an antiquary to become President of the Society of Antiquaries from 1765 until his death in 1768. Lyttleton's arrival at Exeter in 1748 thus coincided with his own developing interest in antiquarian research. For the next fourteen years, working alongside Jeremiah Milles, he researched and restored the cathedral.

Milles came from a less exalted family, being the son of the vicar of Duloe, in Cornwall. Like Lyttleton, he was born in 1714 and educated at Eton and Oxford. In the early 1730s he travelled through Europe with his cousin Richard Pococke, afterwards Bishop of Meath, while his uncle, Dr Thomas Milles, Bishop of Waterford and Lismore, supported his education. Ordained in 1735, Milles first took up positions at Lismore and Waterford cathedrals, although choosing to live in England after inheriting his uncle's fortune in 1740. Marriage in 1745, to the daughter of Archbishop Potter, secured him preferments in the home counties, and his father-in-law's patronage delivered him a precentorship at Exeter in 1747, with a prebendal stall and the emoluments of a canon residentiary. When Lyttleton became Bishop of Carlisle in 1762, Milles took over as Dean at Exeter. He was elected Fellow of the Society of Antiquaries in 1741 and Fellow of the Royal Society in the following year. His election to become the President of the Society of Antiquaries, following Lyttleton's death in 1768, ushered in one of its most energetic and productive phases; working alongside Richard Gough, Milles oversaw the inauguration of the society's journal *Archaeologia* in 1770.

The coincidence of two such notable antiquarian scholars working at Exeter in the middle of the century is instructive, not just for the light their inquiries threw on the history of the cathedral, but also for what their campaign of research and restoration tells us about antiquarian method at this time. After the vicissitudes of the Commonwealth and the repairs undertaken after the restoration of the monarchy, Exeter cathedral had come through the early years of the eighteenth century with little alteration. The most significant restoration projects to take place before mid-century were repairs to Bishop Stapledon's monument in 1733 and to the Chapter House in 1740.[21] Thus, although the Dean and Chapter had made a new post of Surveyor of the Works in 1707, the major eighteenth-century restoration of the cathedral belonged to the second half of the century and was prosecuted under Lyttleton's and Milles's direction.[22] The centre of the great East

Window was repaired and reglazed in 1751, followed by a reglazing programme for most of the cathedral's glass from 1753 to 1760. The pyramidal spire on the North tower was taken down in 1752 and defective medieval timbers in the roof were repaired or replaced. In the 1760s the Elizabethan communion rails were removed, the choir and presbytery re-floored and the choir stalls provided with wainscotting and Gothick arcading. Between 1764 and 1767 the great West Window was replaced with a modern work by William Peckitt, of York, now widely considered to have been the masterpiece of the finest glass painter of his day. The remainder of the great East Window was restored and reglazed from 1767 to 1770. Finally, in the 1780s, the interior of the cathedral was made harmonious through the agency of a uniform programme of colour-washing, with buff yellow for the walls and brown for the columns.[23]

Surviving correspondence of both Lyttleton and Milles clearly shows the enthusiasm they shared in the project of restoring the cathedral. In the earliest letter, dated 4 July 1751, Lyttleton indicates the extent to which he had overcome a recalcitrant chapter.

> I rejoice to find that you are pleased with ye improvements I have made in & about ye cathedral during your absence. Except what I have done with ye muniments, all ye rest would be nothing in any other church where ye Dean had a *Decanal* Power, but as ye Dean of Exeter can do nothing without ye consent of ye Chapter, ye majority of which is sure to oppose every alteration that is attended [with] ye least expence, I take some little merit to myself in what I have done & ye more as you approve of it.[24]

Following Lyttleton's departure for Carlisle in 1762, Milles took over responsibility for the restoration programme and wrote to Lyttleton on 25 August 1764 with an update on progress concerning improvements to the Choir and the great West Window.[25] Milles was understandably optimistic.

> I have accomplished all my wishes in respect to ye Cathedral, I hope to make it compleatly elegant. The Chapter have readily agreed to make a new row of wainscott seats in the place of ye deal ones, which stood outermost, we are to add another seat under mine & ye Chanters stalls, to remove ye Mayor & corporation, to where ye Singing men sit, on one side & to appropriate ye opposite to ye Ladies. The Bp has undertaken to [have] his throne new cleaned repaired painted and sanded & will give us 30£ more towards ye new iron rail for the Western window, so that now ye benefactions will amount to 170£, and ye whole expence near to 500£. I am almost astonished myself to think of ye facility with which I have prevailed on ye chapter to bear this great expence. Snow, & Slack hold back a little Baker does not seem to like it, but no body opposes.[26]

It is important to keep this programme of improvements in mind when reviewing Lyttleton's work on the muniments, for here in this early phase of antiquarian investigation of the fabric, enthusiasm for medieval research could happily co-exist with a programme of modernization of the cathedral.

Indeed, Lyttleton's ordering of the cathedral's library and archives might usefully be regarded as part of that same modernization project, taking the measure of what resources existed and then expending the necessary capital to enhance them. The documents relating to the history of the fabric seem to have been kept in no particular order and Lyttleton set about arranging and cataloguing the books and documents in the cathedral's possession; many of them still bear endorsements in his handwriting today. Exchequer accounts for 1751 list payments for transcribing a catalogue of books and muniments, for cleaning books and cutting off the chains from some volumes.[27] It is, however, that portion of this immense task relating to the fabric rolls that concerns us here, for Lyttleton's steady organization of that resource gave him an unparalleled insight into the surviving documentation of the cathedral's construction. What Hooker had been denied, and Godwin had been too lazy to undertake, Lyttleton now achieved. He must have devoted most of his energies to the task, for he was able to write to Milles, in the summer of 1751, that the task of cataloguing the archive had been completed.[28] It had not, however, been easy work. As he wrote to Sanderson Miller in 1761, looking back on his work with some pride,

> The antient Evidences and Muniments of the Church I found covered with dirt and dust; these to the amount of some Bushells, I cleaned, sorted and endorsed, and having tied them up in little bundles, they are now deposited in the old Exhequer, being a very convenient muniment room.[29]

Lyttleton's use of these records would prove to be decisive, allowing him to provide evidence in place of the conjecture and local tradition on which his predecessors had relied.

Lyttleton's involvement with the work of restoration gave him the chance to examine the fabric in considerable detail, as his workmen made alterations to it; his ordering of the archives provided him with the means to examine all the medieval accounts of its construction that had survived. In the light of Lyttleton's contribution to medievalist research, his access to both sorts of information is crucial. The combination of complementary methods of inquiry, empirical and archival, mark the essay he wrote in 1754 on the history of the fabric, printed posthumously in the Society of Antiquaries' account of the cathedral. He begins by outlining the historiography of the cathedral, from Hooker to Stukeley, to challenge in particular the assumption that the Lady Chapel is a Saxon structure.[30] Crucially, the argument used to refute this tradition is not documentary but visual. Lyttleton's ordering of the fabric rolls would have revealed that their coverage of the new building work begins as summary accounts covering the years 1279–81 and 1285–87, with no rolls at all preserved from 1287–99. The construction of the Lady Chapel is not therefore secured with recourse to archival evidence. Although Lyttleton would use documentary evidence in his essay when he could,[31] here he had only his experience of the stylistic development of Gothic architecture to guide him. Given the rudimentary state of knowledge pertaining to Gothic architecture at this period, his confidence in the authority of visual evidence is striking: 'Not a single stone of [the Lady Chapel] was erected either by that prince [Athelstan] or King Canute; for the style of the pillars, arches, windows, &c. evidently demonstrates that it is some ages posterior to the Norman conquest.'[32] He makes the same stylistic deductions when examining the claim that Bishop Warelwast began the choir, using comparative references to advance his case.

> That Bishop Warelwast began the present choir, I much doubt, the arches being all elliptic, the pillars by no means thick and clumsy, not their capitals hatched dauncette-wise; circumstances which occur in all buildings of that age, as Christ church cathedral in Oxford, Tewkesbury abbey church, &c. The light Gothic ... not prevailing either here, or in other parts of Europe adjoining to England, till about the time of our King Henry II. And even then we find the old Saxon mode frequently intermingled with the Gothic.[33]

Lyttleton's invocation of the 'Saxon mode' here, however, reveals the early date of his essay; its readiness to elide Saxon and Norman architectural styles would not be countenanced a generation later. Notoriously, Lyttleton refers to the two towers that remain of the Norman cathedral as Saxon, and this ascription diminished the value of the essay for his successors.[34] Lyttleton considered that the 'Saxon' (i.e., Norman) fabric must have extended at least as far as the towers, which would have 'flanked the great western door, like those at the Priory church of Worksop in Nottinghamshire, and at Hereford and Chichester cathedrals'. He further drew parallels with Iffley church, near Oxford, and St James's, Devizes, 'both undoubtedly Saxon buildings', in his opinion.[35] But this invocation of Saxon architecture is not as determinate as it would be with later writers and means less than it seems to suggest; it is better understood as the product of an architectural nomenclature still being elaborated at mid-century.[36] Thus Lyttleton can also declare that 'these towers bear evident marks of the Saxon, or early Norman age', as though the terms are in some sense interchangeable.[37] It is also clear that Saxon architecture, as he uses the phrase, includes what we would call Norman. Thus, for Lyttleton, the transition in English medieval architecture from 'the clumsy Saxon mode of building' to 'the Gothic style' occurs between the reigns of Stephen (1135–54) and Henry II (1154–89).[38]

It is unfortunate for Lyttleton's reputation that his terminology was so vague, for the originality of his achievement has been largely diminished in the rush to expose his seeming confusion over the dates of the towers. In fact, his essay is marked throughout by a sophisticated visual analysis, using the evidence of the fabric itself to confront received opinion. Thus, challenging Godwin's assertion that Bishop Quinil (1280–91) had built the towers, Lyttleton is able to demonstrate by the simplest observations that Quinil altered, but indeed could not have built them.

> Both these great windows ... seem plainly to have been made long after the towers were erected, being of a very different form from the other windows in each tower; those being small and round arched, whereas these have both pointed arches. And if we examine the inside wall of the south tower, and the outside of the north tower, we shall plainly discover two old round arched windows (now stopped up,) in the former, which was probably

done when the present great one was made ... And farther, one may perceive the top of the great window in the north tower, cutting the ornamental arched work on the outside wall next the treasury house; which demonstrates that this window was not coeval with the tower.[39]

At this remove, Lyttleton's empirical deductions seem so obvious that there is little in them worthy of comment, but it is important to remember that it is precisely here, in the use of visual testimony, that antiquarian study was coming of age. The antiquarian topographers William Borlase and Richard Gough were also proselytizing for physical inspection of monuments at mid-century as a corrective to text-based study. Borlase, in a letter to Lyttleton, shortly after his arrival at Exeter, had talked of monuments as 'impartial authorities to appeal to', whose 'materials, style, measurement and appurtenances ... are things not to be new moulded by, or made to comply with every fanciful conjecture.'[40] Lyttleton, had he not already been disposed to do so, took the hint in Borlase's remarks: the fabric of the cathedral had an authority of its own, quite distinct from the fanciful conjectures that Hooker and others had entertained. Lyttleton's younger contemporary, Richard Gough, who would become Director of the Society of Antiquaries in 1771, was equally fervent. He had been travelling throughout the 1760s to gather new material for a revised edition of Camden's *Britannia* and was struck by the need to undertake on-site explorations. As he expressed it in 1768,

> Whoever sits down to compile the history and antiquities of a county or a town, should confirm the evidence he collects from books and MSS. by inspection of the places described. The face of the country and the monuments remaining on it, are as interesting as the progress of descents or revolutions of property. Injudicious and sedentary compilers find it much easier to arrange materials put into their hands, than to ramble about, and examine every remnant of antiquity ... nothing is more perplexing than to find no use at all made of many monuments and evidences, obvious to a careful enquirer, but more exposed to the ravages of time and accident.[41]

This attitude, pioneered by researchers such as Lyttleton, would quickly become established as the key methodology that antiquarian research might contribute to historical inquiry. Gough himself was aware that attention to the visible features of Gothic architecture would allow its development to be plotted and a proper assessment of it as an architectural style to emerge. 'Had the remains of antient buildings been more attended to we should before now have seen a system of Gothic architecture in its various areas: we should have had all its parts reduced to rules; their variations and their dates fixed together'.[42] Lyttleton, as one of the first to pay attention to stylistic sequences, could not benefit from the systematic discourse Gough recommended, something that developed through the 1780s and into the next century.[43] His vagueness over the correct terminology to apply to twelfth-century work was, in one sense, precisely what Gough meant when he complained about the lack of system in studying the medieval legacy.

Gough's attempts to provide accurate engravings of medieval antiquities should be understood as part of a growing trend to dignify the study of the middle ages with the same seriousness already allotted to Greece and Rome.[44] This project was materially advanced by Sir Henry Englefield at the Society of Antiquaries, most notably in the decision to publish accurate and large-scale engravings of medieval architecture. At a meeting on 30 March 1792, the Council of the Society resolved 'that it be desireable and useful for the Society to be in possession of Architectural drawings of the different Cathedrals and other Religious Houses in this Kingdom' and that money be set aside to appoint Thomas Richard Underwood as Draughtsman in ordinary to the Society.[45] Englefield's influence is surely detectable here. He had been admitted to the Society of Antiquaries in 1779 and to the Society of Dilettanti in 1781, acting as their secretary from 1781 to 1795. In that position he would have been particularly aware of the Society of Dilettanti's sponsorship of James Stuart and Nicholas Revett at Athens between 1751 and 1753, as well as their underwriting of Revett's exploration of Ionia in 1764, and the ensuing publication, *Antiquities of Ionia* (1769–97), with drawings by William Pars. Englefield had already contributed medieval researches to the Society of Antiquaries, most notably an article in *Archaeologia* on Reading abbey, accompanied with plans and sections.[46] It was evident to Englefield and others that proper visual documentation of medieval architecture would not only provide a secure basis for scholarly investigation, as had happened with classical antiquities, but would also bring the medieval architectural legacy up to some sort of parity with classical remains. What Gough had advocated for so long was about to become a reality. In the light of this new policy, John Carter drew and measured Exeter cathedral as the first of the Society of Antiquaries' projected series of volumes, with Lyttleton's 1754 essay and Englefield's commentary on it accompanying the engravings.[47]

Englefield's essay, written some forty years after Lyttleton's, provides a clear demonstration of the way in which empirical research could now be promulgated as more reliable than text-based authorities. Like Lyttleton, he is keen to show up the inadequacies of post-medieval commentators, from Hooker to Stukeley, but rather than working carefully through their accounts to reveal their shortcomings, as Lyttleton had done, Englefield moves briskly through the extant literature to conclude emphatically, '. . . if the words of these authors are to be taken in a literal sense, it is certain that the accounts they give of the building are inconsistent with the evidence of the structure'.[48] The brusque confidence of this remark ('it is certain') and the use of that telling phrase 'evidence of the structure', are indications of how quickly the pioneering attempt made by Lyttleton in 1754 had matured. Indeed, where Lyttleton had moved with caution, when the fabric rolls could not provide him with detailed information, Englefield relies on an almost forensic scrutiny of detail to advance research. The evidence of the structure is there for those who know how to read it and thus constitutes its own text. Englefield can therefore propose a method of examination that treats architectural details as forms of empirical data. Considering, for example, the irregularities of the image screen at the west end of the church (plates 25 and 26), Englefield declares,

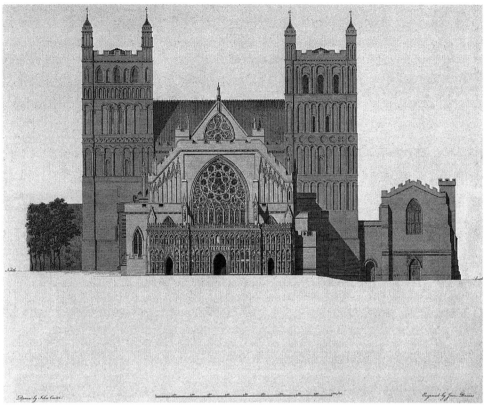

25   James Basire, West Front, Exeter Cathedral. Engraving after drawing by John Carter, from *Plans, Elevations, Sections and Specimens of the Architecture and Ornaments of Exeter Cathedral*, London, 1797. Exeter University Library (Special Collections).

> Perhaps a very minute inspection into the masonry of this screen, and of the Chapter house, might confirm the suspicions of their having been built at different times. It may not be improper to recommend to those who survey or describe our cathedrals, great attention to the courses of the stone, where there is reason to suspect a mixture of work, from the discordancy of style or ornament.[49]

Englefield's ability to rely on stylistic variations as indicators of date was itself made possible by antiquarian research into the historical evolution of Gothic architecture. Publications such as Bentham's *History and Antiquities of the Conventual and Cathedral Church of Ely* (1771) would shortly be joined by Murphy's 'Discourse on the Principles of Gothic Architecture', in his publication on the church of Batalha (1795), and Joseph Halfpenny's *Gothic Ornaments in the Cathedral Church of York* (1795–1800), while the Society of Antiquaries itself was making its own contribution with John Topham's *Some Account of the Collegiate Church of Saint Stephen, Westminster* (1795), whose engravings after Carter had set new standards in accuracy and archaeological importance.[50] Studies such as

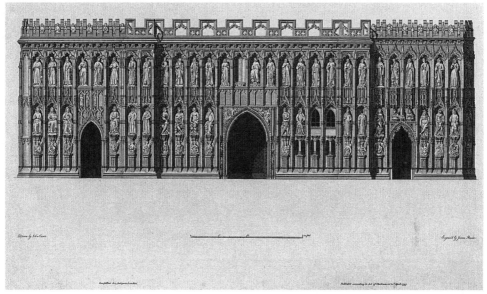

26   James Basire, West Front Image Screen, Exeter Cathedral. Engraving after drawing by John Carter, from *Plans, Elevations, Sections and Specimens of the Architecture and Ornaments of Exeter Cathedral*, London, 1797. Exeter University Library (Special Collections)

these were beginning to supply what Gough had demanded: 'a system of Gothic architecture in its various areas ... its parts reduced to rules; their variations and their dates fixed together'. In the light of such advances in systematic scholarship it is, perhaps, no surprise that Englefield criticized Lyttleton for producing an essay without method or arrangement.[51]

If systematic understanding by the close of the century was becoming regarded as the sine qua non of the route to understanding an architectural style, the provision of accurate visual information was a necessity. The business of recording the medieval legacy would require a scrupulous attention to detail and an absolute refusal to embellish that detail with artistic mannerisms. In the person of John Carter, the Society of Antiquaries had a delineator of medieval antiquities who would not flinch from such a task.[52] Carter had first visited Exeter in 1770 (plate 28) and must have returned again in 1771, judging from the dated drawings now in the British Library.[53] He returned to make numerous studies for the Society of Antiquaries' projected volume in 1792, covering every aspect of the cathedral's structure and ornament (plates 25, 26 and 27).[54] It is a tribute to his project of exemplary accuracy that modern scholars still refer to these drawings, and the engravings produced from them, for information on the cathedral before its next phase of restoration in the early 1800s.[55] Like Gough and Englefield, Carter deprecated the fact that 'whilst so many professional men have presented to the world systematical illustrations of Roman and Grecian Architecture, the study of the Antient Architecture of this country has, in a manner, been wholly disregarded.'[56] As Carter noted, the problem with many of the records that had been made was their infection by stylistic mannerisms. He particularly loathed

27 John Carter, Lower tier of statues in the screen at the west front, Exeter Cathedral, 1792.
Pencil drawing, 23 × 37 cm. By permission of the British Library, Add. MS. 29931, f. 81.

picturesque appearances produced by the skill of the Artist, in a certain
disposal of light and shade toward what is called 'effect' in drawing; an
effect of that kind we perceive when gazing on an object with the eyes
half open, in a sort of dim fascination of the senses, whereby we catch a
momentary gleam of the sublime; such sort of pencilled performances
tending more to accredit the modern Delineator than the antient
Architect.[57]

Carter's method, in place of such embellishment, was to copy the object with
absolute fidelity. Such a procedure, although it had precedents in the illustration
of anatomy and natural history, as well as the delineation of classical architecture,
was still a novelty in the representation of medieval antiquities. Given the
relatively late development of scholarly interest in the middle ages, one might
speculate that only a belief in medieval architecture as rational, organized and
purposeful could support a project of exact representation, whose aim was to
allow the logic of that culture to be perceived. Similarly, only a conviction that
medieval art and architecture constituted one of the highest points of British
civilization could justify the pains taken to record and document its material
record.

    Carter's draughtsmanship was thus conceived as serving knowledge, as a form
of archaeological inquiry, not as an illustrative embellishment to a text: 'not alone
to please the eye ... but to give information and instruction to the rising
generation of Antiquaries and Architectural Professors'.[58] The topographical
engraver John Thomas Smith endorsed Carter's attempt at unswerving accuracy

28   John Carter, View of the north cross aile of Exeter Cathedral (taken 1770). Wash drawing,
28 × 24 cm. By permission of the British Library, Add. MS. 29925, f. 8.

... he justly deserves every remuneration for his perseverance in handing down so rich a mine of antiquity. Many of his plates are etched in a spirited manner, with a close attention to mutilation, a point seldom attended to by Artists. Topographical draughtsmen introduce more than they see, in order to make their productions picturesque; which, however, they may again be tickled up by the engraver, who gives them a silvery effect, are not worth a farthing; and I am sorry to say that engravers in general of antiquarian matters, not only do too much to them, but frequently, in consequence of their ignorance in drawing, endeavour to disguise their defects by high finishing: they give a polish to bodies which never had any, and make no distinction between crumbled stone, wood, linen and metal.[59]

Certainly, by the early nineteenth century the case for exacting visual analysis had been made. The publication of Augustus Charles Pugin's *Specimens of Gothic Architecture* (1821) might well be regarded as the vindication of rigorous observation as an essential prerequisite for medievalist research. Reviewing Pugin's achievement, a contemporary critic remarked that 'studies of this description train the eye to exact and patient observation, thereby enabling us to see far more than we otherwise should.'[60] Proponents of such research were activated by a confident empiricism, a neo-Baconian method, which promoted the accurate record of visual data as a means of amending or even supplanting textual sources.

The recovery of the history of Exeter cathedral from the sixteenth to the eighteenth century can be seen as an exemplary instance of the dialogue between tradition, archive and visual evidence over some two hundred years.[61] It represents a transition in antiquarian thought towards a more rigorous understanding of the complex sequences buried in a building's history, and the means necessary to detect and order them. It also participates in a more general desire to understand the phenomenon of Gothic architecture as a stylistic development, in Britain and in Europe. As antiquarians recognized, for all the confidence expressed in empirical research, close attention to the structure could not, on its own, restore a building's history nor situate that history within larger patterns of architectural development. It was only through the dissemination of reliable research that comparative dating could be established on a secure foundation. The addition of visual material to these accounts rapidly advanced the possibility of a systematic understanding of medieval architecture. The work undertaken on Exeter cathedral in the second half of the eighteenth century can be regarded, therefore, as both witness and beneficiary of the transformation of antiquarian research.

Notes

I am grateful for Bernard Nurse's help in the preparation of this article.

1 The pioneering article in this regard is John Frew, 'An Aspect of the Early Gothic Revival: The Transformation of Medievalist Research', *Journal of the Warburg and Courtauld Institutes,* vol. 43, 1980, pp. 174–85. As will be seen below, while I endorse most of Frew's conclusions, he seems to have overlooked the importance of Lyttleton's deductions from architectural evidence

in his 1754 essay. See also Thomas Cocke, 'Rediscovery of the Romanesque', in *English Romanesque Art, 1066–1200*, London: Arts Council of Great Britain, 1984, pp. 360–4.

2 Lyttleton left Exeter in 1762 to become Bishop of Carlisle, but Milles officiated at the cathedral, when actually resident in the city rather than in London, from 1747 until his death in 1784.

3 To the fabric accounts can be added the Act Books of the Cathedral Chapter Minutes, dating from 1383 to the present. See Audrey Erskine 'The Documentation of Exeter Cathedral: The Archives and their Application', in Francis Kelly (ed.), *Medieval Art and Architecture at Exeter Cathedral*, London: The British Archaeological Association, XI (Conference Transaction for the Year 1985), 1991, pp. 1–3; Audrey Erskine, *The Accounts of the Fabric of Exeter Cathedral, 1279–1353*, two parts, Devon and Cornwall Record Society, New Series, xxiv, xxvi, 1981, 1983.

4 Kelly (ed.), op. cit. (note 3).

5 For a reliable introduction to the history of the cathedral see Audrey Erskine, Vyvyan Hope and John Lloyd, *Exeter Cathedral: A Short History and Description*, Exeter: Exeter Cathedral, 1988.

6 Lyttleton, writing in 1754, believed that Leland's account relied essentially on oral, rather than documentary evidence, 'which no doubt he had from the information of some of the members of the chapter, when he surveyed the church in person'. See Charles Lyttleton 'Some remarks on the original foundation and construction of the present fabric of Exeter Cathedral', in *Some Account of the Cathedral Church of Exeter*, London: Society of Antiquaries, 1797, p. 2. However, Leland records that he visited the cathedral library in 1538. See Lucy Toulmin Smith, *The Itinerary of John Leland*, London 1906–10, vol. 1, pp. 230–1.

7 Thomas Hearne (ed.), *The Itinerary of John Leland the Antiquary*, 3 vols, Oxford 1710–11, vol. 3, pp. 41–2.

8 ibid., p. 42.

9 Examination of the fabric rolls shows that work on the altar began in 1316–17 and was largely completed by 1325, when the final payment for the silver retable was made. See Veronica Sekules, 'The Liturgical Furnishings of the Choir of Exeter Cathedral', in Francis Kelly (ed.), op. cit. (note 3), pp. 172–3.

10 John Vowel, alias Hooker, *The Antique Description and Account of the City of Exeter*, Exeter, 1765, pp. 92–3.

11 As Bishop Lacy was Neville's predecessor, this is, of course, confused. See Vowel, alias Hoker, op. cit. (note 10), pp. 102–3.

12 ibid., p. 12.

13 ibid., p. 99.

14 ibid., p. 102.

15 ibid., pp. 14–15. See also Hooker's further remark on p. 103: 'And albeit, from the time of

K. *Athelstane*, the first Founder, *Anno* 932, until the Death of this *Grandisson*, which was *Anno* 1369, there were 437 Years distant, and in the mean Time this Church builded by sundry and diverse Men, yet so uniformly the same is compact as though it were builded at one Instant.'

16 Robert Hall (pseud. i.e., Peter Heylyn), *An Help to English History* (1641). Heylyn's account was reprinted in various editions until at least 1765. Richard Izacke's account was reprinted in an extended edition by his son Samuel, in 1723.

17 Godwin was a Canon at Exeter from 1586 and sub-Dean from 1587 to 1602, when he was promoted to the see of Llandaff. Lyttleton's essay of 1754 explicitly criticizes Godwin's failure to make use of local resources: 'Such is the history of this cathedral as related by Godwin; who, having been both sub-dean and canon-residentiary thereof, ought to be esteemed a good authority; but upon a strict examination, we shall find that this account of the present fabric is very imperfect, and in some respects not agreeable to truth.' See *Some Account of the Cathedral Church of Exeter*, op. cit. (note 6), p. 1.

18 See, for example, George Oliver's comments on his predecessor as a historian of Exeter: 'He knew that Izaacke's Memorials was reputed a work of authority and credit; and it was reasonable to think, that a man who was Chamberlain of Exeter for thirty years, would have availed himself of the ample means which he possessed to compile a faithful and interesting account of his native city. He had, however, proceeded but a little way, when he discovered that Izaacke is a careless and misleading guide; that he betrays a lamentable deficiency of good taste and judgement; and that to excessive credulity and puerility, he unites no inconsiderable share of dogmatical assurance. Moreover he deserves censure for not acknowledging his great obligations to Mr. John Hoker.' George Oliver, *The History of Exeter*, Exeter, 1821, p. vii.

19 The full inscription reads as follows: 'Hanc Capellam Beatae Mariae Virginis ab Athelstano Rege olim fundatam, in Bibliothecam propriis sumptibus convertit Robertus Vilvaine, M.D. Anno Domini, MDCLVII.' See Alexander Jenkins, *The History and Description of the City of Exeter*, Exeter, 1806, p. 291.

20 George Grenville was Lyttleton's cousin and pressed his claims for advancement to Lord Bute in 1762. See DNB.

21 A drawing by John Carter, from his 1770 visit to the cathedral, copies an inscription on the wall of the Chapter House: 'Begun by Lacey (1455) and finished by Nevill (1465). Damaged by Cromwell. Repaired by Dean and Chapter in 1740.' See British Library Add. Ms 29931, f.12.

22 Strictly speaking, the first holder of this post,

Robert Burrington (1707–30) was titled 'Overseer of the Worke'. His successor, John Weston (1730–42) was the first to be styled 'Surveyor'. Arthur Bradley (1742–59) and John Tothill (1759–99) were the post-holders during the restoration campaigns of Lyttleton and Milles. For their reports on the fabric, see Exeter Cathedral Archive 4700, 4712/1-21.

23 For a summary of eighteenth-century work on the cathedral see Erskine, Hope and Lloyd, op. cit. (note 5), pp. 71–6. The reglazing programme for the Great East Window is detailed in Chris Brooks and David Evans, *The Great East Window of Exeter Cathedral: A Glazing History*, Exeter, 1988. References to these and other improvements can be found in chronological order in the Chapter Act books in Exeter Cathedral Archive.

24 British Library Add. MS 32123.

25 In 1763 James Meffen, mason, was paid 2 shillings and 4 pence per foot to re-lay the choir floor with Purbeck marble and Portland stone. He also repaired the base of the Bishop's throne, the pinnacles of the sedilia and Bishop Oldham's chapel and some edges of tombstones. See Exeter Cathedral Archive 4703, 4710/1-3.

26 British Library Stowe 754, f. 137.

27 The Chapter Act entry for 27 April 1751 records that 'Archdeacon Hole be requested to put the Library in order and that he take Mr. Edwd. Lee the Lay Vicar to attend him'. There were about 6,000 books in the cathedral library at this date, as well as manuscripts and cathedral accounts.

28 'When you have leisure to compare my catalogue of ye muniments with ye muniments themselves, you will judge how laborious a piece of work I have had upon my Hands. Don't forget to look over the Prefatory Discourse I have made in ye first vol. of our Domesday, & then give me your opinion upon it.' Letter dated 4 July 1751, British Library Add. MS 32123.

29 See Lilian Dickins and Mary Stanton (eds), *An Eighteenth-Century Correspondence, being the Letters of the Lyttletons and the Grenvilles ... to Sanderson Miller, esq. of Radway*, London: John Murray, 1910, quoted by Rhys Jenkins in *Devon and Cornwall Notes and Queries*, vol. 15, part 7, July 1929, p. 336.

30 Lyttleton in *Some Account of the Cathedral Church of Exeter*, op. cit. (note 6), pp. 1–2. For Hooker, Godwin and Izacke, see above; Stukeley had reiterated these accounts in his *Itinerarium Curiosum*.

31 See, for example, Lyttleton in *Some Account of the Cathedral Church of Exeter*, op. cit. (note 6), pp. 2, 4, 7, 8, 10.

32 Lyttleton in ibid., p. 2.

33 Lyttleton in ibid., p. 2.

34 See, for example, Englefield in ibid.

35 Lyttleton in ibid., p. 2.

36 The Library of the Society of Antiquaries holds Lyttleton's book of *Drawings of Saxon Churches*, comprising a variety of mid-century views by different hands, and on whose fly-leaf Lyttleton has written: 'This Book contains several original Drawings, for the most part taken from the Door Ways &c. of English Country Churches, (viz) such as are executed in the Style of Architecture which prevailed here in the Saxon & first Norman ages, before the introduction of the Gothick, and which, however confounded with the Gothick by ye generality of our Writers on Antiquity, yet in fact, is no other than a debased and corrupt Roman Architecture.' We might compare Richard Gough's detailed sketch of the south door of Beckett Church, Berkshire, taken in 1766, whose Norman archway is described as ' a Saxon door with rows of lozenges, double zig-zag, and pointed leaves, and demi pillars with flowered capitals supporting zig-zag intermixt with flowers'. Bodleian Library Top. Gen. E.16, p. 206; cited in Frew, op. cit., (note 1), p. 176, n. 13.

37 Lyttleton in *Some Account of the Cathedral Church of Exeter*, op. cit. (note 6), p. 4. Lyttleton's correspondence with other scholars, such as James Bentham, reveals their common interest in clarifying terms. Bentham, for example, declares: 'We have long wanted more distinct terms to express the several kinds & modes of Ancient Buildings that are found among us. Modern writers have used the term *Gothick*, to signify all kinds that deviate from the ancient proportions of the Grecian and Roman Architecture; but Gothick in that sense is a term too vague and general; for it will comprehend all our ancient Architecture, tho' as distinct from each other as any of the regular Orders of the Greeks or Romans. – With more accuracy therefore you use the terms *Saxon, Norman-Saxon*, and what you call strictly *Gothick*, to express the different modes of Building, before the Conquest, immediately after it, & that which next succeeded and continued in use till the Reformation; – & tho' the modes of building are almost infinite, yet perhaps these three terms may be sufficient to distinguish them severally.' Letter from James Bentham to Charles Lyttleton, dated 17 April 1758, British Library Stowe 754, f. 14.

38 Lyttleton in *Some Account of the Cathedral Church of Exeter*, op. cit. (note 6), p. 3. On the fly-leaf of his *Church Notes &c. in divers County's* Lyttleton writes, 'ye round arches, thick Pillars, small windows & hatched mouldings &c. which I denominate *Saxon*, prevail'd both here and in Normandy before and at ye time of W. 1st's invasion of Engd. & continued here till ye end of K. H. 1st's reign & some time later.' Society of Antiquaries MS 153.

39 Lyttleton in *Some Account of the Cathedral Church of Exeter*, op. cit. (note 6), p. 6.

40 Letter from William Borlase to Charles Lyttleton, dated 6 November 1749. British Library Stowe 752 118 LB 50, quoted in P.A.S. Pool, *William*

Borlase, Truro, 1986, pp. 128–9.

41 Richard Gough, *Anecdotes of British Topography. Or, an historical account of what has been done for illustrating the Topographical Antiquities of Great Britain and Ireland*, London, 1768, pp. xviii–xix.

42 Richard Gough, *Anecdotes of British Topography*, p. xx. For Gough, see Rosemary Sweet, 'Antiquaries and Antiquities in Eighteenth-Century England', *Eighteenth-Century Studies*, vol. 34, no. 2 (2001), pp. 181–206.

43 The transition might be characterized as starting with James Bentham's *History of the Conventual and Cathedral church of Ely* (1771) and reaching maturity with Thomas Rickman's *An Attempt to Discriminate the Styles of English Architecture from the Conquest to the Reformation* (1817) and Augustus Pugin's *Specimens of Gothic Architecture* (1821). For requests to Lyttleton to write or promote such a survey, see British Library Stowe 753, ff. 91–2 (George Ballard, 19 October 1748); Stowe 754, f. 15 (James Bentham, 17 April 1758).

44 Wood's *Ruins of Palmyra* and *Ruins of Balbec* were published in 1753 and 1757 respectively. Stuart and Revett's *Antiquities of Athens* began publication in 1762.

45 See Joan Evans, *A History of the Society of Antiquaries*, Oxford: OUP, 1956, p. 206.

46 Englefield became Vice-President of the Society in 1799 and would have been President in 1811, had Lysons and others not disputed his election. See Evans, op. cit. (note 45), pp. 196, 219–20.

47 Carter had resigned his position as Draughtsman to the Society and was elected FSA in 1795. He had already produced very fine drawings of the Palace of Westminster for the Society of Antiquaries, published in 1795. In 1796 he was commissioned to produce similar investigations of Gloucester and Tewkesbury cathedrals and produced the drawings for the Society of Antiquaries' publications on Bath (1798), Durham (1801), Gloucester (1809) and St Alban's (1813). For his Exeter drawings he was paid £100 expenses for 152 days' work. See Evans, op. cit. (note 45), pp. 206–14.

48 Sir Henry Englefield, 'Observations on Bishop Lyttleton's Account of Exeter Cathedral', in *Some Account of the Cathedral Church of Exeter*, op. cit. (note 6), p. 13.

49 ibid., p. 15. The original paper, read to the Society of Antiquaries on 6 April 1797, adds to this passage the recognition that empirical observation requires refinement: 'But from the most painful attention something will ever escape, & repeated surveys can alone discover all.' Society of Antiquaries MS 52.

50 See M.E. Roberts, 'John Carter at St. Stephen's Chapel: a Romantic turns Archaeologist', in

W.M. Ormrod (ed.), *England in the Fourteenth Century*, Proceedings of the 1985 Harlaxton Symposium, London, 1986, pp. 202–12. See also J. Mordaunt Crook, *John Carter and the Mind of the Gothic Revival*, London: Society of Antiquaries, 1995.

51 See Englefield in Lyttleton, *Some Account of the Cathedral Church of Exeter*, op. cit. (note 6), p. 13.

52 For an overview of the use of images in understanding Gothic architecture, see Sam Smiles, *Eye Witness: Artists and Visual Documentation in Britain, 1770–1830*, Aldershot and Brookfield, VT: Ashgate, 2000, especially chap. 3.

53 See ff. 7 and 8, 14 and 15 in British Library Add. MS 29925, dated 1770 and 1771 respectively.

54 See British Library Add. MS 29931, ff. 38–142. This manuscript volume is inscribed by Carter 'A Selection of Sketches of subjects relating to the Antiquities of this Kingdom, taken from the real objects in 1792.'

55 See, for example, J.P. Allan and S.R. Blaylock 'The west Front: I The Structural History of the West Front', and Eddie Sinclair 'The West Front II – The West Front Polychromy', in Francis Kelly (ed.), 1991, op. cit. (note 3), pp. 94–133.

56 John Carter, *The Ancient Architecture of England, including the orders during the British, Roman, Saxon and Norman eras; and under the reigns of Henry III and Edward III*, (1795, 1814), London, 1837, n.p.

57 J.C., 'Publication of Cathedrals by the Antiquarian Society', *Gentleman's Magazine*, vol. 73 (1803), I, pp. 106–7.

58 ibid.

59 J.T. Smith, *Ancient Topography of London*, London, 1815, p. 1.

60 *Magazine of the Fine Arts*, vol. 1, no. 4, February 1833, p. 323.

61 In the nineteenth century Lyttleton's pioneering research would be supplanted by the work of George Oliver, a local historian and antiquarian, whose understanding of the cathedral was indebted to Lyttleton's combination of archival and visual research. See George Oliver's *History of Exeter*, op. cit. (note 18); and his *Lives of the Bishops of Exeter, and a History of the Cathedral*, Exeter, 1861. The growing awareness of the need to study the archives in conjunction with the fabric is neatly demonstrated in the origins of the first widely published survey of the cathedral, John Britton's *The History and Antiquities of the Cathedral Church of Exeter* (1826). Britton, like Hooker three hundred years earlier, was denied access to the records and relied primarily on Oliver for archival information. See Britton, pp. i–iii.

7

Every Man is Naturally an Antiquarian: Francis Grose and polite antiquities

Stephen Bending

It is unpardonable to be inaccurate in a work, in which one
nor expects nor demands anything but fidelity.

Horace Walpole (1779)[1]

Horace Walpole's attack on the inaccuracy of popular antiquarian publishing and its cavalier attitude towards the illustration of historical remains in the late eighteenth century aligns him with an influential strand of antiquarian thinking; it also misrepresents the nature of much antiquarian publishing in the period.[2] Walpole conjures up the image of a static, knowable past which can be recorded and represented as such, and indeed which requires to be recorded in the face both of physical decay and the depredations wrought by a swiftly changing modern world. However, what I will be exploring in this essay is some of the ways in which that neat model of separation between past and present is resisted and I will be doing so with the aid of the popularizing antiquarian Francis Grose. What makes Grose a figure of note is that his large-scale publishing ventures set about repackaging the ancient as a form of modern novelty, to be consumed in a burgeoning commercial market even as they repeatedly insist on the stasis of antiquity and on the pastness of the past. It is Grose, I will argue, who comes closest to recognizing and acting on antiquarianism's awkward closeness to other contemporary commercial ventures.[3] He represents a popularizing strand of antiquarian publishing in the late eighteenth century, and his massive output – around 1,000 antiquarian images – is often dismissed as the trivia of a jobbing hack: unscholarly, unsophisticated, inaccurate. What I want to argue, however, is that it is exactly those qualities which should allow us to see him as part of an early national heritage industry, of an industry which relies on the commodification of the past as an occasion for nostalgia.

The reputation of antiquarians in the eighteenth century is now well known.[4] The membership of the Society of Antiquaries grew from around 300 in the middle of the century to about 800 by its end, and antiquarian prints and publications had an increasingly large market; but the most popular image of the antiquary was that of the pedantic fool, the man who cherishes the minor and the forgotten, who wastes his time on trivia and becomes lost in the past. In this guise the antiquarian is set against, and indeed often sets himself against, the Enlightenment figure of the 'historian', who, armed with rationality and system, explores past cultures in order to improve society's understanding of the present, who discards the local, the quirky, the unusual, for the general, the abstract, the fundamental principle.[5] Thus, where the historian searches for the abstract idea, the antiquarian collects the physical object; he treasures those things from the past which have been forgotten or lost, but forgotten or lost perhaps for good reason. The distinction we might make is between a historian whose business is ultimately the present and the antiquarian who loses sight of the present in his attachment to the past. As Horace Walpole remarks in a letter to his friend the Reverend Cole, 'We antiquaries are a little apt to get laughed at for knowing what everybody has forgotten, and for being ignorant of what every child knows.'[6] The dismissive tone of Walpole's comment is characteristic of antiquarian self-deprecation; however, he was also acutely aware of antiquarianism's attraction, and one part of that attraction was as the occasion for nostalgic reverie and the evocation of a simpler, purer and less troubled life. Indeed, Walpole suggests that antiquarianism's particular attraction lay precisely in its ability to remove one from the present, and by the late eighteenth century that present increasingly meant the threatened loss of empire and the possibility of invasion. Writing to Cole in 1778, Walpole remarks:

> Our empire is falling to pieces; we are relapsing to a little island. In that state, men are apt to inquire how great their ancestors have been; and when a kingdom is past doing anything, the few, that are studious, look into the memorials of past time; nations, like private persons, seek lustre from their progenitors, when they have none in themselves, and the farther they are from the dignity of their source.[7]

In the last few years there has been an attempt to recuperate antiquarianism, to see it not simply in those rather easily dismissive terms of the eighteenth century, but to explore its cultural significance and to map it into some of the wider interests of eighteenth-century society.[8] One aspect of this has been the recognition of antiquarian research as part of that larger project to create and assert an independent national identity, the kind of identity of which Walpole is only too aware in the 1770s. As Gerald Newman and others have noted, the antiquarian fascination with Britain's medieval past keeps company with similar endeavours in philology, linguistics and ethnic research, in the production of literary histories and dictionaries, in the creation of national academies of art and music. The antiquarian attempt to possess the past is, then, as Newman argues, part of a large-scale 'expansion of national self-study'.[9] However, as I have already suggested, for all that we can make these very general moves and place antiquarianism within that much larger, but also rather vague, cultural movement of 'nationalism', the eighteenth-century antiquary remains something of an awkward outsider. What I want to do here is explore in rather more detail some of the connections between antiquarianism and the culture it inhabits: how do we square that increasing popularity of antiquarian prints with the popular image of the antiquarian as an unworldly obsessive?

101

One of the problems for the eighteenth-century antiquary was that it was always tempting to adopt that very rhetoric of foolishness, to admit that an interest in apparent trivia was itself trivial; and so one of the characteristics of much antiquarian writing is that it sways between a kind of bullish self-defence and an admission of its own sheer lack of consequence. Thus, we find Grose writing in the preface to his *Antiquarian Repertory*:

> It has long been the fashion to laugh at the study of Antiquities, and to consider it as the idle amusement of a few humdrum, plodding fellows, who wanting genius for nobler studies, busied themselves in heaping up illegible Manuscripts, mutilated Statues, obliterated Coins, and broken Pipkins; in this the laughter may perhaps have been somewhat justified, from the absurd pursuits of a few collectors ... I trust I shall be able to prove, that without a competent fund of antiquarian Learning, no one will ever make a respectable figure, either as a Divine, a Lawyer, Statesman, Soldier, or even a private Gentleman, and that it is the *sine quâ non* of several of the more liberal professions, as well as many trades; and is besides a study to which all persons in particular instances have a kind of propensity, every man being, as Logicians express it, *Quoad hoc*, an Antiquarian.[10]

What antiquarians claim to share is their attempt to preserve the monuments of the past. What they are less certain about is just what it is they are preserving, what they are preserving it for, or, indeed, for whom they are preserving it.[11] For all of Grose's grand claims, it would be difficult to imagine a lawyer, a statesman or a soldier being aided greatly in their professions by the letter-press accounts he adds to his engravings. Indeed, in the preface to his *Antiquities of England*, he takes care to note that he does not 'pretend to inform the veteran antiquary; but has drawn up these accounts solely for the use of such as are desirous of having, without much trouble, a general knowledge of the subjects treated of in this publication ...'.[12] Nevertheless, in making claims for preservation, Grose seems to align himself with one of the key figures of the Society of Antiquaries, Richard Gough, who repeatedly insists on the value of antiquarian engravings as a means of preserving the past.[13]

In his *Sepulchral Monuments*, Gough bewails the difficulty of getting good draftsmen for antiquarian work, and continues:

> But as some may think indifferent representations, even those in the *History of Northumberland* and [Francis Grose's] *Antiquarian Repertory*, better than none at all (though I must ever beg leave to hold a different opinion), and they may not be displeased with verbal descriptions, it may be worth while to supply the great deficiency of such descriptions, and to suggest certain rules and examples for this method of preserving monuments.[14]

For Gough, attempts to preserve the past revolve around the question of fidelity: in Gothic architecture, what 'scholarly' antiquarians such as Gough require is accurate representations of the traces of the past, representations which make use of the recently formulated language of stylistic analysis in order to produce readable images of a building's history. The complaint about lack of accuracy in Grose and other popularizers, then, is that they are not producing representations of the right kind of history; they are not producing images which can be read in the right way. Characteristically, Horace Walpole thought Grose's work 'dull and silly', while his friend Cole dismissed the *Antiquities* as a 'mere picture book' full of 'old women's stories and vulgar tradition'.[15] As John Frew has noted, in histories of antiquarianism Grose's work tends to be sidelined as 'rambling and anecdotal' and it would be tempting, I suppose, to align oneself with this kind of scholarly stance and to dismiss Grose as nothing more than a jobbing hack.[16] But there is something else happening here because, for all that Grose offers us inaccurate images and old wives tales, he finds himself a huge market for antiquarian prints. The issue turns, that is, on the question of what kind of history and what kind of audience the antiquarian might be addressing, on how an antiquarian account of the past might be engaging with a commercial present. In this context Grose's publications articulate an uneasy division as they defend antiquarian scholarship against its own abuses and the abuse of others; insist on the innate value of the past; but nevertheless recognize and exploit the past's commercial potential as a marketable commodity. In this they partake in what Neil McKendrick has termed the democratization of consumption.[17] What marks out popular antiquarian publishing, then, is that novelty, a sense of the new and desirable, has to be created from the very things which appear to be out of fashion.

In some respects, as we have seen, antiquarianism seems to involve the rejection of the present in its search for the past; and certainly a characteristic ploy in antiquarian writing is to distinguish its own set of values from current commercial activity. In the Supplement to the *Antiquities*, Grose discusses Netley Abbey, and the actions of a Mr Dummer, who had prevented further depredations from taking place. He writes,

> The great care taken by Mr. Dummer for the preservation of the remains of this venerable pile, claims the acknowledgements of every lover of antiquities; and both reflects an honour on his taste, and exhibits an example worthy of the imitation of all possessors of such buildings, many of whom too inconsiderately suffer their stewards or tenants to demolish them for the sale of the materials, not reflecting that they thereby deprive their estates of very striking ornaments; ornaments which, in other countries, are preserved with the utmost attention; and that without any material benefit, as the cost of demolition generally amounts to nearly the value of the materials so gained. The gentleman above named has not only preserved these, by inclosing them with a wall, but, by a judicious management of the trees, which have spontaneously sprung up among the mouldering walls, has greatly improved the beauty and solemnity of the scene, hereby rendered as well worthy visiting, as any object of that kind in Great Britain.[18]

What Grose is doing here is marking out a distinction between profit and ornament, and marking also, therefore, a distinction between an aestheticization of the material past and the pressures of contemporary commerce. Dummer is held up as an example for the rest of society, and it is here that we can see claims being made for the value of a national heritage, claims which seem to rely crucially on a disjunction between money and value. Dummer is preserving the nation's past by resisting commercial pressure and as a private landowner he acts in the interests of the nation. Grose, in turn, claims to offer his own form of preservation – the antiquarian print – and thus claims also to be serving the national interest. However, as a publishing antiquarian in a fashionable market Grose has to work hard to align himself with such public disinterestedness. He of course offers his services for a fee and if his published works seek to establish a distinction between public service and commercial gain, they also suggest that such a distinction is not easily maintained. Thus in the final lines of this passage, when he turns to the management of trees and the pleasures of visiting, Grose naturalizes the image and moves it away from commerce – with that spontaneous growth of trees – but then recommends it to those with the income to take part in the newly forming leisure industry of picturesque travel, and offers his subscribers the possession of three separate plates (at sixpence each).

In fact, Grose was to take this apparent separation of commerce from anti-quarianism a stage further with his *Guide to Health, Beauty, Riches, and Honour* (1785), which turns to that key innovation of commercial culture, the advertise-ment, in order to satirize a belief in money as a source of value or happiness.[19] The advertisements he includes are mostly about making money or borrowing it. We find false teeth, infallible methods of winning the lottery or making millions, hairdressing, cosmetics and Mr Graham's 'medico-electrical apparatus' which 'visibly displays . . . the various faculties of the material soul of universal and eternal nature', all in the space of a few pages. In the preface to the volume Grose writes,

> Although the great encrease of knowledge in this kingdom is in general known, yet few who live remote from the capital are able to form an adequate idea of the vast improvements made within this century, not only in the more abstruse sciences, but also in the arts and conveniences of life . . . Justice here makes it necessary to observe and commend the spirit of philanthropy reigning among the several ingenious professors of the different arts, sciences, and callings, who . . . labour solely pro bono publico: in short, we seem to be the wisest, wealthiest, and may if we please be the happiest people under the sun, as we are the most generous and disinterested. But lest foreigners should doubt the truth of these assertions, and deem them the vain boastings of a man endeavouring to raise the honour of his native country, I have in evidence of my position selected a few advertisements from the many daily offered to the publick, containing invitations to Health, Beauty, Vigour, Wives, Places, Pensions and Honours, all which may be had for money . . . (p. i)

Thus, the *Guide to Health* seems to reject those instant remedies on offer in a culture which relies on exchange value and the immediate gratification of desires. Grose is satirizing a discourse based on money which claims to provide happiness: the implication, of course, is that all of this is reliant on gullibility and foolishness, but also that these claims are tainted by their relationship with money. A satire on

HISTORY preserving the Monuments of Antiquity

29 Frontispiece to Francis Grose, *The Antiquities of England and Wales*, New Edition (London, 1773–87).

false hopes of future happiness becomes also a means of deflecting attention from Grose's own investment in a form of happiness only generated from the past. What is important here is that Grose is effectively trying to divorce the book trade and the publishing of antiquarian scholarship from the contemporary commercial publication of advertisements. The implicit claim, then, is that prints are not a commodity but represent some other kind of value, that they have an intrinsic worth because they represent the past.

Of course, prints *are* also part of an exchange economy, and thus I would suggest that for all Grose's attempts to maintain a distinction between the commercial world and the antiquarian past, he relies on the collapsing of any such distinction for the success of his own publications. The objects of consumer desire may be different, but the culture of British antiquity, and the culture of Health, Beauty, Riches and Honour – with all its claims to instant gratification – share a desire for commodities both physical and aesthetic. As I have already suggested, Grose's prints are aimed at the cheaper end of the market, and the attractions of cheapness are made much of by the popularizers of antiquity. While Gough's desire for accuracy results in expensive plates and aligns him with the largely patrician establishment of the Society of Antiquaries, Grose and the popularizers champion cheap pleasures and easy knowledge. Even a relatively up-market work, such as *The Virtuosi's Museum*, with designs by Paul Sandby, received the following puff in its preface:

> the student, as well as the admirer of the ingenious art of sculpture, will be supplied with elegant engravings from the designs of one of the first artists of this kingdom at the very moderate price of One Shilling for each plate, instead of the usual demand of, from 2s. 6d. to 4s. made for landscapes of inferior merit.
>
> What a cheap and rational amusement then will these Gentlemen possess monthly, for the same consideration that is given for one night's admittance to the pit of the theatre! and in the course of a year, what a beautiful addition will be made to the furniture of their apartments, for less than the value of a masquerade ticket![20]

In *The Virtuosi's Museum*, then, the activities of polite culture are set in direct competition with the antiquarian print, but are also crucially recognized as a part of that same culture of aesthetic commodities and are explicitly made available to a wide audience. This is a move which is repeated again and again. What is at issue can be explained in part with the help of two images, the frontispiece to Grose's *Antiquities* and that to Alexander Hogg's *Picturesque Views of the Antiquities of England and Wales*, a plagiarized edition of Grose produced in 1786.[21] Like many others, Hogg (publishing under the pseudonym of Henry Boswell) claims that his purpose is 'to rescue, preserve and illustrate ... venerable Piles of Splendour and Magnificence from the Ravages of Time' and he suggests that,

---

30 (opposite) Frontispiece to Henry Boswell (pseud. Alexander Hogg), *Historical Description of New and Elegant Picturesque Views of the Antiquities of England and Wales: being a Grand Copper-Plate Repository of Elegance, Taste, and Entertainment* (London, nd [1786]).

Drawn by J. Hamilton.

Engraved by Noble.

EXPLANATION

The figure seated in the foreground represents HISTORY Recording an Account of the Original & present state of the ANTIQUITIES of England & Wales. She is also engaged in resisting the Ravages of TIME, who advances to destroy those beautiful Monuments of Antient magnificence. The figures viewing the Monument of an illustrious Warrior, the Monastic Edifice behind them, together with a distant glimpse of Stonehenge, and the other parts of the plate very properly point out the general nature of this Useful & Entertaining Work.

Published according to Act of Parliament by Alex.r Hogg Nov. 24 1786.

hitherto, none except the Affluent have been able to purchase Works of this kind, which (though in many Respects very defective and ill-executed) have nevertheless be sold at most extravagant Prices. Therefore to accommodate all sorts of Readers whatever, the present Publication is undertaken on the most elegant, cheap, and desirable Plan; a Plan which must be acknowledged absolutely unobjectionable, being calculated much more for public Advantage than private Emolument; as it is adapted to all Pockets and Dispositions, and affords Persons of every Description in the Kingdom (Poor as well as Rich, and the middle Class of the World), an opportunity of being possessed of a valuable Work – which will at once improve their Minds, please their Taste, Ornament their Libraries, decorate their Apartments, and in various Ways afford Sentiments of Pleasure and Delight to all around them. (p. iii)

If this is strikingly similar in its claims to the very advertisements ridiculed by Grose in his *Guide to Health*, it is also very close to Grose's own antiquarian publications, with Boswell largely paraphrasing the *Antiquities*. What we can see here is a publication acutely aware of an appropriate and appropriating language. We are offered an extended sales pitch and central to that pitch is the stress on cheapness and availability to a wide audience (the rich, the poor, and everyone in between), with its stress on the multiple pleasures it will engender. The past is offered to us as a form of present gratification.

When we then turn to the two frontispieces, the original from Grose's volume and the copy from Boswell's, what we are offered in each case is an allegory of 'History preserving the monuments of Antiquity' (plates 29 and 30). In the middle distance of both is Lindisfarne, in the foreground a female figure of 'History' fending off Father Time with his scythe. In Grose's original image there is little more than this generalizing allegory of preservation, but it is that notion of preservation which needs to be explored. We may be offered a recognizable Lindisfarne but we would be hard pressed to work out the history of its construction from the details we are given by Grose. This, emphatically, is not an image which adopts the detailed architectural language required by Gough, and when we turn to Boswell's edition, this becomes even more clear. Indeed, in true antiquarian fashion, Boswell makes something new out of the old by merging Grose's frontispiece with the smaller engraving from his adjacent title page (which shows two gentlemen inspecting the remains of a tomb in a decaying gothic abbey); he then adds a dubiously narrow spire; a further 'gothic' structure in the background; and a distant view of Stonehenge for good measure. If, as a work of accuracy and fidelity, Boswell's image becomes suspect, as a work engaging with the popular imagination, it does not. By including Grose's title-page engraving of two gentlemen tourists in his frontispiece, Boswell effectively acknowledges the role of the individual in the creation of the historical past. That is, the accretion of chronologically and geographically disparate subjects points to a clear awareness of both the popular market at which his volume is aimed and the imagination of history that market requires. While lip-service is paid to the accurate preservation of monuments through illustration, Boswell's volume finally has its eye not so much on preserving the past as on marketing the past to the present. Like Grose before him, Boswell nods at the responsibilities of preservation but offers the enjoyments of history as a theme park.

One way of making sense of this move is to turn to Susan Stewart's account of antiquarian engagements with the past. Stewart has argued that an antiquarian account of the past is fundamentally aesthetic: it seeks to erase the actual past in order to replace it with an imagined past which is made available for consumption.[22] As we have seen, part of the attraction of antiquarianism is that it looks back to an apparently more 'primitive' culture from the position of a complex commercial present. Thus, while Gough wants scholarly accuracy, Grose and his popularizing contemporaries are producing images which are expansive in their assumed audience; which offer a language of the past wholly saturated by the present; and which turn not to the dryness of detail but gesture towards an imaginative engagement with the past through its physical remains. Offered in series, what marks prints out is that they also imply a sense of collecting with all its interest in ownership. Modern consumerism, which is driven by the replaceability of objects, is thus transformed into a means of ownership, not just of the print as an object but of an imagined national past with which its owner can engage. In this prints are the products and the occasion of nostalgia. As Stewart has noted, nostalgia is narrative in its operation: it is for the individual to make their own connection between a lost past and their own complex present. The print's owner must construct their own narrative in order to link that imagined past with their own lives and in these terms nostalgia looks not simply to the past but is fundamentally defined by and takes part in defining the present.

Grose sold his engravings for sixpence and what I am arguing is that for sixpence middle-class consumers could begin to write themselves into the nation's history. At sixpence a plate, the owning of antiquarian prints is also an owning of the nation's past. The sixpenny print offers the chance of imagining one's place in the nation and of doing so without the aid of land or rank, and without the need to take action in the political arena. If prints transform the objects of the past into a commodity, buying into those representations of the past – the transformation of the physical into the aesthetic products of consumerism – is also, then, the chance to buy into a shared national heritage, into the beginnings of a national heritage industry. In this sense, the popular antiquarian print offers its owner access to the nationally significant through domestic acquisition and consumer aesthetics. Grose's account of the past emerges from scattered fragments, random traces, from old wives' tales and vague gestures. What is at stake here is not scientific accuracy or the certainty of system, but the value of myths, the value of a view which fails to see clearly but which offers imaginative access to the past. If that view gives shared access to a national past, it gives also, in the egalitarian marketplace of the consumer, a shared place in the national present.

Notes

1 Letter from Horace Walpole to Rev. William Cole, 18 February 1779, reproduced in the *Yale Edition of the Correspondence of Horace Walpole*, vol. 2, p. 146.

2 In this volume see especially Smiles and Lolla.

3 This essay develops ideas first explored in my 'The true rust of the Barons' Wars: gardens, ruins, and the national landscape', in *Producing*

the Past: Aspects of Antiquarian Culture and Practice 1700–1850, eds M. Myrone and L. Peltz, Aldershot and Brookfield, VT: Ashgate, 1999, pp. 83–93.

4 See, for example, Myrone & Peltz, Producing the Past op. cit. (note 3).

5 For a fuller discussion of this see Sam Smiles, The Image of Antiquity: Ancient Britain and the Romantic Imagination, New Haven and London: Yale University Press, 1994, especially chap. 2, and Sam Smiles, Eye Witness and Visual Documentation in Britain, 1770–1830, Aldershot, and Brookfield, VT: Ashgate, 2000.

6 Letter from Horace Walpole to Rev. William Cole, 11 November 1780, reproduced in Correspondence of Horace Walpole, op. cit. (note 1), vol. 2, p. 238.

7 Letter from Horace Walpole to Rev. William Cole, 1 September 1778, reproduced in ibid., p. 117.

8 Notably, see Myrone & Peltz, Producing the Past, op. cit. (note 3).

9 Gerald Newman, The Rise of English Nationalism: A Cultural History 1740–1830, London, 1987, pp. 111–12.

10 Francis Grose, The Antiquarian Repertory: A Miscellany, intended to preserve and illustrate several valuable remains. Adorned with elegant sculptures, 4 vols, London, 1775–84, vol. 1, p. iii.

11 In this volume see especially Lolla.

12 Francis Grose, The Antiquities of England and Wales, new edn, London, 1773–87, vol. 1, p. iv.

13 For a discussion of Gough's concerns with preservation, see Smiles in this volume.

14 Richard Gough, Sepulchral Monuments in Great Britain Applied to Illustrate the History of Families, Manners, Habits, and Arts, at the different periods from the Norman Conquest to the Seventeenth Century. With Introductory Observations. Part I. Containing the first four centuries, London, 1786, p. 7.

15 Letter from Horace Walpole to Cole, 24 November 1780, and William Cole to Walpole, 30 December 1779, reproduced in the Correspondence of Horace Walpole, op. cit. (note 1), vol. 2, pp. 245, 182.

16 John Frew, 'An aspect of the early Gothic Revival: the transformation of Medievalist research', Journal of the Warburg and Courtauld Institutes, vol. 43 (1980), pp. 174–85, p. 175.

17 For the broader ramifications of a 'consumer culture', see Neil McKendrick, John Brewer and J.H. Plumb, The Birth of a Consumer Society: The Commercialization of Eighteenth-Century England, London: Hutchinson & Co., 1982, the phrase appears p. 23.

18 Grose, Antiquities of England and Wales, op. cit. (note 12), supplement, vol. 2, pp. 209–12.

19 Francis Grose, A Guide to Health, Beauty, Riches, and Honour, London, 1785.

20 The Virtuosi's Museum; containing Select Views, in England, Scotland, and Ireland; Drawn by P. Sandby, Esqr R.A., London, 1778, Preface.

21 Henry Boswell (pseud. Alexander Hogg), Historical Description of New and Elegant Picturesque Views of the Antiquities of England and Wales: being a Grand Copper-Plate Repository of Elegance, Taste, and Entertainment ..., London, nd (1786).

22 Susan Stewart, On Longing: narratives of the miniature, the gigantic, the souvenir, the collection, Baltimore: Johns Hopkins University Press, 1984; rpt Durham: Duke University Press, 1993, p. 143.

8

Voyage: Dominique-Vivant Denon and the transference of images of Egypt

Abigail Harrison Moore

> In the year 1804,[1] Monsieur Denon's grand publication detailing the antiquities of Egypt became public. The novelty displayed throughout these fine specimens of art, calling to the recollection so distant a portion of ancient history, gave rise and life to a taste for this description of embellishment.[2]

In 1826 George Smith, the English cabinet-maker, described the impact that the publication in 1802 of Dominique-Vivant Denon's *Voyage dans la Basse et la Haute d'Egypte* had on English interior design. This illustrated journal of his travels through Egypt established the importance of Denon in disseminating the Egyptian revival in salons across Paris. He achieved a position of such standing in France at the beginning of the nineteenth century that he was able to act as an arbiter of taste for both Bonaparte and his ministers in all artistic matters, a position that allowed his English counterparts access to his designs, particularly through an English edition of *Voyage*, published first in 1803. The fact that an English edition appeared only one year after *Voyage*'s original publication in France is evidence of its great popularity on both sides of the Channel. By 1806, this edition was described as having affected 'many articles of interior decoration [which have become] the present prevailing fashion' in Regency England.[3]

Over the last thirty years, texts published on the Egyptian Revival have tended to place it within a simple series of stylistic changes.[4] As such, few have analysed or even referred to it in terms of the 'Orientalist' project that has been part and parcel of contemporary cultural studies. This is acutely demonstrated by the use of the term 'Egyptomania' in a number of these studies. The dictionary definition of a mania is 'an obsessional enthusiasm',[5] which, when applied to the Egyptian Revival, suggests a compulsion, rather than a deliberate action within a political hegemony. The rationale for the use of this term, as illustrated by the 1994 exhibition *Egyptomania*, held in Paris, Ottawa and Vienna, rests on the tautology that Western artists looked to ancient Egyptian motifs because ancient Egypt itself was intrinsically so alluring.[6] The 'Egyptian Revival' has been discussed simply in terms of style, likening it to the 'Gothic Revival' or 'Neoclassicism', and placing it within the dialectical structure that marks many histories of architecture and furniture.

It is only recently that a new phase of analysis has begun – that of the 'Egyptian' style as a political tool.[7] By using the example of Denon's *Voyage* and theorizing it by way of resources provided in the work of Roland Barthes, this essay aims to explain some of the processes that reconfigured the image of Egypt in France and England at the beginning of the nineteenth century.

Denon published *Voyage* on his return from expeditions to Syria and Egypt in 1798 to 1801, during which the archaeological mission, as directed by Bonaparte, had been to document and collect historic Egyptian artefacts. In his preface to the 1802 edition, Denon stated that his principal aim in recording his journey was the presentation of a paper to the Institute of Cairo on his return. He intended to deliver 'an account of my travels in Upper Egypt … to read extracts from the journal *intended to accompany* the drawings I have brought from France'.[8] This statement reveals his intention to publish a visual account of his travels, with the text as a secondary feature. 'I was engaged in travelling through a country which was known to Europe by name only; it therefore became important to describe everything … I have made drawings of objects of every description.'[9]

Image/Text

Visual images have always played an important part in the construction of history. We look for visual signs to confirm written statements and in isolation these visual signs have a powerful effect on our imagination when it seeks the 'truth'.[10] Denon reconstructed Egypt's archaeology using a scientific system of standardization, a legible language of signs recognizable to both his French and

31   Dominique-Vivant Denon, Profile of the Sphinx near the Pyramids, plate IX from *Voyage*.

32   Dominique-Vivant Denon, Plan and Elevation of the Portico at Latopolis, from *Voyage*.

English audiences. We can see evidence of this process of occidentalizing the views of Egypt if we examine Denon's engraving of the sphinx (plate 31), an image that continues to function as a key sign of Egypt in the Western psyche. The figures, trees and animals, and general landscape contextualizing the sphinx illustrate the intended 'picturesque' qualities of the scene.[11] Denon was also at pains to link this image of Egypt visually and textually to the classicizing aims of architects, designers and artists of the eighteenth century and to give it revivalist credence:

> I had only time to view the sphinx ... if the head wants what is called 'style', that is to say, the straight and bold lines which give expression to the figures under which the Greeks have designated their deities, yet sufficient justice has been rendered to the fine simplicity and character of nature which is displayed in this figure.[12]

Denon's accompanying text explains the image by applying a Western painterly construct, that of the classical, picturesque landscape. In his *Philosophy of Fine Arts*, Hegel postulates that Egyptian art was especially ambiguous because, for him, Egypt was one of the earliest examples of a society consciously using images and artefacts in order to represent itself, internally and externally. It could accrue a certain stability of meaning through its setting and the expectations of the public. For example, he suggested that the meaning of a pyramid may appear open-ended, but

113

when placed in a church would clearly signal the trinity.[13] The meaning of an image of the sphinx is altered depending upon its context of use. Denon's sphinx was intended to have a specific meaning for the new French society.

The process of transcribing a historic site creates something that is at once removed from its original situation and, thus, Denon can impose order onto the ruins of Egypt by using a recognizable linguistic language and a universal science of recording. The engraving of the *Plan and Elevation of the Portico at Latopolis* (plate 32), for example, illustrates Denon's habit of creating ground plans for the Egyptian buildings, even though, as he admits in the text,

> the moving sands, or a defect in the foundation, have caused partial sinkings, by which several of the columns are thrown out of the perpendicular, and the ceiling of the portico is much damaged. I made a plan, however, of the building, in order to gain a clear idea of the distribution of its parts.[14]

As Denon indicates, the plan is an artistic construction and the building's ruined state was artificially reconstructed in an attempt to apply traditional methods of recording architecture that date from the popularization of Palladio's *I Quattro Libri dell'Architettura*.

In *Voyage* Denon has provided his audience, both French and English, with specifically recognizable images. This is akin to Benjamin's observation that 'for every image of the past that is not recognized by the present as one of its own concerns threatens to disappear irretrievably'.[15] Here, Denon aimed visually to link nineteenth-century France to the time of Egyptian rule, to use the past to define the present.

Cultural Annexation/Reappropriation

Voyage established the Egyptian style as representing not only the most fashionable taste in France but also as a link between the present empire builders and the most long-lived period of rule in history. The advertisement provides us with an indication of Denon's aims for his archaeological mission:

> The author [Denon], a member of the Institute of Cairo, and an excellent draftsman, was selected to accompany the troops designed for the conquest of Upper Egypt, that under the protection of a military escort he might have an opportunity of examining those stupendous remains, and eternal documents of the ancient civilization of the country, to which its unsettled state had denied a peaceable admission.[16]

Why did Bonaparte want a cultural record of this conquered country? The dedication of *Voyage* allows us an insight into Denon's political ambitions as an expeditionary force of and for the new Empire, and indicates the political capital to be gained from the establishment of a new artistic order in France.

To Bonaparte,
To combine the lustre of your name with the splendour of the Monuments of Egypt, is to associate the glorious annal of our time with the history of the heroic age, and to reanimate, the dust of Sesostris and Mendes, like you Conquerors, like you Benefactors.
Europe, by learning that I accompanied you in one of your most memorable expeditions, will receive my work with eager interest. I have neglected nothing in my power to render it worthy of the hero to whom it is inscribed.[17]

This statement presents two key factors in the establishment of the Egyptian revival in France – that of the heroic age, to which Napoleon was eager to associate himself visually, and the idea of France as a cultural benefactor, bestowing upon Europe its knowledge of fashion and taste through its collections and the visual records of them. The notion of benefaction also acted as a foil to the blatant raiding of the archaeological artefacts of Egypt, and many other conquered lands, which were brought back to France with much pomp and celebration. Said sees such collections as maintaining the image of Western superiority over the Orient, under the general heading of increasing knowledge of the Orient and within the 'umbrella of Western hegemony over Egypt' during the period from the end of the eighteenth century.[18] Through publications such as

33   Dominique-Vivant Denon, Various Fragments of Egyptian Architecture, plate XXIX from *Voyage*.

Denon's, there emerged a complex archaeology and history in and of the conquered lands. In their construction, the illustrations in *Voyage* adapt a European precedent and each has a didactic quality. Plate XXIX (plate 33) depicts fragments of Egyptian architecture and is designed to act as a resourceful image for architects busy designing buildings appropriate for the new Empire and its metropolis. Here Denon deliberately replaces the Grecian bias of previous pattern books with Egyptian architecture and aims to support the vitality of these designs by linking them visually and textually to the classical orders.

> In viewing such variety of form, uniting such richness of ornament, with elegance of outline, one may well be surprised that the world has allowed the Greeks, on their own assertion, the merit of being the inventors of architecture, and that all the truths of this art are to be sought for in the rules of the three Grecian orders. Might we not suppose that if some history, like that of the urn of the priestess of Corinth, were attached to each of these capitals, they would each have acquired equal celebrity.[19]

Thus, by adopting and attempting to usurp the domination of Grecian design, Denon posits Egyptian design as suitable for study in the academies, for display in the museums, and for illustration in historical theses about mankind which discussed ideas of ancient development useful for those involved in cultural, national or personal 'revolution'. As such, Denon follows an established pattern of borrowing foreign and historical culture and making them applicable, if not essential, for European designers and artists. The revolution which had begun with Rome would be consolidated with Egypt.

The Language of Signs I

Western domination over the Orient was translated, through works such as *Voyage*, into France's domination over her European competitors. Vitally, these texts used a recognizable cultural language in order to achieve this. Previous regimes had turned to revivalism and its powerful aura of the past to support their hegemonic activities in the present. The presentation of the past within a recognizable visual taxonomy was an acknowledged way of securing power. We can begin to question the language of signs that Denon employs in *Voyage* by analysing and explaining the meanings that it may have had for its French and latterly English audience.

Voyage presents a link between past and present Empires in order

> to articulate the past historically [which] does not mean to recognise it 'the way it really was' ... All rulers are the heirs of those who conquered before them. Hence, empathy with the victor invariably benefits the rulers. Historical materialists know what that means. Whoever has emerged victorious participates to this day in the triumphal procession in which the present rulers step over those who are lying prostrate.[20]

It is this that allows us to explore the various readings of this association.

In the *Dedication*, Denon indicates the need to 'Associate the glorious annals of our own time with the history of the heroic age'.[21] The cultural objects of ancient lands are of crucial importance to the cultural ideology of their new rulers.[22] The establishment of collections of the bounty of war resonates with political significance. In France the ruling classes forged 'an equation in the public eye between careful conservation of valued art treasures and good government ... the equation grew in importance ... to a point where, during the Revolution, the museum was used to counteract perceptions at home and abroad of social and political turmoil.'[23] The French commitment to the collection and conservation of ancient artefacts at the turn of the century was extended to justify the appropriation of art confiscated in the conquered lands. By representing itself as a politically and culturally superior nation, France claimed to be uniquely qualified to safeguard the world's treasures for the benefit of mankind. This action, however, accompanied by texts such as *Voyage*, that codified and academicized such practice, was undertaken specifically for the benefit of France and its new rulers. This *myth* allowed Denon (and others like him) to appropriate Egyptian artefacts in such a way as to emphasize their responsibility as the cultured class, charged with protecting such treasures while, at the same time, acknowledging their financial worth.[24]

The Language of Signs II: Revivalism

Understanding the cultural importance of *Voyage* requires some knowledge of revivalism in general and, more specifically, of the revival of ancient Egyptian motifs. The commissioning and collecting of revivalist objects has been perceived as a method by which we can create our public persona, but also – and as importantly – as a way of understanding ourselves and the world in which we live by helping us to define our social surroundings. We purchase and collect goods in part because of their semiotic significance. Historicism in design allows the purchaser and designer to attach him- or herself to a notion of worldliness and intellect. From the 1730s onwards, revivalism signified a scholarly approach to the arts. With the popularity of the grand tour and archaeological findings, Europe saw a rise of interest in the artefacts and philosophies of ancient Greece and Rome.

The appropriation of ancient Egyptian culture and art enabled the new republic to separate itself from the previous, much despised aristocratic taste in visual culture. The new style maintained vital psychological links with the past, but its visual culture was different enough to satisfy the self-consciousness of its new ruling classes. Egypt was revealed as a seemingly inexhaustible source of new design ideas. Importantly for those who wished to connect themselves to some notion of the Enlightenment, archaeology began to reveal that Egyptian society was a literate society with its own recorded history. Through the continuing discovery of more ancient history, it became clear that Egypt had been a highly sophisticated society, with its own distinct character. Above all, Egypt's status as a powerful empire, that enabled it to maintain its development over twenty-five centuries, appealed to the nationalistic tendencies of post-Revolutionary France.[25] The classical collections of the European world, particularly those of ancient Greece and Rome, had for many years constituted both proper thought and good art. The culture of ancient Egypt both supported and supplemented this idea, allowing a new generation of connoisseurs to make statements on their own personal taste and link them with a great and ancient culture. Fourier's 'Preface Historique' to the monumental text *Description de L'Egypte,* published under the auspices of Napoleon from 1809 to 1828, connects the two distinct ancient cultures.

> Placed between Africa and Asia, and communicating easily with Europe, Egypt occupies the centre of the ancient continent ... Homer, Lycurgus, Solon, Pythagorus and Plato all went to Egypt to study the sciences, religion and the laws. Alexander found an opulent city there, which for a long time enjoyed commercial supremacy and witnessed Pompey, Caesar, Mark-Anthony and Augustus deciding between them and the fate of Rome and the entire world.[26]

The publication of plates illustrating the orders of architecture had been established in the pattern books of the eighteenth century as a way of demonstrating an understanding of Graeco-Roman design. It signified the author's classical learning and professional ability. Denon chooses his illustrations to highlight the ability of the Egyptian architect: 'Shortly after, Denderah taught me that it was not in the Doric, Ionic, and Corinthian orders alone, that the beauties of architecture were to be sought; wherever a harmony of parts exists there beauty is to be found.'[27] Through illustrations such as Plate XXIX (plate 33), Denon asserts that not only was Egyptian architecture as important as Graeco-Roman but that it pre-dated the classical designers: 'The Egyptians have copied nature, such as it appears in their own country, this the Greeks have borrowed from them, and have added to it nothing but fable.' The Greeks are reduced in status to mere copiers and this has important implications for confirming the status of the new republic in the light of the previous aristocracy and their cultural bias.

It has been pointed out elsewhere that Fourier's *Description of Egypt* was the most authoritive document of the Egyptian campaign, 'the urtext of French Egyptology'.[28] Like Denon's *Voyage,* it embraces the historicizing ideology of its Western sources. Throughout its twenty-one volumes, the premise of the *Description* is a cyclical history of civilization that insists on the fundamental role of Egypt, documenting its capture by the Romans and its destruction and decadence under Muslim rule.[29] Modern France is seen as promising Egypt's renewal through examination, documentation and publication. In his 'Préface historique', Fourier explains that since the passing of the Pharaonic dynasties, Egypt has not ceased to be 'subjugated by foreign domination',[30] but, unlike Muslim Egypt's depravity, modern France's control will remake Egypt as the theatre of Napoleon's glory.[31]

Why did the French decide to revive an ancient culture for the purposes of supporting their contemporary history? Society had already established a connection between revivalism and ideas of beauty, truth, genius, civilization, form, status, taste, etc. By re-inventing the Egyptian past, a privileged minority could retrospectively justify its role as the ruling class. Napoleon and his cultural attachés were seeking to find a new truth in the antiquities of ancient Egypt. By turning from Graeco-Roman artefacts and ideas, they could distance themselves from the previous French aristocracy and yet still link themselves to the intellectual and cultural power of an ancient world. As with all artistic histories, the empowered classes could utilize this ancient history to support its own present struggle. Denon confirms such an aim when he narrates the process of bringing *Voyage* into the public realm.

> On my arrival at Paris, my friend Citizen Legrand, an excellent architect, and a zealous promoter of all the arts connected with his profession, emboldened me to give to the public all the plans and architectural fragments ... Being apprehensive that Citizen Pere would not have it in his power to complete the operations that he had been charged by the Commission of Arts in Egypt, I no longer hesitated to add all that my feeble means would furnish to so desirable an object; and the reader, in waiting for the immortal work on this subject undertaken by the government a work which will be as colossal a monument of the arts as the originals themselves, may be gratified with observing a few of the elegant and significative forms of these capitals.[32]

Voyage is posited as a vital bridge between the campaigns and the publication of the *Description de L'Egypte,* bringing Egyptian design into the public realm in France as rapidly as possible after its author's return to Paris. As one commentator put it, 'We should not lose sight of the irony. As military actions go, the Egyptian campaign was a failure, but it was a triumph on the walls of the Napoleonic salons ... the Egyptian campaign was a founding myth in Napoleon's rise to power.'[33]

French imperial expansion into Egypt acted as a diversion from the after-effects of the French Revolution and was vital for Napoleon's control of society. In 1797 Bonaparte was supposed to be extending the liberation of Europe across the Channel. The invasion of Egypt, rather than England, was undertaken, according to Talleyrand, 'in order to deflect revolutionary ideas from over-whelming the whole of Europe'.[34] Napoleon also reasoned that conquering Egypt would weaken the British by cutting off their access to India, a key part of its imperial expansion. Napoleon's plans were destroyed on 1 August 1798, when Nelson conquered the French fleet at Abouker Bay. Napoleon quickly left for France, while the news reports still favoured him. His other victories in Egypt helped to propel him to power in November 1799, in the Coup of Eighteen Brumaire, despite the fact that the occupational army he left to govern Egypt surrendered to the British in August 1801.

Although it was a loss in military terms, the Egyptian campaign was represented in France as one of the most glorious moments of the Napoleonic era. Part of this perception is due to the intellectual programmes inherent in the campaign. Napoleon had taken 164 of France's most important thinkers with him to Egypt, including scientists, mathematicians, astronomers, engineers, linguists, architects, draftsmen and painters. The resulting publications, including the *Description of Egypt* and its precursor *Voyage*, disguised Napoleon's losses and presented Egypt as a political and social success story.

Denon saw Egypt as a literate society, an association with which could only bring benefit for France.

> In these latter journeys I visited the tombs of the kings, to the end that in these secret depositories I might form an idea of the art of painting among the Egyptians, of their utensils, arms, furniture, musical instruments, ceremonies and triumphs. It was also on these occasions that I assured myself, that the hieroglyphs sculptured on the walls were not the only books of that learned nation. After having discovered on the bas-reliefs the representations of persons in the act of writing. I made the additional discovery of that roll of papyrus, of that unique manuscript which has already engaged your attention. This fragile rival of the pyramids, this invaluable pledge of a preservatory climate, this monument which time has spared, in the most ancient of all books, and boasts the duration of forty centuries.[35]

Denon aggrandizes his own publication through association with the most ancient texts. He publishes engravings of many of the hieroglyphic symbols that he has encountered on his journeys (plate 34) and refers to scholarly investigation into the ancient language that was taking place in France.

> I entirely abandon all theoretical conjecture to the luminous investigation of those learned men who are employed in this species of enquiry; I shall feel myself sufficiently honoured by having been able to furnish new subjects for their learned researches.[36]

The texts of ancient Egypt, whether on papyrus or carved on walls, act as signifiers of a distinct set of social and cultural values for the researchers, Denon and his followers. They are 'language objects' appropriated and given a new historical and cultural specificity. The past could validate and explain the present and support Denon's aesthetic and cultural objectives. France's belief in its cultural superiority over the rest of Europe meant that it saw itself as the inheritor of the mantle of ancient Egypt. Denon's work functioned in the self-conscious construction of a culture which represented and enhanced current beliefs and values. Antiquity was appropriated and re-used as 'an invented memory with an ideological end'.[37] The invented memory of an ancient past allowed writers and artists, such as Denon, to create an ordered image of a timeless culture in support of the present,

> Napoleon ... wanted nothing less than to take the whole of Egypt, and his advance preparations were of unparalleled magnitude and thoroughness. Even so, these preparations were almost fanatically schematic ... Napoleon had been attracted to the Orient since his adolescence ... and it is evident from all his writings and conversation that he was steeped ... in the memories and glories attached to Alexander's Orient generally and to Egypt in particular.[38]

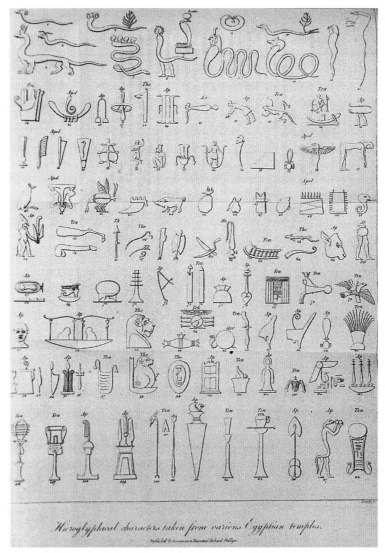

34 Dominique-Vivant Denon, Heiroglyphical characters taken from various Egyptian temples, from *Voyage*.

Before Napoleon and Denon set out on their mission to conquer and record Egypt, there was already in place an 'invented memory' of the ancient civilization which allowed them to manipulate its historiographical benefits for the new empire. Denon uses Egypt as a paradigm for French world rule; 'I saw at length the portico of Hermopolis, the huge masses of the ruins . . . on each of the blocks of which this edifice was composed, I fancied I saw the words posterity, eternity.'[39] (plate 35) Egyptian architecture surrenders to and then signifies *'liberté, fraternité, egalité'*. This notion of an 'invented memory' can be read through Barthes's interpretation of ideology, an interpretation based in his enthusiasm for Marx and Engel's *The German Ideology*. Barthes's ideology, like Marx's and Engel's, 'refers to the distortion of thought which both stems from and conceals social contradictions. This distortion takes the form, specifically, of an inverted consciousness of reality.'[40] Denon is using such an inversion to link Egypt with the rhetoric of nineteenth-century bourgeois liberalism, dominated by words such as 'freedom' and 'equality'. As Barthes suggests in *Mythologies*, however, if one delved beneath this manifest level of discourse to the latent social realities of the period then, 'This apparent individual equality and liberty disappear and prove to be inequality and unfreedom.'[41] Ideology is perceived as a society's subjective representation of its objective position.[42]

The most fundamental *image renversée* for Barthes, following Marx and Engels, is the one that turns culture into nature, the historical into the eternal. Myth, the signifying aspect of ideology, is the perfect instrument for this task, making 'Ancient Egypt' a fundamental signifier of eternity and a powerful aspect of Napoleonic rule.[43]

The Language of Signs III: Archaeology and the Ordering of Knowledge

35   Dominique-Vivant Denon, Ruins of the Temple of Hermopolis, plate XIV from *Voyage*.

On opening the two volumes, we are immediately greeted with a map of lower Egypt, plus a chart of astronomical positions and a detailed key. If we combine this plate with the images of architecture that appear later in the text, we can see one of the visual patterns used by Denon. Take the engraving of the *Ruins of the*

Temple of Hermopolis (plate 35), for example. Here the reader is presented with an elevation of the building, but is also provided with a ground plan that appears to be to scale. Why has Denon included this detail? The provision of ground plans gives the buildings a scientific aura. Combine this with the frontispiece of the map and we can build an image of an inquiry that tries to give itself the status of science by providing a 'scientific classification' for the ancient architecture. Denon himself allies his work with

> the sciences of arts, united by good taste; have decorated the Temple of Isis; there astronomy, morals and metaphysics, assume shape and figure, and these figures and shapes decorate the ceilings, friezes and bases, with at least as much taste and grace as our slight and insignificant paintings in fresco which ornament the modern cabinets.[44]

This is a rare moment, where Denon attempts to explain the visual images because, throughout *Voyage*, the text generally takes second place to the visual images. Denon provides us with 'An Explanation of the Plates' at the end of each volume, but rarely places these in the text of the journey itself, unless he aims to highlight the importance of an image. He explains that he saw his main duty to be recording the visual nature of Egypt: 'I have made this multitude of drawings, frequently too small because our marches were too precipitate to enable me to seize the details of the objects, the aspect and ensemble at least of which I was determined to bring away with me.'[45]

In his essay 'The Plates of the Encyclopaedia', Barthes looks at the ways in which separating the image from the text created an 'autonomous iconography of the object'.[46] The representation that presents the 'object', in our case Egyptian architecture, adds to the encyclopaedia's didactic purpose by giving the object an aesthetic order and a scientific classification.

The use of invented ground plans reminds us of the great classical architectural pattern books, particularly the popularity of the orthogonal presentations of buildings in Palladio's *I Quattro Libri dell'Architettura*. Surely this is a deliberate, self-conscious visual link provided for the reader by Denon. When describing the aesthetic effect of the Temple of Hermopolis, Denon stresses its link to classical architecture,

> Is it the Egyptians who have invented and brought to perfection such a beautiful art? This is a question that I am unable to answer; but even on first glimpse of this edifice we may pronounce, that the Greeks have never devised nor executed any thing in a grander style.[47]

His aim seems to be to utilize the format of rendering classical architecture to underline both the links with, and the superiority over Grecian architecture, that he finds in Egypt. Denon has mapped his images of Egypt against the development of an architectural language of the late eighteenth century where buildings are reduced to a schemata of plan and elevation. He changes the history of Egypt, and his images of it, to suit the needs of the French.

In this way Denon does not democratize his images of Egypt in *Voyage*. The intellectual and scientific stance that his engravings take means that they can only be understood to possess a meaning which is determined by their position in relation to a self-referential system of signifiers, especially those of a specific class, the bourgeoisie. If we analyse the artistic bias of other images from *Voyage*, we can see a similar pattern of reproduction for a specific audience. The majority of the architectural engravings assume a picturesque stance, where the temples, ruins and pyramids of Egypt are surrounded by figures, horses, dogs, trees and a landscape that reminds one of the Reverend William Gilpin's picturesque views of England (plate 31). By employing an artistic language associated with Western architectural and landscape prints, an attempt has been made to create Egyptian scenes that would be understood by a French, and latterly English, audience. The way in which Denon represents the plans scientifically and the elevations picturesquely gives the illustrations a Straussian totemic character and fulfils the need for Denon to show that they 'belong' in a certain French society. *Voyage* becomes a signifier of an invisible network of relations of belonging and exclusion, i.e., class.

A number of images of Egyptian culture and its ancient people are also featured. We are provided with examples of a noble lady, an engraving of *Egyptian Ladies* and *A Scene in an Egyptian Hot Bath* (plate 36) which is thematically reminiscent of the paintings of Ingres and the academic tradition of celebrating the other. This demonstrates how Denon seems to be orientalizing the culture for his own ends, representing one race for the benefit of another. It reminds one of another great piece of orientalizing literature, *Salammbo,* and how Flaubert's encounter with an Egyptian courtesan produced a widely influential model of the oriental woman, hidden behind her veil, who never spoke for herself but was instead represented by the author, the Westerner. Said suggests that Flaubert is representative of the pattern of relative strength between East and West and the discourse about the Orient that it enabled.[48] Denon also seems to adopt this stance.

Denon's sketches of the native Egyptian peoples, including 'Egyptian Ladies', 'A Santan', 'A Caravan Driver from Darfur', 'A Noble Lady' and 'Local Arabs from Rosetta', were used as resources and as 'scientific evidence' for commemorative paintings of the Egyptian campaigns. For example Pierre-Narcisse Guérin used Denon's 'Local Arabs from Rosetta' as models for the faces in his *Bonaparte Pardoning the Rebels in Cairo* (1808). Porterfield describes Guérin's painting as an exercise in intertextuality rather than a first-hand account.[49] Its meaning and legitimacy were produced through the citation of antecedent authorities. It is not an image of the East, but an image of the East translated through the plates in *Voyage*. Denon's pattern book of images was appropriated by a great number of painters commissioned to produce images of French victories in Egypt.[50] It was a vital resource in the mythological promotion of a victorious Napoleon against the facticity of setback and defeat.

In his images of Egyptian motifs culled from ancient architecture, Denon conforms to an established European method, that of the architectural and furniture pattern book (plate 33). Denon makes comparisons between ancient cultures in his Preface: 'Shortly after Denderah (Tentyris) taught me that it was not in the doric, ionic and Corinthian orders alone, that the beauties of architecture were to be sought; wherever a harmony of parts exists there beauty is

36   Dominique-Vivant Denon, Scene in an Egyptian hot Bath, plate XVI
from *Voyage*.

found.'[51] The majority of pattern books including Chippendale's *Director* and
Sheraton's *Drawing Book*, began with a visual reminder of the orders of
architecture. Here Denon provides us with an alternative explanation of the
development of the orders in his description of his illustration (plate 33):

> Here, the calyx of a flower, supported by the stem, has furnished the form
> of the column, its base, and its capital; the lotus has afforded the first
> model ... as a homage of gratitude to Isis, who presided over this
> bountious gift: as goddess of the earth, they have also dedicated to her the
> other productions of the foil, the reed, the palm, the vine.[52]

We are presented with page on page of Egyptian motifs and patterns, often on
large sheets folded into the text. Denon is creating a history of Egyptian design
that predates Greece and Rome, even in its key design motifs, and thus creates the
ideal taste of and for a new republic. The presentation of these in terms of familiar
formulae made them accessible and easily adaptable for use in design schemes.

As presented in his essay on 'The Plates of the Encyclopaedia', Barthes's
categories provide us with a useful lexical reference for reading Denon's various
approaches to the printed images. Barthes sees the actual object as apprehended
by the image on three levels and we can apply all these levels to the images in
Voyage. On the anthological level, the actual object is isolated from its context
and presented as a representation of itself. Denon provides us with anthological
readings of Egyptian architecture when he uses the pattern-book method of

supplying sheets of designs such as columns and entablatures (plate 33). On the next level a genetic image offers us the trajectory from raw substance to finished object. Denon highlights actual construction processes in Egyptian architecture by creating imaginary ground plans in his pseudo-scientific interpretations of the buildings (plates 32 and 35). Finally, on the anecdotic level, the object is 'naturalized' by its insertion into a grand-scale *tableau vivant*, such as we find in Denon's picturesque images of Egypt (plate 31). Each of these visual levels allow Denon to 'show how we can produce things from their very nonexistence and thus to credit man with an extraordinary power of creation'. For example, in Denon's image of the sphinx (plate 31) several figures seem to be considering the object, measuring it and surveying it. As in the plate of the Giant's Causeway in the *Encyclopaedia*, the 'mass is stuffed with humanity … reduced, tamed and familiarised.'[53]

In Denon's depiction of the sphinx, French soldiers and archaeologists are shown climbing over the Egyptian monolith and thereby claiming it. The image underlines a new familiar ownership: Barthes stresses that this ability to place man within the image means that a catalogue of pictorial views can never be neutral, it allows the artist to appropriate the landscape and, thus, *Voyage* becomes a 'huge ledger of ownership'.[54] France's annexation of Egypt is illustrated and codified by Denon. *Voyage* is constantly concerned with the familiarization of Egypt and the humanization of the images by all three Barthian levels, which implies an intellectual system that had important ideological implications for the European reader.

Denon uses his publication to reproduce images of Egypt for the purposes of disseminating information about this culture in France, but not in order to democratize these images – his aim was to create a taste that would support the domination of the ruling classes in Paris. The cultural hierarchy, as represented in the designs of Denon, claimed republican ideals and enlightened goals, but was simply sustaining itself through such publications, and did not aim to open up the arts to 'the people', only to a limited people. In this way, Denon attempts the opposite of Benjamin's insistence on democratization of the image in the age of mechanical reproduction. Instead of *withering* the aura of the work of art, here Denon's key aim is to give his Egyptian motifs a new, invented aura, as a part of the creation of the paradigm of French rule. The parallaxical relationship between what Denon saw on his travels and how he represented it undermines the notion of democratization and, instead, provides the actual archaeological objects with a new status. Although it would seem easy to link Denon's publication to what Benjamin describes as 'the desire of the contemporary masses to bring things "closer" spatially and humanly', and the visual needs of 'contemporary mass movements',[55] the language of the visual images turns away from a mass audience to a cultured, limited one. It was the fate of subsequent publications, heavily indebted to Denon's, to achieve a wider acceptance for Egyptian motifs. In France, Percier's and Fontaine's role as architects to Napoleon guaranteed a popular following after they published the *Recueil de Décorations Intérieures*.

By acknowledging the semiological importance of images of Egypt in France, we can also begin to understand the popularity of this style in England at the beginning of the nineteenth century. This is the subject of another essay in itself, but suffice to say, the Egyptian revival was used by its supporters in England to signify an admiration for the styling of France, the symbol of a culture of difference associated with the court of the Prince of Wales. French culture and its objects were adopted by certain political groupings around the Prince, predominantly associated with the Whig politics of Charles James Fox. Simultaneously, it symbolized a move away from the majority who, led by Prime Minister Pitt and George III, were concerned about French influence on English life at a time when France was perceived as the closest enemy and a threat to the safety of English society. While many fought to make England less permeable to French influence and commodification, the collecting practice of the Prince of Wales and his followers created a sense of opposition to the traditional structures of power, as art and cultural consumption fulfilled a social function of legitimizing social differences.[56] This was reflected in the Prince of Wales's choice of designers and the interiors of both Carlton House and the Brighton Pavilion. Consumer habits that signified his opposition politics were particularly noticeable during his younger years, when, as Prince of Wales, he established a base of opposition ideology at Carlton House. This was at a time when the 'pretentious Frenchifying' of the cabinet-maker's vocabulary was criticized by the *Gentleman's Magazine,* who complained that, 'words entirely foreign have been greatly pressed into service, not by philologists and lexicographers, but by cabinet-makers and auctioneers, to give dignity to tables and chairs, to exalt cupboards and bracketts.'[57]

The rise and progress of the English edition of *Voyage* is recorded in magazines and architectural publications such as *A Collection of Architectural Designs for Mansions*, by Randall in 1806. Thomas Hope experimented with motifs culled from the prints in his Duchess Street house and in the bibliography of *Household Furniture,* he mentions *Voyage* among the works most useful to him. George Smith's comments in his *A Collection of Designs for Household Furniture and Interior Decoration* attest to the popularity of Denon's 'embellishments' on this side of the Channel.

The influence of the Egyptian revival style and Denon's work was not universally celebrated, however, and a divergence between scholarly and popular interest led to C.A. Busby's comment in 1808 that, 'the travels of Denon have produced more evil than the elegance of the engravings and the splendour of his publication, can be allowed to have compensated.'[58] That said, Denon's popularization of the Egyptian as a semiotically charged style was vital in France and England for those wishing to establish a new cultural order. As such, we can theorize the processes that reconfigured the image of Egypt in France and England at the beginning of the nineteenth century, in order to map visual culture against political culture, to offer a new reading of Denon's *Voyage.*

Notes

All plates are reproduced by kind permission of the Earl and Countess of Harewood and the Trustees of Harewood House Trust.

1 The English edition of *Voyage* was actually published first in 1803, a year after the original French publication in 1802.

2 Ralph Fastnedge, *English Furniture Styles, 1500–*

1830, Harmondsworth: Penguin, 1962, p. 261. George Smith, cabinet-maker and upholsterer, published *A Collection of Designs for Household Furniture and Interior Decoration* in 1808. The work contained 158 plates in colour, some showing approved schemes of decoration for whole rooms. Smith was advertised as 'Upholder Extraordinary to his Royal Highness the Prince of Wales'. Most of Smith's information on the Egyptian style was culled from Denon's *Voyage* leading to his comment, quoted from 1826, but referring to when Smith first published in 1808.

3 Randall, *A Collection of Architectural Designs for Mansions*, London, 1806.

4 Any study of Egyptomania would begin with the catalogue of this exhibition, and would include standard texts such as: Richard G. Carrott's *The Egyptian Revival: Its Sources, Monuments and Meaning, 1808–1858*, Berkeley, CA: University of California Press, 1978 and James Stevens Curl's *The Egyptian Revival: An Introductory Study of a Recurring Theme in the History of Taste*, London: Allen and Unwin, 1982 and *Egyptomania: The Egyptian Revival*, Manchester: Manchester University Press, 1994.

5 *Collins Paperback English Dictionary*, Glasgow: Collins, 1990, p. 511.

6 Todd Porterfield, 'Egyptomania', *Art in America*, vol. 82, no. 11, November 1994, p. 86.

7 See ibid., p. 88.

8 *Voyage*, 'The Preface', p. i. my italics.

9 ibid., p. ii.

10 See D. Arnold's essay in this volume.

11 In the text of *Voyage* Denon frequently refers to the picturesque elements of his journey and the views he encounters. 'On viewing the fine banks of the Soane [*sic*], and the picturesque scenes of the Rhone', pp. 18–19. He utilizes this term when describing the Egyptian scenes and does not draw any distinction between European and Asian views and their 'picturesque' content. This term had specific currency in early nineteenth-century France and England, and it seems that Denon used it purposely to give credence to his artistic endeavours, to support the idea of his identity as a man of culture and to highlight his didactic purposes in producing the images in *Voyage*.

12 *Voyage*, p. 171.

13 G.W.F. Hegel, *Philosophy of Fine Arts*, trans. F.R.R. Osmaston, 4 vols, London: G. Bell and Sons, 1920, p. 14.

14 *Voyage*, p. 186.

15 Walter Benjamin, 'Thesis on the Philosophy of History', *Illuminations*, ed. Hannah Arendt, trans. Harry Zohn, London: Fontana, 1973, p. 247.

16 *Voyage*, p. i.

17 ibid.

18 Edward Said, *Orientalism*, Harmondsworth: Penguin, 1991, p. 7.

19 *Voyage*, p. 266.

20 Benjamin, 'Thesis on the Philosophy of History', op. cit. (note 15), p. 248.

21 *Voyage*, Dedication, p. 1.

22 Benjamin, 'Thesis on the Philosophy of History, op. cit. (note 15), p. 248.

23 Andrew McClellan, *Inventing the Louvre: Art, Politics and the Origins of the Modern Museum in Eighteenth Century Paris*, Cambridge: Cambridge University Press, 1994, p. 7.

24 See Roland Barthes, *Mythologies*, trans. A. Lavers, London: Jonathan Cape, 1967.

25 Susan Pearce, *On Collecting*, London: Routledge, 1995, p. 347.

26 *Description*, vol. I, p. 1.

27 *Voyage*, 'Preface', pp. v–vi.

28 Todd Porterfield, *The Allure of the Empire; Art in the Service of French Imperislism, 1798–1836*, Princeton, New Jersey: Princeton University Press, 1998, p. 30.

29 See Linda Nochlin, 'The Image of the Orient', *Art in America*, May 1983, p. 123, when she discusses the broken tiles in Gérômes's *Street in Algiers* where, 'neglected, ill-repaired architecture functions, in nineteenth century orientalist art, as a standard *topos* for commenting on the corruption of contemporary Islamic society and the vice of idleness frequently commented upon by nineteenth century Western travellers'.

30 Fourier quoted in Porterfield, 'Egyptomania', op. cit. (note 6), p. 30.

31 ibid., p. 30.

32 *Voyage*, p. 267. Denon is describing the need for his images of architectural fragments in Egypt and in the 'Explanation of the Plates', refers specifically to Plate XXIX (fig. 32).

33 Porterfield, 'Egyptomania', op. cit. (note 6), p. 8.

34 Charles-Maurice de Talleyrand, Napoleon's Foreign Minister, quoted in ibid., p. 44.

35 *Voyage*, 'Preface', p. vii.

36 ibid., p. 286.

37 Dana Arnold, *The Georgian Country House*, Stroud: Sutton, 1998, p. 107.

38 Said, *Orientalism*, op. cit. (note 18), p. 80.

39 *Voyage*, 'Preface', pp. v–vi.

40 Andrew Leak, *Barthes' Mythologies*, London: Grant and Cutler, 1994, p. 24.

41 ibid., p. 24, quoting Marx. Here Barthes uses Marxist theory to underline his notion of the ideological use of myth.

42 ibid.

43 Barthes wrote *Mythologies* at a period when France was struggling with its colonies, particularly those in North Africa. This creates a specific backdrop of official discourse in a language whose principal device is the inversion of reality, where the 'destinies' of France and Algeria were portrayed as mysteriously wedded. See Roland Barthes, *Selected Writings*, ed. Susan Sontag, London: Fontana, 1983, p. xi.

44 *Voyage*, 'Preface', p. vi.

45 ibid., p. v.

46 Roland Barthes, 'The Plates of the Encyclopaedia', in *Barthes, Selected Writings*, op. cit. (note 43), p. 218.

47 *Voyage,* p. 240.
48 Said, *Orientalism*, op. cit. (note 18), p. 6.
49 Porterfield, 'Egyptomania', op. cit. (note 6), p. 73.
50 See Porterfield for a detailed discussion of these images.
51 *Voyage*, 'Preface', p. vi.
52 ibid., p. 266. Here Denon supports the notion posited in Riegl's *Stilfragen* (1893) that the lotus motif led directly to the acanthus motif of Graeco-Roman design, and thus traces a direct link between Egypt and Classical design, with Egypt as the precursor.
53 Barthes, 'The Plates of the Encyclopaedia', op.

cit. (note 46), p. 222.
54 ibid.
55 Benjamin, 'The Work of Art in the Age of Mechanical Reproduction', op. cit. (note 15), pp. 215–17.
56 See Pierre Bourdieu, *Distinction*, London: Routledge, 1997, p. 2.
57 *Gentleman's Magazine,* September 1802, quoted in Geoffrey de Bellaigue, 'English Marquetry's debt to France', *Country Life,* 13 June 1968, pp. 1594–8.
58 C.A. Busby, *A Series of Designs for Villas and Country Houses*, London, 1808, pp. 11–12.

9

Specimens of Antient Sculpture: Imperialism and the decline of art

Andrew Ballantyne

In 1809 the Society of Dilettanti published a volume of very fine engraved prints illustrating examples of antique sculptures, with a commentary by Richard Payne Knight. It was always intended that there would be a second volume, but in the event that did not appear until 1835, well after Knight's death. This second volume had a commentary that was hostile to Knight, but it nevertheless included (as an appendix) an essay by Knight that he had intended as its introduction and commentary, as well as specimens of sculpture which had belonged to him. There are also remarks which are attributed to him in the 'official' commentary, so his name appears with greater frequency in the second volume, which is therefore still stamped with his imprint. The two volumes together make a problematic whole, as the second volume includes specimens of sculpture and engraving which would not have been approved in the earlier book, as well as some remarks that distance the writer from identification with Knight's views.[1] The matter is further confused by the fact that the introductions to both volumes were presented anonymously, whereas Knight's second essay went out under his own personal name, which gives the views presented the air of being personal opinions, in contrast with the lofty authority that seems to attach to the voice without personality that introduces the volumes. There is apparent continuity in the anonymous voice from one volume to the next, but Knight is displaced to a less authoritive position in the second volume, and it is only then that it is officially announced that his had been the 'authoritive' voice in the first volume.

The project was without doubt inspired by Winckelmann's account of ancient art, and by its shortcomings. The engraved plates are of a far higher quality than those which Winckelmann managed to commission – the plates of *Specimens of Antient Sculpture* match the high standards set by the Society of Dilettanti's earlier publication of the *Antiquities of Athens*, by Stuart and Revett, and they have the same large folio format, so they make an apparent continuation of the same series. Knight's introductory essay to the second volume was an exposition of 'The Symbolical Language of Antiquity', which sought to interpret the symbolic aspects of antique art in general, and which again can be seen as marking a step forward from Winckelmann's often successful attempts to decode the meaning of ancient images. Winckelmann made progress by taking images of groups of figures found in Rome and matching them not to Roman myths (as had previously been done) but to Greek ones, which they fitted with greater felicity, helping to establish the importance of Greek culture in the Roman art world.[2] What Knight did in his commentary was to take the images to be emblems from Greek religion, symbolically coded, and this gave him a feeling that there was a vast wealth of arcane knowledge to be uncovered from them. His interpretations are not always convincing. They can sound over-elaborate, but sometimes, when an image does not make sense in a straightforward way, his method comes into its own. Knight had already published the essay 'The Symbolical Language of Antiquity' (without illustrations) at a time when it must have been clear to him that the second volume of *Specimens of Antient Sculpture* would not be coming out during his lifetime, maybe never at all. In fact, Knight's essay was to be reprinted not only in *Specimens of Antient Sculpture*, but also later – the only one of his many books to appear in a new edition after his death, before the revival of interest in him during the twentieth century. The essay revisited the theme of his very first publication – *A Discourse on the Worship of Priapus* – which had also been published by the Society of Dilettanti, for private circulation, in 1786.

So the two volumes of *Specimens of Antient Sculpture* were to represent a significant step forward in scholarship, both in producing images of a high quality, and in producing a commentary which would enable them to be understood properly. The commentary to the first volume was concerned to establish a chronology and to establish the superiority of Greek over Roman work. It specifically excluded discussion of the symbolic aspects of the sculpture, because this would be treated in the second volume. The tone of the writing is lofty and pedantic, but an argument is shaped here that clearly has behind it some passionate feeling, and it comes as a surprise to find just how vehemently Roman culture is deplored in these pages, and how the grounds for the denunciation connect with the political events of the day. The story presented in the text goes that in the well-regulated city states of ancient Greece, perfection had been achieved, so that it was necessary for art not to deviate at all from Greek practice. Deviation could only lead to vice and extravagance.[3] Knight described the coming of the dominion of Rome as 'a great and disastrous change in the affairs of mankind, which brought all the learned and civilized nations of the earth under the hard dominion of one military republick; and, in its consequences, plunged them into barbarism and utter darkness.'[4] The remarks reflect the anxieties of Knight's own day, being written at a time when the rise of Napoleon was yet to be checked – the battles of Trafalgar and Waterloo lay in the future, and there was no saying whether Britain too might not fall to Napoleon's imperial ambition. Elsewhere Knight showed his characteristic general scorn for the middle ages – in the manner typical of Enlightenment thinkers – seeing it as a dark age of superstition and ignorance. This is only to be expected from someone with his general cast of mind. What is far from commonplace, even among determined radicals, is the way in which Knight here projects medieval attitudes (or more precisely an Enlightenment caricature of medieval attitudes) back into the culture of Imperial Rome, so that the onset of medieval vice is not to be found beginning suddenly with the fall of Rome to the barbarians in the fifth century AD, but much much earlier – in the second century BC. It was then, Knight observed, that 'art, having reached its summit, began gradually to decline.'[5] Superstition – always a bad thing in Knight's view – was rife among the Romans,[6] as it would continue to be during the middle ages. Knight thoroughly approved of the ancient religion of the Greeks, which he saw as using the poetic images of gods as the personification of the forces of nature. It was, therefore, in his view rational. The images were fanciful, but they demonstrated scientific truths – 'it conveyed abstract ideas under visible forms.'[7] In this line of thought Knight followed the Baron d'Hancarville and the earlier attempt by Francis Bacon to decode ancient symbolism in *The Wisedom of the Ancients*.[8] Knight would, he said, explain this fully in the introductory essay to the second volume. Here, in the first volume, he explained that in Roman art 'the mystic system, though degraded and corrupted, was not yet extinct, and the meanness of the characters, poverty of the drapery, and feebleness of the action, all indicate an expiring effort of the art.'[9]

Knight tended to follow the moral teaching of Epicurus, who advised that it is best to gratify the appetites of the body, avoiding any tendency to excess, and aiming to limit the appetite so that it could very readily be gratified and would not make one its slave.[10] He saw the medieval Christians as losing sight of the benefits of this teaching, so that the monastic virtues of fasting, celibacy and abstinence were, from his point of view, simply perversions.[11] Again this view was normal among Enlightenment intellectuals. It is not usual to find the same charges directed against the pre-Christian Romans, but in Knight's mind the decline of the arts was caused by the same mechanism: education and prevailing opinion taught the Romans to oppose 'the gratifications of pride and ambition to those of ease and sensuality; and thus deprived death of its terrors by depriving life of its enjoyments'.[12] The state of moral as well as artistic decline meant that life was devalued along with art, and ambition was such that of the twenty emperors who succeeded Septimus Severus, and 'who followed each other in the brief period of seventy years, only one died a natural death; and he after a reign of only two years.'[13] The decline of art is portrayed as a symptom which correlates with the decline of society in a more general way. And the decline is associated not with the adoption of Christianity – as it was in Gibbon's *Decline and Fall of the Roman Empire* – but with imperialism. Indeed, the decline of art is linked deliberately with the rise of the very idea of imperialism, which began with the Macedonian king Alexander the Great in the fourth century BC. It was precisely in Macedonia that Knight located the point where civilization began to decline:

> Art, having thus reached its summit, began gradually to decline. Through the weakness of some of the Macedonian dynasties, the tyranny of others, and the ambition and extravagance of all, revolts and dissentions were excited; and the funds which had been applied to nourish genius and develope [*sic*] talent, applied to less salutary purposes; to spread desolation, or pamper ostentatious vanity, or sordid luxury.[14]

Plainly, in Knight's view, art could not achieve the highest merit in such circumstances. He followed Winckelmann in making a strong connection between the ideal life of the ancient Greeks and the excellence of their art,[15] and in his practical involvement with politics he was guided by an ideal of liberty and the desire to see culture as a totality: the ideal way of life would be conducive to the production of the best possible art. Hence the recurrent theme of the commentary which continually links political history with connoisseurship. It is certain, in Knight's view of the matter, that work of the highest merit must have come from free Greece, and could not have come from despotic imperialistic Rome. It is therefore unfortunate for Knight that he did not entertain a higher opinion of the Parthenon sculptures when Lord Elgin brought them from Athens.[16] Firstly, it is clear that he did not like Elgin, which led him to make ungenerous remarks out loud – plainly he intended to hurt. Secondly and more importantly, the sculptures did not fit his idea of what the finest sculpture would be. The pedimental sculptures were badly damaged, and had lost the surface, which was what would have given the sculptures their expressivity – there are many remarks on the pages of *Specimens of Antient Sculpture* drawing attention to the intactness of surfaces, which it is true can patinate to take on the apparent texture of skin. However, Knight believed that the pedimental sculptures were Hadrianic replacements, not the original work from the fifth century BC, and they are not mentioned at all in this book. He did not originate that idea, but he maintained it. He was wrong, and from the time that he was known to be wrong, his reputation as an authority on Greek sculpture was blasted. That is why the second volume did not appear during his lifetime.

Knight believed that architectural sculpture would never have been the best sculpture of an age, and therefore excluded it from the highest rank of art. Friezes and metopes would be decorative art, but it would be as much a mistake to look for signs of genius in them as it would to do so in the work of an interior decorator. The only architectural sculpture to be illustrated in the first volume of *Specimens of Antient Sculpture* was included not as a formal plate, but as an illustrative endpiece to the essay (plate 37).

> The most antient monument of Grecian sculpture now extant is unquestionably the broken piece of natural relief in the ancient portal to the gates of Mycenae, which is probably the same that belonged to the capital of Agamemnon, and may therefore be at least as old as the age of Daedalus. It represents two lions rampant, sufficiently entire to afford a very tolerable idea of the style of the work. The plate of it given in the tail-piece to this discourse, is engraved from a sketch made upon the spot, and corrected by admeasurement, by William Gell, esq. And though this does not afford any very accurate information as to the details of the work, the three compositions of the engraved gem given with it are perfectly competent to supply such information; they being in exactly the same style and having been found in the same country by the same intelligent and industrious traveller.[17]

This sculpture had special significance, as it came from the age of Homer and his historical-mythical heroes. (A measure of its prestige was that it was adopted as the insignia of the Royal Institute of British Architects.) A more polished rendering of the

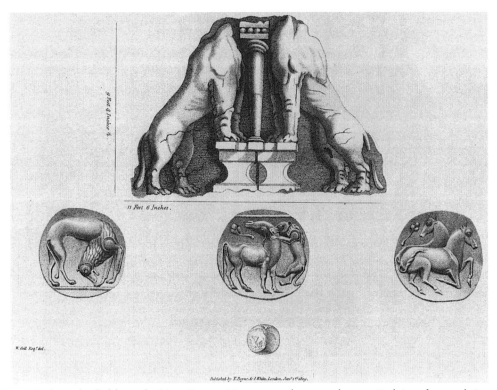

37   Sculptural relief from the Lion Gate at Mycenae, and engraved gems. Endpiece from vol. I of *Specimens of Antient Sculpture*. By permission of the British Library.

same sculpted panel was included in the second volume, this one the work of a Mr Hawkins (plate 38). The commentary notes that properly this sculpture should not be included in the volume, because it is not in a British collection.[18] The exceptional historical interest here uniquely outweighed the feeling that architectural sculpture did not merit inclusion. At the other end of the scale, the sculpture from the Parthenon which was certainly of the highest class was the cult image of Athena by Phidias himself. Unfortunately, this statue had been destroyed. It was made of bronze, covered in ivory and gold (which could usefully be melted down) and could not have been absorbed into any merely decorative scheme when the building was turned into a church. However, Thomas Hope owned a large marble copy of the statue, made in ancient times. He was on the Society of Dilettanti's publication committee for the book, and the statue so impressed that it was included twice, once in each volume. It was the only specimen of ancient sculpture to reappear in this way – there were only two other repetitions, one of them being the improved representation of the panel at Mycenae, the other the Earl of Egrement's *Apollo* where the first artist had made the sculpture look awkward (see below). Hope's *Athena* was alone in being adequately represented in the first volume, and then included in the second for the sheer joy of it (plate 39).

It was thought that this statue was the work of the studio of Phidias, even perhaps by the great man himself,[19] and it enjoyed a glamour and celebrity which has vanished from it forever, now that it is believed to be a Roman copy. Of all the antiquities sold

38 Sculptural relief from the Lion Gate at Mycenae, plate III of vol. II of
Specimens of Antient Sculpture. By permission of the British Library.

from Hope's collection in 1917, this was the one which fetched the highest price –
6,800 guineas (£7,140). In 1933 it was auctioned again, and was bought in by Sotheby's
at £200 – a spectacular fall from grace following reattribution.[20] Knight's account of
the production of Greek sculpture contrasts with that of Roman. The Roman artists
were expected to make portrait images of tyrants, so 'Instead of giving appropriate
form and character to abstract perfections or poetical images, the artist was thus
degraded to the mean and irksome labour of copying the features and embellishing the
form of some contemptible despot.'[21] How different from the Greek practice: for the
Greek artists 'all the charms of beauty, grace, majesty, and elegance, which the human
mind can bestow on the human form, were vigorously conceived and most correctly
executed.'[22] Slavish imitation of superficial appearances was not the point – that
would be merely a mechanical skill – the great artist would work apparently from an
exalted and well-stocked mind.

> It was not by copying individual nature in their works that they gave to
> those works a character so much above it; but by previously studying and
> copying it in detail till they had become completely possessed of it, and
> were enabled to decompose and recompose it as they pleased by memory
> only, so as to trust imagination in refining embellishing, and exalting it,
> without incurring the risk of any other deviation from truth. Thus they
> exhibited the forms, as the great father of poetry has exhibited the minds
> and actions of men, only differing from those of which we have daily
> experience, by being upon a more exalted scale, and employing a more
> vigorous and perfect organization.[23]

135

39 *Athena*, in the collection of Thomas Hope, plate XXV of vol. I of
Specimens of Antient Sculpture. By permission of the British Library.

The general view of the Greeks was that they could do no wrong, and that their sculptural works had never been excelled. However when it came to matching this view with the evidence to support it, Knight repeatedly ran into trouble. Many sculptural works which Knight took to be from Classical Greece are now thought to be Roman copies of Hellenistic work, and when he was faced with genuinely Classical work, he did not always see in it the exalted value which he theoretically believed should have been there. Lord Elgin had brought the statuary from the Parthenon to London in 1806, and it was eventually bought for the nation in 1816, so its eventual whereabouts was uncertain when *Specimens of Antient Sculpture* was being written. It is nevertheless surprising to find that its presence on this island was not so much as mentioned, though the works were discussed, and denigrated. He referred the reader not to the collection of sculptures, but to the Society of Dilettanti's publication, *The Antiquities of Athens* (compiled by Stuart and Revett). He avoided mentioning the large statues from the pediments, which he continued to think were Hadrianic (from the second century AD) and explained that the frieze and metope panels did not belong to the highest class of art – being architectural decoration, executed by 'workmen scarcely ranked among artists, and meant to be seen at the height of more than forty feet from the eye'.[24]

Specimens of Antient Sculpture therefore cannot any longer be taken as an authoritive account of the works which are presented, but it is a valuable document for understanding the taste and the preoccupations of its time. For example, the sculpture which Knight singled out for the highest praise of all is now virtually unknown. Perhaps unsurprisingly, it was in Knight's own collection. He knew that most of the antique marble statues around were Roman copies of Greek originals, and part of the project of *Specimens of Antient Sculpture* was to identify genuine Greek work. He found it, most excellently, in a small brass figure: an Apollo Didymaeus, or androgynous personification of Apollo (plates 40 and 41). 'For taste and elegance of design,' he said,

> grace and ease of action, and delicacy and skill of execution, it is perhaps the most perfect work of human art now extant. The countenance expresses a mind seriously though placidly intent on the action; to which every limb and muscle spontaneously co-operate, without any particular effort or exertion; so that, from whatever point the figure be viewed, its attitude and posture are as easy and natural, as they are graceful, elegant and beautiful. The unperverted influence of a dignified and exalted mind upon a free and unrestrained body, appears in every limb, joint, and feature; in which the skill of consummate art has united the truth and simplicity of individual, with the abstract perfection of ideal nature. It has every characteristic of the original work of a great artist, and is certainly not unworthy of Praxiteles himself.[25]

Clearly, Knight would have loved to have been able to attribute the work to a named artist, but he had no evidence to allow the attempt to be plausible. Winckelmann himself had attributed one of Townley's sculptures to Polykleitos,[26] but wrongly, as Knight and Townley knew by the time they selected which specimens they would include in the volume – otherwise this sculpture would certainly have been included. That Knight should have singled out this particular Apollo as worthy of such extraordinarily high praise, and indeed the fact that he praised by means of the particular terms of approbation he used, shows that he had adopted from Winckelmann the idea that the most perfect kind of bodily beauty was androgynous – having elements of both masculine and feminine qualities, here confined to secondary characteristics. It can be found in other neoclassically inspired works, such as David's *Death of Bara* (1794) – and also Richard Westall's *Orpheus* (1812), painted for Knight.[27] Knight left his collection to the British Museum, where the sculpture of

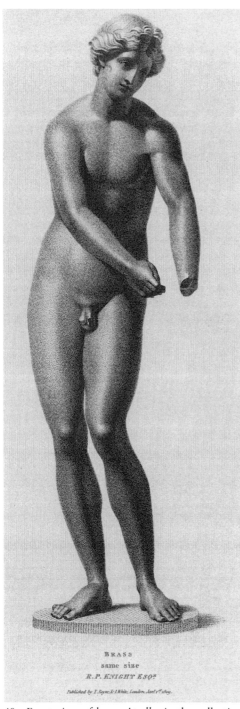

BRASS
same size
R.P. KNIGHT ESQᴿ

Published by T.Payne, & J.White, London, Jan.¹ ¹ᵗ 1809.

40 Front view of brass *Apollo*, in the collection of R.P. Knight, plate XLIII of vol. I of *Specimens of Antient Sculpture*. By permission of the British Library.

Apollo is now, sometimes on display, but often not. It is, of course, completely eclipsed by the Elgin Marbles, which also upstaged the collection of marbles assembled by Charles Townley – who had been one of Knight's closest friends, and whose collection figures prominently in the *Specimens of Antient Sculpture*. He collaborated on the volume, even though he had died before it was completed. Townley and Knight shared the same ideas about the symbolic significance of ancient art, which they imbibed from Pierre François Hugues, who went by the name of 'Baron' d'Hancarville – best known now as the publisher of Sir William Hamilton's collection of Greek vases. Townley and Knight had shared the considerable cost of publishing his researches, and of keeping him – when he lived with Townley in London. Townley and d'Hancarville are shown together in Zoffany's famous portrait of Townley surrounded by his collection. This collection was left to the British Museum, then in its infancy, and it formed the core of its display – these statues were its principal exhibits. The acquisition of the Elgin Marbles saw them lose their eminence, and they are now displayed in a basement, not so much as an example of the finest antique art as of an eighteenth-century collection. One of the peculiarities which Knight and his contemporaries shared with Winckelmann was that their knowledge of antique sculpture, and their ideas about it, derived mainly from works of Imperial Rome – which is to say, relatively late Roman works. They eulogized the Classical age of Greece but they did not authoritively know how to recognize its art works. Knight was not alone in making mistakes in this area, but his mistake became very public knowledge and in the public mind his authority was discredited.

Specimens of Antient Sculpture is a useful means of understanding the state of knowledge and taste of its time, and it remains a folio of beautiful prints. Knight's text repeatedly draws attention to the fact that we are not faced with mechanical renderings of the works of art under consideration, but are looking at one artistic production representing a second. It is unusual to find this sort of commentary. In a modern book the photographic illustrations of statues are normally presented as if they were neutral indications of the appearance of the works. In the illustrations to Winckelmann's *Monumenti antichi inediti* the illustrations are so plainly in their own idiom – relying heavily on outlines – that the question of correspondence hardly arises: they show the iconography clearly enough, but do not attempt to render the material qualities of the objects under discussion – they are presented simply as images, ready to be decoded, rather than as sculpted stones with sensuous surfaces. In *Specimens of Antient Sculpture* there is often complete satisfaction with the way the work of art is depicted – rendering further descriptive comment superfluous. So, for example, in the commentary for Plate XXXIX, identified as a head of Bacchus in the possession of the Earl of Upper Ossory (plate 42), we find the observation that 'The character of the countenance is that of mildness, amenity, and hilarity mixed with dignity, which is faithfully rendered in the print.'[28] However, the more interesting comments are interpolated when Knight saw shortcomings in the rendition. For example, the most severe remarks concerned a statue of Apollo belonging to the Earl of Egremont (plate 43).

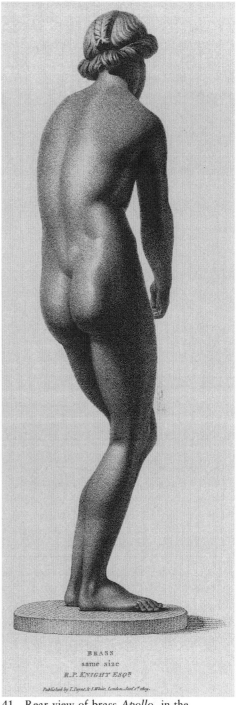

BRASS
same size
R.P. KNIGHT ESQ.ʳ

Published by T. Payne, & I. White, London, June.ʳ 1809.

41 Rear view of brass *Apollo*, in the collection of R.P. Knight, plate XLIV of vol. I of *Specimens of Antient Sculpture*. By permission of the British Library.

42 *Bacchus*, in the collection of the Earl of Ossory, plate XXXIX of vol. I of *Specimens of Antient Sculpture*. By permission of the British Library.

43 *Apollo*, in the collection of the Earl of Egremont, plate LXII of vol. I of *Specimens of Antient Sculpture*. By permission of the British Library.

Our duty to the public obliges us to acknowledge that justice has not been done in the print either to the truth of the proportions, the elegance of the limbs, or the grace of the action in this fine figure of Apollo. The head is too small, the legs too large, and the posture too erect.[29]

The reservations about this image were such that a different artist was commissioned to try it, and this more successful attempt was included in the second volume.[30] These remarks concern the mechanical accuracy of the artist's transcription. Other remarks sketch out a theory of good practice for the artists engaged in this activity of presenting sculpture in prints. In these circumstances Knight strongly disapproved of 'picturesque' effects, which in other circumstances he would be very ready to praise. The point of the illustrations was not to make decorative works of art, but to enlist the artists' technique in the service of presenting the sculpture – the work of art to be depicted. Therefore, when the

effects of light and shade became interesting, they were a distraction from the beauty of the sculpture. 'The artist who made the drawing' of a laughing faun, from Charles Townley's collection (plate 44), 'though he had in general a very just feeling for antient sculpture, was rather too fond of introducing effects of light and shade, properly belonging to painting, into his imitations of it; and this fault of refinement is retained in the print, which is otherwise perfectly accurate.'[31] This discussion is characteristic of Knight, whose theory of the picturesque was fully explained in his *Analytical Inquiry into the Principles of Taste* of 1805. 'Picturesque', he said, meant *after the manner of painters*, and the thing which particularly characterized the manner of painters was the principle of 'massing' – using broad sweeps of colour or shade rather than picking up every visible detail in the rendering of an image.[32] Sculpture operated by different principles, and it was the duty of the artist who was illustrating sculpture to convey the impression of the original sculpture, rather than make a brilliant pictorial image. In his remarks about another of Charles Townley's sculptures, depicted by the same artist (I. Brown, plate 45) he says:

44 *Faun*, in the collection of Charles Townley, plate LIX of vol. I of *Specimens of Antient Sculpture*. By permission of the British Library.

this head of the Didymaean or androgynous Apollo appears to be a fragment of a statue of extremely fine sculpture. It is quite entire, with the surface perfectly preserved; and is very accurately represented in the print; though the artist has introduced too much of the painter's beauties of play of light and shadow, and glitter of effect; which, how fascinating soe'er in the sister art, sculpture does not admit of; and which therefore ought not to be employed in the imitations of it; since fidelity of representation, and not beauty of effect, is the excellence required in such secondary productions of art.[33]

The artists are therefore cast as characters in the production of the book, and are not merely invisible artisans, though as illustrators they are kept firmly in their place as artists of a second division of artistic production. There was, as is clear from the critical remarks, an expectation that the illustrators should be able to catch something of the grace and expression of the statues, and that this might require something beyond a mere slavish transcription of the form of the works: some sympathy and feeling also seems to have been needed. However, if the artist started to let pictorial beauties (rather than sculptural beauties) become evident in the illustration, then that overstepped the mark and was grounds for criticism. The accurate imitation of superficial appearances was clearly something to be valued in the secondary production of illustrative work, and Knight opened his essay at the beginning of *Specimens of Antient Sculpture* by explaining that imitation makes for the basis of all society:

every present generation imitating the improvements of the past, without precluding itself from adding others of its own; so that every acquired faculty, whether of mind or body, became instantly naturalized; and every incidental invention of the individual expanded itself into a common property of the whole race: for, though invention be transitory and occasional, and usually arising from the necessity of the moment, imitation is permanent and uninterrupted; and proceeds spontaneously and regularly without the incentive of any external stimulus.[34]

Invention makes for progress, but imitation is more widespread, consolidating and naturalizing the new, indeed making the progress possible – because without it we would simply be faced with a continual starting-again. It is necessary for both principles to operate if civilization is to arise in the first place, and if it is to develop at all. The aesthetic theory being proposed in Knight's text is that in ancient Greece invention occurred as a matter of course, simply and unaffectedly, because the genuine artists tried to capture in bronze or marble the trace of a mental state – an image formed in the mind, and then externalized. By contrast, the portrait busts of the Romans showed a preoccupation with the servile copying of superficial appearances, work which was mechanical, pedantic and demeaning. It is a view of art which seems to be calculated to resist the idea of mechanical reproduction – certainly it is not threatened in the least by the camera's ability to capture superficial likenesses. We think most readily of the camera as capturing an image by mechanical means, but that was not a possibility in Knight's day. The

45 *Androgynous Apollo*, in the collection of Charles Townley, plate LXIV of vol. I of *Specimens of Antient Sculpture*. By permission of the British Library.

reproduction of three-dimensional objects by means of casting was, however, widespread, not only where casts of antique sculpture were concerned but also for more routine purposes. It is worth remembering that Knight's fortune was one of the first of the great fortunes of the Industrial Revolution – made by his grandfather's ironworks – and cast iron would be one of the early means used in mass-production. He was also a great collector of coins, which were perhaps the earliest type of mass-produced object, and which included representational images. Knight's version of neoclassicism gave overwhelming priority not to the particular forms of Greek art, but to the idea of the spontaneous and inspired link between mind and action. We see Knight at the beginning of the nineteenth century already investing particular value in something he saw being driven out of the modern world – the all too human activity which could never be replaced by mechanical efficiency or pedantic measurement. It would be possible to cast in iron perfectly proportioned Ionic columns, but such a way of working would have by-passed what Knight saw as valuable in Greek work. He saw the ideal state as having existed in ancient times, in the independent city states of Classical Greece, and he saw its decline to date from the inception of the idea of empire. The attempt to sustain a link between the existence of an ideal society and the production of perfect works of art was romantic and flawed, but the idea persists – now linking with the Parthenon marbles, rather than the examples which Knight and Townley selected. The most valuable part of Knight's view of ancient Greece, though, is his desire to see the transient spontaneities of the mind snatched from the air and transmitted across time, so that the greatest works of art are not those which show the greatest mechanical skill, but those which have drawn on an artist's superb technique in order to pass on to us traces of the great artists' mental life – felt not as a dazzling technical performance, but as an inspirational breath wafted across aeons of time.

Notes

1 *Specimens of Antient Sculpture*, 2 vols, published by the Society of Dilettanti (hereafter *Specimens*). Neither gives an author on the title page, but vol. 1 is by Richard Payne Knight (1809). Vol. 2 (1835) is clearly a continuation of the initial project, despite the intervening years. Many of the plates are by the same artists as in the first volume, and production of them could have been steady. Presumably the reason for completing the publication in 1835 was that there was a sizeable stock of high-quality illustrative material at the Society's disposal, and indeed commissioned at the Society's expense. The new introductory essay, by J.B.S. Morritt, was followed by the essay by Knight on 'The Symbolical Language of Antiquity', as promised in the first volume. It had in the meantime been published as an independent volume in 1818 – at which point it must have been evident to Knight that the second volume would not see the light of day during his lifetime, the purchase of the Elgin Marbles in 1816 having brought to an end his reputation as an authority on these matters. See Michael Clarke and Nicholas Penny, *The Arrogant Connoisseur: Richard Payne Knight 1751–1824*, Manchester: Manchester University Press, 1982, p. 149.

2 Johann Joachim Winckelmann's principal publications were *Gedanken über die Nachahmung der griechischen Werke*, translated by Henry Fuseli as *Reflections on the Painting and Sculpture of the Greeks*, London, 1765; and *Geschichte der Kunst des Alterthums*, 1st edn Dresden, 1764; 2nd edn Vienna, 1776, translated by G.H. Lodge as *The History of Ancient Art among the Greeks*, London, 1850. His *Monumenti antichi inediti*, Rome, 1767, presented specimens of ancient sculpture. Knight made some critical and no appreciative remarks about Winckelmann, but his whole view of ancient Greece was shaped by his reading of

Winckelmann, whose works he would have known from Fuseli's translation and from the French editions, to which his footnotes sometimes refer.

3 *Specimens*, vol. I, p. lii (sect. 90).

4 *Specimens*, vol. I, p. liii.

5 *Specimens*, vol. I, p. li.

6 *Specimens*, vol. I, p. lix.

7 *Specimens*, vol. I, p. i.

8 'Baron d'Hancarville' was the fraudulently adopted name of Pierre François Hugues, author of *Recherches sur l'origine et les progrès des arts de la Grèce*, 3 vols, London, 1785. See Andrew Ballantyne, *Architecture, Landscape and Liberty: Richard Payne Knight and the Picturesque*, Cambridge: Cambridge University Press, 1997, especially pp. 89–94 and footnotes. Francis Bacon, *De Sapienta Veterum* (1609), translated by Arthur Gorges as *The Wisedome of the Ancients* (1619).

9 *Specimens*, vol. I, p. lxxix.

10 Ballantyne, op. cit. (note 8), pp. 22–7.

11 ibid., and Richard Payne Knight, *The Landscape* (1795 edn), bk. I, lines 395–8.

12 *Specimens*, vol. I, p. lxi.

13 *Specimens*, vol. I, p. lxxix.

14 *Specimens*, vol. I, p. li.

15 Winckelmann, *History of Ancient Art*, vol. I, p. 286. Ballantyne, op. cit. (note 8), pp. 40–5.

16 Ballantyne, op. cit. (note 8), pp. 45–58.

17 *Specimens*, vol. I, pp. vii–viii.

18 *Specimens*, vol. II, p. xix.

19 *Specimens*, vol. I, commentary for plate XXV.

20 Geoffrey Waywell, *The Lever and Hope Sculptures*, Berlin: Gebr. Mann Verlag, 1986, p. 67.

21 *Specimens*, vol. I, p. li.

22 *Specimens*, vol. I, p. xxxviii.

23 *Specimens*, vol. I, p. xxxix.

24 *Specimens*, vol. I, p. xxxix.

25 *Specimens*, vol. I, commentary for plates XLIII

and XLIV.

26 B.F. Cook, *The Townley Marbles*, London: British Museum Press, 1985, p. 11.

27 Jacques-Louis David, *The Death of Joseph Bara*, 1794, is reproduced in Abigail Solomon-Godeau, *Male Trouble: A Crisis in Representation*, London: Thames and Hudson, 1997, p. 135. Richard Westall, *Orpheus*, 1812, is reproduced in Ballantyne, op. cit. (note 8), p. 178.

28 *Specimens*, vol. I, commentary for plate XXXIX.

29 *Specimens*, vol. I, commentary for plate LXII.

30 *Specimens*, vol. II, plate XLV.

31 *Specimens*, vol. I, commentary for plate LIX.

32 Richard Payne Knight, *An Analytical Inquiry into the Principles of Taste*, 1st edn, London, 1805; 4th and final edn 1808, p. 150.

33 *Specimens*, vol. I, commentary for plate LXIV.

34 *Specimens*, vol. I, p. ii.

Index

Printed and bound by CPI Group (UK) Ltd, Croydon, CR0 4YY

15/12/2023

08209260-0001